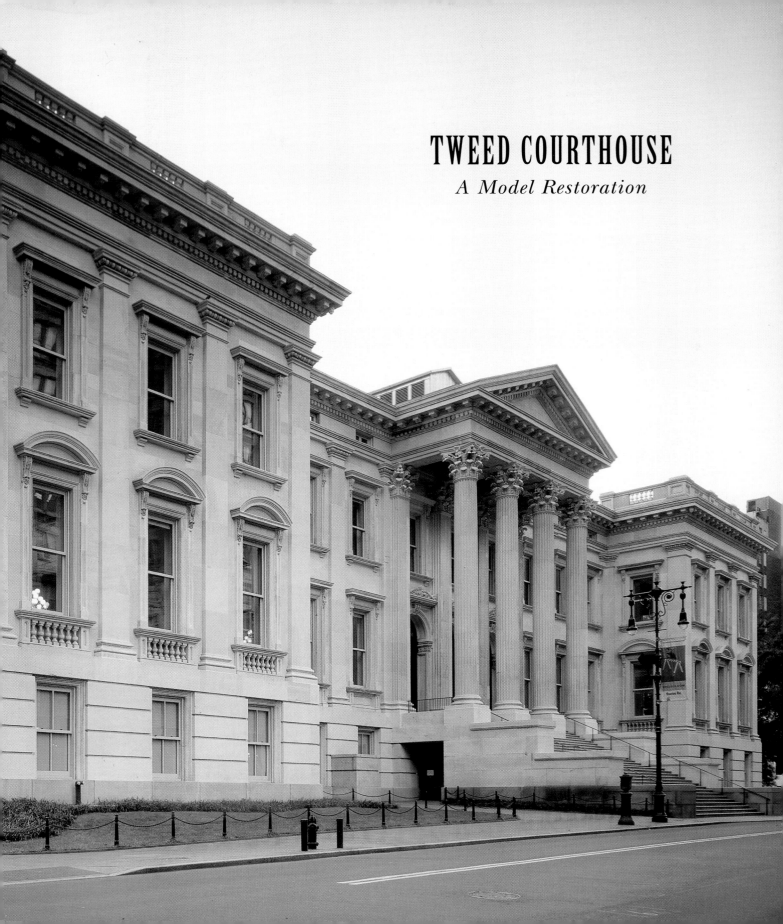

TWEED COURTHOUSE

A Model Restoration

Preceding page: The Chambers Street elevation. Photograph by Lily Wang

Restored exterior from the north east. Photograph by Michael Rogol

Restored exterior. The exterior of the courthouse, constructed of Tuckahoe and Sheffield marbles, was completely restored. More than 1,500 pieces of stone were repaired or replaced across the entire building facade. The entire 1,220-foot-long cornice, along with 335 modillions, was replaced. The monumental Chambers Street stairway, which was removed in the 1940s for the widening of Chambers Street, was rebuilt as the main entrance to the building. Along with the re-establishment of the three double-doorway entrances on the main floor, the restored stairway provides code-complying egress for the new uses of the building. Photograph by Michael Rogol

A cross-section of the building rendered in watercolor was prepared by the architects to illustrate the recommendations of the feasibility study. All of the major elements of the restoration, which would come to fruition a decade later, are shown in the rendering. They include the rebuilding of the Chambers Street staircase, restoration of Rotunda and laylight, and the restoration of the original courtrooms including replication of historic lighting fixtures and color schemes. Also shown was the utilization of the original ventilation shafts for the new HVAC system. Watercolor by Mesick•Cohen•Waite Architects.

Top: Rotunda before restoration.
Photograph by Lily Wang

Above: Rotunda during restoration.
Photograph by Lily Wang

Above: Restored laylight over rotunda.
Photograph by Lily Wang

Opposite: Restored rotunda showing underside of main-floor glass tile flooring. In the event of fire, smoke and combustion gases are collected in the upper section of the rotunda and extracted directly to the exterior by large fans located at the attic level.

Restored rotunda and ground floor. The glass tile flooring allows light to enter the basement.
Photograph by Lily Wang

Opposite: Rotunda after restoration.
Photograph by Michael Rogol

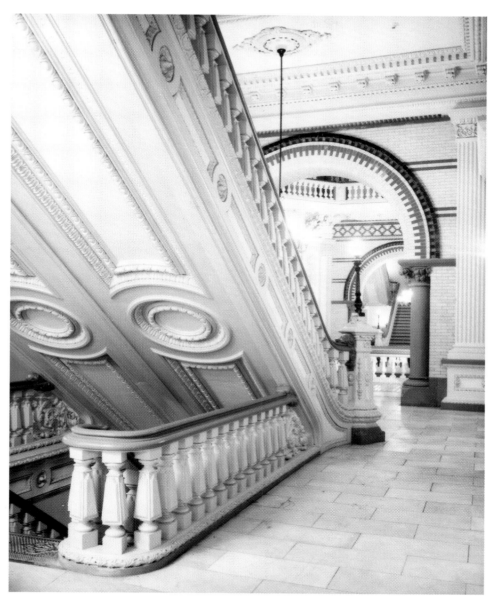

Opposite: Main stairway at the main floor after restoration. The stair is constructed entirely of cast iron, including the paneled underside of the stair runs. Photograph by Lily Wang

Above: Main stairway after restoration. Photograph by Lily Wang

Left: Main courtroom in south wing after restoration. Designed by Leopold Eidlitz, the masonry was cleaned and restored, the tile floor repaired, the historic lighting fixtures replicated, and a new bronze overmantel installed.

Top: Chamber of the Board of Supervisors, showing the opulent furnishings and light-colored walls. From Manual of the Corporation of the City of New York, *1868.*

Above: Restored original courtroom designed by John Kellum. The historic lighting fixtures have been replicated, the decorative plaster ornamentation has been restored, and modern office furniture was installed to accommodate offices for the Department of Education. Photograph by Lily Wang.

Leopold Eidlitz–designed courtroom on main floor of south wing during restoration.

Right: Restored Leopold Eidlitz–designed courtroom on third floor of south wing. The polychromed decorative brickwork had been coated with over a dozen layers of paint and the space had been subdivided into many offices. Photograph by Lily Wang.

Original third-floor court-room photograph showing restoration prior to installation of new finished floor.

Right: Restored original third-floor courtroom with replicated historic lighting fixtures and color scheme.
Photograph by Lily Wang

TWEED COURTHOUSE

A Model Restoration

John G. Waite

WITH

Nancy A. Rankin and Diana S. Waite

W. W. NORTON & COMPANY

NEW YORK • LONDON

For information about permission to reproduce selections from this book, write to
Permissions, W. W. Norton & Company, Inc., 500 Fifth Avenue, New York, NY 10110

Manufacturing by Quebecor World Kingsport
Book design by Abigail Sturges
Production manager: Leeann Graham

Library of Congress Cataloging-in-Publication Data

Waite, John G.
Tweed Courthouse: a model restoration / John G. Waite with Nancy A. Rankin and Diana S. Waite.
p. cm.
Includes bibliographical references and index.
ISBN-13: 978-0-393-73123-1
ISBN-10: 0-393-73123-5
1. Buildings—Repair and reconstruction—New York (State)—New York. 2. Tweed Courthouse (New York, N.Y.)
—Conservation and restoration. 3. Historic buildings—New York (State)—New York—Conservation and restoration.
4. Architecture—United States—19th century—Conservation and restoration.
I. Rankin, Nancy A. II. Waite, Diana S. III. Title.

TH3401.W35 2006
690'.515—dc22

2005057232

W. W. Norton & Company, Inc., 500 Fifth Avenue, New York, N.Y. 10110
www.wwnorton.com

W. W. Norton & Company Ltd., Castle House, 75/76 Wells Street, London W1T 3QT

0 9 8 7 6 5 4 3 2 1

CONTENTS

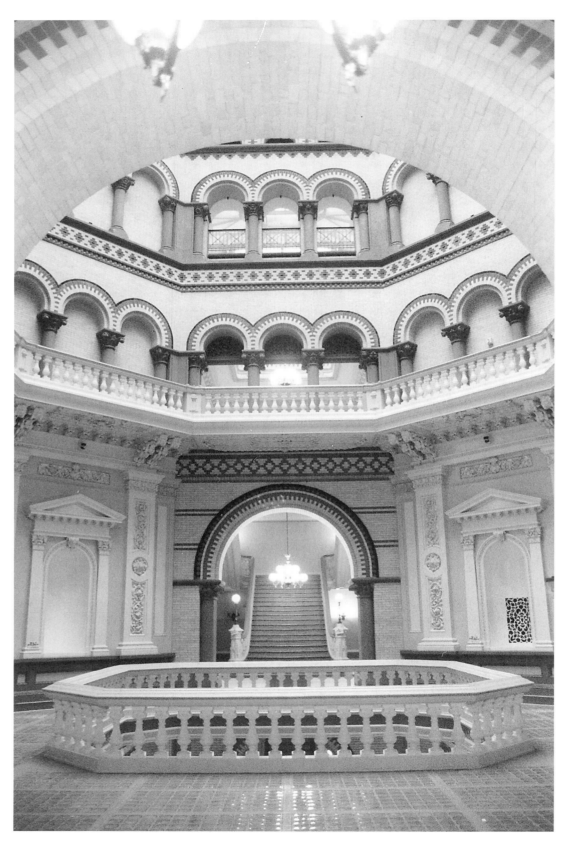

Restored rotunda at main floor. The masonry and cast iron were cleaned and repaired, the glass floor tiles replaced, and the historic paint scheme replicated.

PREFACE

The Old New York County Courthouse, better known as Tweed Courthouse, is one of New York City's great civic monuments. Built between 1861 and 1881, it is the creation of two of the city's most prominent nineteenth-century architects, John Kellum and Leopold Eidlitz. The courthouse is the legacy of Tammany Hall "Boss" William M. Tweed, who controlled the initial construction. While notorious for his corrupt political machine, Tweed did in fact impact the city in positive ways by re-instituting home rule (returning the right to govern itself back to New York City from the State legislature), providing jobs for immigrants, and advancing many public construction projects.

Grandly scaled and richly decorated, Tweed Courthouse is among the most significant public buildings constructed in the United States during the third quarter of the nineteenth century. First intended to be the "New City Hall," it has served many purposes: as county courthouse, city courthouse, and municipal office building. Despite all these changes in use, the building has retained its original spatial arrangement, encompassing thirty monumental courtrooms and a five-story central rotunda. The immense cast-iron structural and decorative elements in the rotunda and courtrooms are unparalleled in any American public building.

Although the courthouse was threatened with demolition as late as the 1970s, its significance has been recognized by governmental agencies at the local, state, and national levels. It was listed in the National Register of Historic Places in 1974, and two years later designated a National Historic Landmark by the U.S. Department of the Interior. In 1984 the New York City Landmarks Preservation Commission honored the building with exterior and interior designations.

In 1989 the restoration of the building began when the city commissioned Mesick•Cohen•Waite Architects, a predecessor of the firm of John G. Waite Associates, Architects, to prepare a feasibility study for the building's preservation and reuse. In 1999 New York City Mayor Rudolph W. Giuliani directed the New York City Economic Development Corporation to proceed with a $90 million comprehensive restoration of the building. Under Mayor Michael Bloomberg the building was fitted out in 2002–3 as the headquarters for the new Department of Education.

The restoration of Tweed Courthouse was a complex and intricate process. A large team of architects, engineers, construction managers, architectural historians, archaeologists, conservators, artists, and contractors was assembled to carry out the design and construction work. Because the work was so extensive and because it had to be done within a two-and-one-half-year period, the architects and construction manager established full-time offices on the site. At any one time some parts of the project were under construction, while the architects were preparing working drawings for other parts, and planning was under way for still more. This integrated approach allowed the project to be completed on schedule and within budget. Ultimately the restoration involved more than one hundred separate contracts and hundreds of construction workers.

Tweed Courthouse was a model restoration project in several respects. Through the leadership of the Economic Development Corporation, the usual municipal procurement processes were streamlined, allowing an accelerated design and construction schedule without sacrificing stringent cost controls. The management techniques utilized for the Tweed Courthouse project can be applied to the restoration of other large public buildings.

Because of the comprehensive nature of the courthouse restoration, state-of-the-art building-conservation practices were applied to a wide spectrum of construction technology and materials problems. The stabilization and restoration of the exterior stonework and the introduction of new utilities systems especially required innovative solutions. The scope and extent of the project allowed the development and utilization of these techniques to an extent not realized in other recent preservation projects in the United States. The individual technical procedures, and the process for their integration, can be utilized in many public building restoration projects.

ACKNOWLEDGMENTS

From the architects' standpoint, the restoration of Tweed Courthouse was an ideal historic preservation project. Not only is the building of major architectural and historical significance, but it is prominently located and houses an important and highly visible public agency. The restoration was carried out with a tight but adequate schedule and with sufficient funding to address the many problems that had accumulated over the building's 140-year history.

The restoration had the full support of the mayor's office and the cooperation of the various city agencies having jurisdiction over the project. The Economic Development Corporation provided very effective leadership for the project, streamlining the usual city construction-procurement system. This arrangement allowed the architects to develop a comprehensive approach to the restoration of the building and to utilize management techniques that assured having qualified contractors for all aspects of the work. Historical research and building-fabric investigations were fully integrated into the design process to provide the information necessary to make sound design decisions for the long-term preservation of the building.

The restoration project was also unusual in that it was a complete project under the direction of a single architectural firm. Often large governmental projects are fractured so that separate architectural firms are responsible for design, historic preservation, contract-document preparation, and construction administration. Because of the special circumstances of the Tweed Courthouse restoration, John G. Waite Associates, Architects was responsible for the entire construction project.

The organization of this book reflects that of the overall restoration project. There are chapters on the history of the building, the planning of and approach to the restoration, and technical sections on the analysis and restoration of all the components of the building, including interior elements, exterior features, and building systems.

As with the restoration of Tweed Courthouse, many people contributed to the preparation of this book. The history was researched and written by Diana S. Waite. Leo Hershkowitz, professor of history at Queens College, and Kenneth R. Cobb, former head of the Municipal Archives of the City of New York, provided special help with the historical research.

The sections on developing a restoration plan, interior restoration, exterior restoration, building systems, and conclusion were written by John G. Waite and Nancy A. Rankin, with major contributions by the following: Douglas G. Bucher: paint, hardware, lighting; Nicholas Cates: plaster, tile floors, stone floors, etched glass, interior and exterior wood doors, reconstruction of Chambers Street stairs, wood and cast-iron windows, hardware; William G. Foulks: exterior stone; Lee Pinckney III: exterior stone; Andrew Sniderman: decorative masonry, cast iron, paint, lighting, laylights, roof and skylights.

John Chester, Imtiaz Mulla, and Christopher Marrion assisted in the preparation of the building-systems chapters. The design team's general participation in the restoration is demonstrated in this arrangement. All of the sections were reviewed by Douglas G. Bucher and edited by Diana S. Waite.

Special assistance in the production of this book was provided by Chelle Jenkins and Evelyn Gutierrez of John G. Waite Associates, Architects. Other staff members who provided production assistance were Jennifer R. Breslin, Carrie Britt, Janessa Francoeur, M. Grace Jukes, and Christen Kelley.

Finally, Nancy Green of W. W. Norton patiently directed the development and publication of this book.

RESTORATION TEAM 1999–2002

JOHN G. WAITE ASSOCIATES, ARCHITECTS

NEW YORK OFFICE
Nancy A. Rankin
Nicholas A. Cates
John P. Chester
Lee Pinckney, III
Andrew G. Sniderman
Roimon Hepburn

ALBANY OFFICE
John G. Waite
William Brandow
Douglas G. Bucher
Michael Curcio
Chelle M. Jenkins
Clay S. Palazzo
William P. Palmer
Robert A. Petito, Jr.
Stephen F. Reilly
Daniel Wilson

CONSULTANTS

MECHANICAL, ELECTRICAL,
PLUMBING AND FIRE ENGINEERING

ARUP
Imtiaz Mulla (also with Meinhardt USA)
Christopher E. Marrion
David Richards
Jaime Birman
Aidan O'Dwyer
Marc Gateau

STRUCTURAL ENGINEERING
Robert Silman Associates
Robert Silman
Karina Tribble

CIVIL ENGINEERING
Langan Engineering and Environmental Services
Gerald McDonnell

LIGHTING DESIGN
Fisher Marantz Stone
Hank Forrest

SPECIFICATIONS
Preservation Specs Group
Dede Nash

VERTICAL TRANSPORTATION
CONSULTANT
Van Deusen & Associates
Richard Sayah

EXPEDITER
JAM Consultants
Christopher Hazell
Orlando Diaz

ARCHEOLOGY
Hartgen Archeological Associates
Karen Hartgen
Carol A. Raemsch

HISTORICAL RESEARCH
Mount Ida Press
Diana S. Waite

COST ESTIMATOR
Nasco Construction Services
Robert Rubenstein

STAINED GLASS
Cummings Studios
William Cummings

SIGNAGE
Solsaa Design
Trish Solsaa

PHOTOGRAPHY AFTER CONSTRUCTION
Lily Wang

CONSTRUCTION MANAGER

BOVIS LEND LEASE LMB
Robert Bradshaw
Denise Cox
Glen Crandall
Donald Curtis
Rosario Davi
Andrew Faulds
Vincent Galleto
Joan Gerner
William Hickman
Beth Leahy
Laura Lunsford
Robert MacDougal
Wilbert Oliver
Michael Orlando
John Santoro
Roz Shapiro
Raymond Stokes
Holly Ulses

PROFESSIONAL STAFF 1989–1995

MESICK·COHEN·WAITE ARCHITECTS
John G. Waite
Douglas G. Bucher
Michael Curcio
William G. Foulks
Chelle M. Jenkins
Robert A. Petito, Jr.
Nancy A. Rankin

Charles E. Barthe, Jr.
James A. Comegys
Vladimir Kalivoda
Kyle Larabee
Wei Li
Siobhan McGrath
William P. Palmer
Lee Pinckney, III
Laurence F. Wilson

CONSULTANTS

MECHANICAL AND ELECTRICAL
ENGINEERING
Goldman Copeland Batlan, P.C.

STRUCTURAL ENGINEERING
Robert Silman Associates

VERTICAL TRANSPORTATION
CONSULTANT
Calvin L. Kort, P.E.

MASONRY CONSULTANT
Norman R. Weiss

CITY OF NEW YORK

2002–2003
Michael Bloomberg, Mayor

Patricia Harris, Deputy Mayor

Joel I. Klein, Chancellor, Department
of Education

Martha K. Hirst, Commissioner, Department
of Citywide Administrative Services

1999–2001
Rudolph W. Giuliani, Mayor

Jennifer Raab, Chair, New York City Landmarks
Preservation Commission

Anthony P. Coles, Deputy Mayor for Planning,
Education and Cultural Affairs

Robert M. Harding, Deputy Mayor for Economic
Development and Finance

John S. Dyson, Chairman, Council
of Economic Advisors

Ronny A. Livian, Acting Deputy Commissioner,
New York City Department of Buildings

NEW YORK CITY ECONOMIC DEVELOPMENT
CORPORATION
Michael G. Carey, President

Melvin A. Glickman, Executive Vice-President

Terri E. Bahr, Senior Project Manager

Sandra Tomas, Senior Project Manager

TWEED COURTHOUSE
RESTORATION PROJECT COMMITTEE
Melvin A. Glickman, Chairman

New York City Economic Development Corporation,
Terri E. Bahr

New York City Office of the Mayor, Jean Ross, Lt.
Donald Henney

New York City Landmarks Preservation Commission,
Kim Hoyt, Brian E. Hogg

New York City Department of Citywide
Administrative Services, James Zethraus

Museum of the City of New York, Robert R.
MacDonald, Ed Henry

John G. Waite Associates, Architects,
Nancy A. Rankin

Bovis Lend Lease LMB, Donald Curtis

Opposite: The completed court-house, looking southeast along Chambers Street, photograph by J. S. Johnston, c. 1888. Collection of The New-York Historical Society, neg. 72309.

CHAPTER ONE

"Unimpeached in Anything Except Cost"

The Construction of Tweed Courthouse

Despite the blustery weather, a large crowd gathered in City Hall Park on the day after Christmas in 1861, eager to witness a long-awaited ceremony: the laying of the cornerstone for the new county courthouse. At the same time, but in quite comfortable quarters next door at City Hall, officials were assembling to form a proper procession. Stepping out of the rear door of City Hall and into the wind, they threaded their way across the frozen ground through an opening in the rough construction fence and took their seats on a sheltered platform at the northeast corner of the foundations, just south of Chambers Street.

Displayed before the spectators was an impressive tableau. Construction had begun only in September, but already laborers had hauled away more than 71,000 loads of excavated earth and stone and masons had laid 650,000 bricks and 38,000 cubic feet of stone foundation walls. Overhead, a large American flag fluttered from the derrick waiting to maneuver the cornerstone. The stone itself measured 38 inches square and was, like the foundation walls, made of Kips Bay granite.[1]

After the invocation the chairman of the Board of Commissioners in charge of the building read aloud the list of items that had been deposited in the protective metal box set inside the cornerstone: a copy of the U.S. Constitution, city directories, newspapers, literary and scientific journals, maps, and a zinc plate engraved with the names of city officials, as well as the most recent payroll, which listed all of the construction workers. As more observers gathered, Mayor Fernando Wood used a mallet and trowel to secure the cap for the cornerstone, a massive block of white marble from Westchester County. The next hour and a half was filled with speeches by the mayor, the presiding justice of the state supreme court, and the president of the Board of Supervisors. The *New York Times* reported that the audience listened attentively, "with exemplary order."

In lofty ceremonial language Mayor Wood expressed the wish that the "historical associations of the new building may be no less auspicious than those which belong to its predecessors," the city's other public buildings. Even though the building was being erected during the "times

of trial" of the Civil War, he hoped that "within these walls we may reasonably expect to trace the increasing prosperity of the great Metropolis, and the preservation of that system of jurisprudence by which both individual freedom and public order are maintained." One can only wonder at the thoughts of William M. Tweed, surely sitting on the platform beside his fellow supervisors that afternoon and hearing those words. Tweed was already intimately involved with the construction of the courthouse, but little could he, or any of the others present that afternoon, have predicted that, although it was exceptionally well built, its cost would precipitate an enormous scandal. The courthouse would become the infamous Tweed Ring's greatest fraud. It would become the venue for Tweed's own trial and eventually carry his own besmirched name.

From Pasture to Park

At the cornerstone-laying ceremony Mayor Wood reminded the audience that the courthouse was situated in a his-

toric part of Manhattan, at the upper edge of City Hall Park, an open space that had long been a public domain. The Dutch had called this area the *vlacte*, or flat, to distinguish its topography from the island's many rocky outcroppings and low-lying marshes, and they had used it as a public pasture for their cattle. In 1686, under English governor Thomas Dongan, the area officially came under municipal stewardship. Known as the Common, it remained remote from the settled tip of Manhattan and undeveloped until the mid-eighteenth century. The Common was the site of executions, and by 1713 a burial ground for blacks had been established near its northern reaches. A little farther north, amid forest, was the Collect, or Fresh Water Pond, a spring-fed lake sixty feet deep, its shoreline heaped with oyster shells that had been pried open by Indians.[2]

Meanwhile, the European population was expanding steadily northward toward the Common. Pine, Cedar, Liberty, and John streets were laid out in 1692. A 1731 map, the first to be printed in New York City, shows the east boundary of the Common delineated by the Post Road to

Boston, which ran south past the Collect and then diagonally along the present line of Park Row to meet Broadway at today's Vesey Street. The map also shows a ropewalk along the west edge of the Common, where workers spun out long lengths of cordage, uninterrupted, for hundreds

of feet. In 1760 a city surveyor staked out a 50-foot-wide extension to Broadway that ran north and formed the west boundary of the Common. Its north boundary remained unfixed until 1796, when the Common Council authorized the opening of Chambers Street.[3]

"A Plan of the City and Environs of New York as they were in the Years 1742, 1743 & 1744," drawn by David Grim, 1813. The Common appears as the open area above the triangular intersection of Broadway *and the Post Road leading northeast to Boston, and the pond known as the Collect is the large body of fresh water to the north.* Collection of The New-York Historical Society, image 3046.

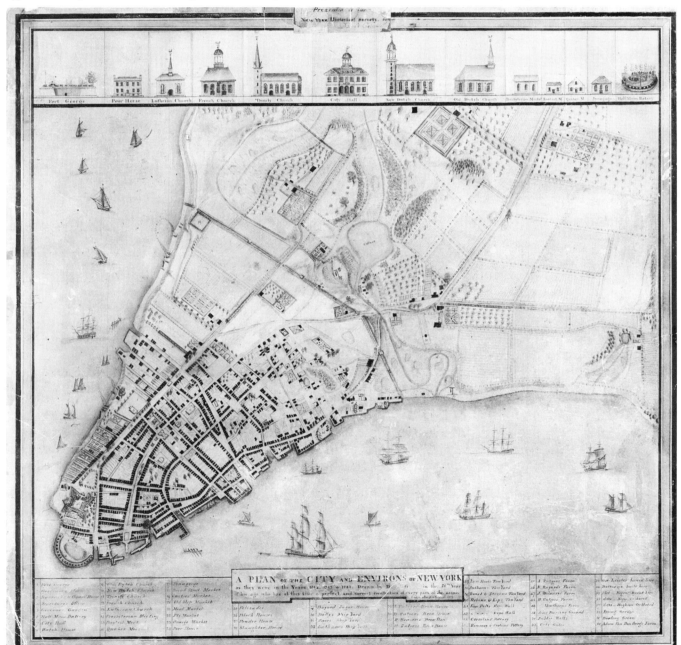

"The Second Almshouse," watercolor by Arthur J. Stansbury, c. 1825. This view, looking southeast across the intersection of Chambers Street and Broadway, shows the second almshouse (left, then occupied by the American Museum), which burned in 1854 and was then demolished to make way for the new courthouse. Just beyond the almshouse is the domed roof of the art gallery known as the Rotunda. South of the almshouse was the New Gaol, center, and City Hall, right. Museum of the City of New York, 52.100.16.

Before the Revolution much of the Common north of Murray Street had already been developed. By 1731 a house had been built opposite the ropewalk, and in 1740 the Common Council ordered the installation of a fence to separate this property from the recently completed almshouse, a two-story structure, 56 feet long, which stood on the site of the present City Hall. The purpose of the almshouse was to care for the city's poor and ill, including widows and children; it was part infirmary and part workhouse, where more able-bodied residents learned weaving, shoemaking, and other trades.[4]

Several other substantial buildings were erected near the almshouse during the late 1750s. The first, a two-story, forty-room structure known as the upper barracks, was only 21 feet wide but 420 feet long; located north of the almshouse, it stood on the site now occupied by Tweed Courthouse. To the east of the almshouse was the "new gaol," a three-story stone structure with a vaulted dun-geon, and to the southeast was a powder magazine. In 1775 another stone jail, known as the Bridewell, was built to the west of the almshouse; it reportedly held eight hundred prisoners in 1777.[5]

By the 1790s the character of the Common was again changing. The portion south of Murray Street appeared on a 1797 map as "The Park." The upper barracks was demolished, and a second almshouse was built on the site. The first almshouse was then torn down to make way for the new City Hall, begun in 1803. After facilities for the ill and poor were moved to Bellevue at 23rd Street and the East River in 1816, New York Institution took over the almshouse on Chambers Street, which now sheltered cultural groups, including the New-York Historical Society, the Academy of Arts, and the Lyceum of Natural History. An art gallery, circular in plan and known as the Rotunda, was built along Chambers Street in 1818 to showcase painter John Vanderlyn's panoramas. An iron fence for the perimeter of the park was imported from England in 1821.[6]

By the mid-1820s there was more interest in turning the former Common into a promenade grounds. New Yorkers now partied in the park on the Fourth of July; the Marquis de Lafayette was feted there; and the opening of the Erie Canal and the arrival of water for the city from Croton were celebrated. Along with these more refined civic uses, the former "new gaol" was remodeled in 1830 into a hall of records and municipal office building, complete with classical porticoes. The Bridewell was demolished. A combination dispensary and firehouse was built at the northeast corner of the park. Across Chambers Street, at the corner of Broadway, A. T. Stewart opened a spectacular marble-fronted emporium in 1846. In 1852 a new city courthouse was tucked in between the Rotunda and the former almshouse, which twenty years earlier had been converted to a federal courthouse. The old almshouse burned in 1854.[7]

Planning the New Courthouse

Planning for the new county courthouse actually began as planning for a new city hall. By the mid-1850s the existing city hall was too small to accommodate the offices needed to serve the city's burgeoning population, which had more than doubled in two decades. More and more people were moving uptown, and Mayor Wood proposed that a bigger city hall be constructed farther north and that the old one be converted to courts.[8]

In the spring of 1857 the New York State legislature enacted a law authorizing the construction of a new city hall behind the existing one, on the north portion of the block bounded by Broadway and by Chambers and Centre streets. Funding would come from the sale of what would be called City Hall stock. The law provided for the appointment of four commissioners, who were charged with securing plans and overseeing construction; but before making any commitments they were to consult with federal authorities to determine whether space might be wanted in the building for a post office or courtrooms. The city would then convey or lease to the United States the land on which its part of the building would stand, provided that the federal government would pay for its share of the construction. The new building would have not only mixed use but also mixed ownership.[9]

When the Common Council failed to raise the authorized funds for the new building, the state legislature repealed the 1857 law and passed another, in April 1858. This time there was no provision for a federal partnership. Instead, the new structure, still called the "New City Hall," would be filled entirely with facilities for the commissioner of jurors, the district attorney, a law institute, and no less than seven different state and municipal courts.[10]

Under the 1858 law, up to three Commissioners of the New City Hall were to be appointed to "decide upon the plans and specifications," solicit proposals, enter into contracts, erect the building, and furnish it, all in a manner most conducive to the administration of justice and to the preservation of the city's public records. For funding, the commissioners were directed to call upon the Board of Supervisors of New York County to issue stock, at six percent interest, up to the sum of $250,000, the anticipated cost of construction.[11]

Two of the commissioners, Wilson G. Hunt and John B. Corlies, had taken office in November 1858. They began their work by interviewing judges and other officials about the types and amounts of space they would need in the new building. The commissioners submitted a detailed inventory of their findings to the Board of Supervisors in January 1859. The sheriff, they reported, would need a large main office, a private office, and twelve smaller rooms for his deputies, while the state supreme court justices alone wanted "two rooms for Circuit Court, with two rooms for juries adjoining, one General Term room, one room for Chambers, with a private room attached for the Judges, and one room for Special Term." Altogether, the commissioners estimated, it would take a two-story building with a raised basement and cellar—containing ninety-seven rooms and measuring 375 by 131 feet in plan—to accommodate the stated needs. The new building would be more than four times larger than the city hall, and it should be fireproof, to protect the "numerous important books, documents and papers" to be kept inside. The commissioners suggested including facilities for the Board of Supervisors and the register, even though they had not been mentioned in the legislation. Furthermore, the commissioners warned, even more space would be needed in the future, because the "business of all these courts and offices is continually increasing proportionately with the rapid growth of the trade and population of the city." The new building, they concluded, should be "well calculated, not only in its size, but as to its arrangements, to afford the necessary accommodation, present as well as prospective." Moreover, it should "in its architectural style and beauty" be "in harmony with the other public edifices of the city, as well as commensurate with the wealth and importance of this metropolis."[12]

Because the commissioners considered the $250,000 authorization woefully inadequate, they had not yet bothered to secure detailed plans or specifications from any architects. However, they had obtained three preliminary estimates from contractors: a brick building with wood beams and floors would cost $737,006; a fireproof building of brick, $840,000; and a fireproof building with marble facades, $940,870. The Board of Supervisors adopted

Certificate for New York County Court House stock, issued to finance the construction of the new courthouse, 1864. Under the authority of the New York State Legislature, the County Board of Supervisors issued new stock as more funding was needed. Courtesy of Leo Hershkowitz.

the commissioners' recommendation to seek a state appropriation of $1 million and to erect a marble-front structure.[13]

When the legislature in Albany refused this appeal, the supervisors decided to force the issue: in May 1859 they directed the commissioners to "proceed, immediately, to discharge the duties incumbent upon them." In response, the commissioners took a new approach: they proposed to erect the building in sections over a period of several years, as funding became available. When the commissioners sought an attorney's opinion about whether they should proceed, the advice was not encouraging: not only were they forbidden to build just a part of the structure; they needed the consent of the Common Council, not just a directive from the state legislature, in order to build within City Hall Park. The Common Council, it appeared, was unlikely to cooperate. Furthermore, the commission-

er's attorney pointed out, the Board of Supervisors had no authority to issue stock for construction, nor did they have any property to back the capital of investors. Stymied, the commissioners turned in a report in June 1859, concluding, rather sadly, that they had spent hardly any money, only $100 for legal advice and $150 for some preliminary architectural plans by Thomas Little. The supervisors decided to table the report.[14]

Wrangling continued into 1860. Some citizens petitioned the state senate to move the city hall to Madison Square. The Board of Supervisors confirmed Mayor Wood's appointment of James Salmon to fill one vacancy on the Board of Commissioners, but the mayor now proposed that the commission turn its attention to building a large new city hall farther uptown. It would include space for courtrooms, thus making a new courthouse in the park redundant.[15]

In 1861 the logjam was finally broken. On April 10 the state legislature passed a new law specifically empowering the Board of Supervisors to move ahead with the project. The supervisors were directed to take whatever land they deemed necessary and to be responsible for erecting the new building. The land was to be appraised, and what was now called "Court House stock" was to be issued, this time at seven percent interest and redeemable in ten years. The interest was to be paid from a tax on the real and personal estates of people residing in the city.[16]

Within two weeks the supervisors decided to shift their responsibility for decision-making to a select committee made up of five supervisors. On May 7 the supervisors voted unanimously to select an area of City Hall Park fronting on Chambers Street as the site for the new building: a lot that extended along Chambers Street for 320 feet and was 200 feet deep. The site was appraised at $450,000.[17]

In July Supervisor William M. Tweed began pushing the Board of Supervisors to move ahead with the design of the courthouse. Finally, on August 30, the supervisors passed a resolution directing a special committee on constructing the courthouse to "employ a suitable architect to prepare plans and specifications" and to proceed with construction "with all possible dispatch." This committee was to purchase the building materials and "to build such portion thereof by contract or 'days' work' as they may deem for the best interests of the County." Vendors' contracts were to be presented to the full board for approval, and the comptroller was then to pay the bills once the committee had issued the proper approvals. On September 7 a state supreme court justice gave official approval to the site in City Hall Park. The special committee wasted no time: within nine days they had acquired title to the land and started excavation.[18]

Construction Finally Begins

After more than four years of dickering, ground was broken on September 16, 1861, even though the authorized budget of $150,000 was entirely inadequate to complete construction. According to the president of the Board of Supervisors, William R. Stewart, the board had, "after mature reflection," determined that the only way to prevent further delays was to have a committee of their own members direct the work and to start immediately. They would pay vendors under a system of day labor; otherwise, if they waited for complete plans and specifications to be prepared and then awarded construction contracts, work could not begin until the following spring. In any case, Stewart explained, no responsible contractor would have entered into a contract, since funding for only part, not

all, of the building had been authorized. By beginning right away, the supervisors could also take advantage of the current business climate and the "exceedingly low" price of labor and building materials.[19]

Two of the supervisors assigned major tasks to themselves: Stewart would serve as the general superintendent, and Thomas Little would be the architect. Little's design called for the courthouse to extend 244 feet along Chambers Street; the main block would be 112 feet deep, and there would be two wings, each 144 feet deep. The building would be "surrounded on three sides by a wide courtyard," which would run south nearly to the back of City Hall. "Many fine trees" in the park would have to be cut down. The supervisors hired Cummings H. Tucker, a respected mason, to oversee the project, and he promised to have two stories finished by the end of the year. The *New York Times* reported to its readers that even though construction had begun, "no estimate of the total cost has been made."[20]

The Special Committee immediately set about finding appropriate building materials. On October 24 they told the supervisors that they had invited the "principal marble-dealers in this City" to submit proposals for huge marble blocks, which would weigh on average three tons each; they were to be "quarried to specified sizes" and then delivered to the site. Five dealers bid on this work: the two highest would charge $2.00 a cubic foot, and the two lowest came in at $1.25. Committee members then inspected the quality of the marble from the two lowest bidders and decided to award contracts to both of them, because so much stone was needed and because the committee members wanted to be able to build "as far as possible by next spring."[21]

One of the low bidders, the Eastchester Quarry Company, had been supplying large slabs of white marble from its Westchester County quarries for monumental buildings in New York City ever since the 1820s, and its owner, John Masterson, was well known to the city's leading architects. The other low bidder, the Sheffield Quarry Company, had been operating since the late 1830s. What the Special Committee's report did not mention was that John R. Briggs, a supervisor and one of the members of the Special Committee, was an owner of the Sheffield operation; it would later be revealed that Supervisor Tweed was also involved with that quarry.[22]

In addition to masonry, construction of the basement of the courthouse would require 10,000 running feet of 9-inch iron beams. The committee determined that only two companies in the country were capable of manufacturing them: the Trenton Iron Company, located in New Jersey, and the Phoenix Iron Company in Philadelphia. The committee accepted the lower bid of the Trenton firm.[23]

Meanwhile, even as the foundations were being dug, Mayor Wood asked the corporation counsel, Greene C. Bronson, for an opinion about whether the Board of Supervisors had exceeded its authority by actually undertaking construction. Bronson found that the board had "not the power to build"; according to his interpretation of the law, the work instead should be directed by the Commissioners of the New City Hall. Bronson added that he had made his determination very reluctantly, because he did not want to retard the progress of the badly needed courthouse. Accordingly, the supervisors voted unanimously on November 2 to transfer power to the three commissioners: Wilson G. Hunt, John B. Corlies, and James Salmon. The supervisors then requested the sum of $25,000 to begin work.[24]

By now the perimeter of the construction site had been enclosed with a high board fence, 300 feet long and 200 feet wide, which was intended "to keep idlers and loafers away from the work." In December 1861 the fenced area was extended westward, reaching to within 20 feet of Broadway and then running south 150 feet. A temporary roof was installed over this new section in order to accommodate the marble cutters, who were expected to arrive soon and continue work through the winter. The *New York Times* commented that so far the weather had been "so favorable" that the "Commissioners have been enabled to push on the work beyond their expectations, and the amount of labor already performed shows how much can be accomplished by many hands judiciously employed."[25]

A few adjustments had been made to the architectural design during the weeks after the September groundbreaking, probably at the direction of the newly appointed "suitable architect." The height of the building had been raised by 8 feet. Its overall length had been increased by only about a foot, to 245 feet, but the wings had been lengthened by about 4 feet, to 148 feet. In plan, the north-south dimension of the main block of the building remained at 112 feet, and the wings were to measure 53 feet east to west. The height from the sidewalk to the top of the parapet was to be about 78 feet. Steam heating was to be incorporated. Together, the U-shaped plan and the large windows would provide a "due proportion of light to all the rooms."[26]

The courtyard that had been described in September news stories was not mentioned in the December accounts, but now there would be a dome based on the one at St. Peter's Basilica in Rome; it was intended to "highly ornament and beautify the exterior." Positioned over the central rotunda, the dome would measure 50 feet in diameter at its base and be surmounted by a "massive gilt ball," fully 100 feet above ground level. Overall, the design for the courthouse would follow the "full Corinthian style of architecture," and there would be two

William M. "Boss" Tweed. From *Dictionary of American Portraits* (New York: Dover Publications, 1967).

main entrances, one on Chambers Street and the other from the park, both through impressive porticoes. The *New York Times* reported that "in its style of architecture, the edifice will be the only classical one (except the somber Tombs) belonging to the City."[27]

Inside the courthouse, six large rooms and four smaller spaces on the ground floor would house the valuable records of the surrogate, county clerk, and register. On the two upper stories would be twelve large courtrooms and eight smaller ones, as well as "two fair-sized rooms, to be used either for libraries or Grand Jury rooms." The structural system would consist of masonry bearing walls and floors constructed of iron beams and brick arches; the stairs and the roof were to be made of iron; and the halls would be paved with marble—all to ensure fireproof construction. The ventilation of the building was also of prime importance: it was reported that "no pains will be spared to obviate the criminal neglect in this respect, which has characterized most of our courtrooms heretofore." Furnaces housed in the basement of the new building would supply warmed air, with a "never failing supply of oxygen."[28]

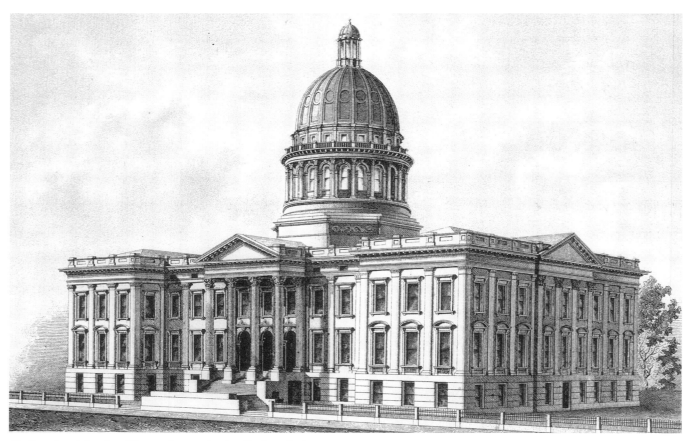

North and west facades of the courthouse, showing the dome that was never constructed over the rotunda. From *Manual of the Corporation of the City of New York*, 1868.

Thomas Little had prepared plans for the courthouse in 1859. He had earlier designed the New England Congregational Church in Brooklyn and commercial buildings on Duane Street, all in the Italianate style, but probably most importantly for the courthouse he was a member of the Board of Supervisors. However, in August 1861, when the supervisors directed the committee in charge of the construction to engage a "suitable architect to prepare plans and specifications," they chose John Kellum. His name was inscribed after Little's on the metal box that was deposited in the cornerstone in December 1861.[29]

Kellum, then fifty-two, had been trained as a carpenter. During the 1840s he became a partner in the Brooklyn architectural office of Gamaliel King, and in the late 1850s he formed the firm of Kellum and Son. Before being chosen to work on the courthouse, Kellum had already designed the Cary Building at 105 Chambers Street, one of the first cast-iron facades in New York; the Friends Meeting House on Gramercy Park; and several commercial buildings on Broadway, including a new iron-fronted department store for A. T. Stewart at Broadway

and Tenth Street. While construction at the courthouse was under way, Kellum was also busy with commissions for two cast-iron ferry houses in lower Manhattan, more commercial buildings, an opulent residence for Stewart on Fifth Avenue, and houses and public buildings in Garden City, a model community being developed by Stewart on Long Island. In 1866 Kellum was said to stand "at the head of his profession."[30]

Cummings H. Tucker had supervised the construction work at the courthouse since September 1861. The *New York Times* called him "one of the best mason builders in the country," and he was credited with using the latest construction technology, including valuable "labor-savers and time-economizers." Like Kellum, Tucker and his clerks had an office inside the fence around the construction site. He worked full time on the courthouse, and his duties were described as being "very onerous: he employed all the men, purchased materials, weighed, measured and inspected all the materials received, so that the County should only pay what was actually received, superintended all the finishing of all the marble which was delivered under the contract in the rough, and directed the whole building process." He was paid a percentage of the construction costs.[31]

During the fall of 1861 usually 450 men were employed at the construction site, and by the end of the year nearly all of the foundation walls had been laid. The *Times* reported that the joints between the foundation stones were being "formed with lead, so as to prevent displacement by washing out of mortar" and assured readers that "none of the foundations have been laid in frosty weather." An old, 34-foot-deep well, directly in the line of the new foundations, had to be filled in before construction could proceed. By mid-January, it was expected, the walls would all extend above grade. To the reporter from the *Times* the progress appeared to have been "unusually rapid," but an editorial writer foresaw the construction as an "enormous additional burden" that would result in higher taxes and a "movement for effectual reform in our City affairs." In 1860 and 1861 the sum of $150,000 had been raised by tax revenue for construction of the courthouse, and by the close of 1861 a total of $87,000 had been expended.[32]

Favorable weather early in 1862 made it possible to resume construction by mid-March, and the commissioners, who now carried the name of Commissioners of New City Hall for Building a Court House, requested an appropriation of $38,000.25, all that then remained in the

comptroller's accounts for the building. In April 1862 the supervisors decided to issue $700,000 in county stock for the courthouse. Of that sum, $450,000 would be paid to the city for the land in the park, and the balance of $250,000 used to complete the building.[33]

The Board of Supervisors immediately asked the commissioners to prepare specifications for the remaining work and to advertise for proposals from contractors. By early June the *Times* reported some progress (the building was beginning "to assume definite proportions") and predicted that, when complete, it would be an "ornament to the city." The foundation walls had been "finished some time since, and the marble walls of the front begin to show themselves above the high board fence which surrounds the space in which the workmen are employed."[34]

Mayoral Stalemates and New Contracts

James Salmon resigned as a commissioner in the spring of 1862. Mayor George Opdyke used the resulting vacancy to veto payments for construction expenses, claiming that the commission had to be at full strength, with all three members. The supervisors, however, refused to approve the mayor's nominee, Timothy G. Churchill, and authorized the commission to consult with an attorney about the best way to move forward with the construction. Mayor

John Kellum. From Deborah S. Gardiner, "The Architecture of Commercial Capitalism: John Kellum and the Development of New York, 1840–1875" (Columbia Univerrsity Dissertation, 1979).

Request by John Kellum for payment for architectural services, 1864. The statement was certified by Cummings M. Tucker, who supervised the construction of the courthouse. Municipal Archives, New York City.

*Looking east across Broadway, with Chambers Street at left, showing
ground-floor walls of the courthouse under construction, c. 1863.*
Collection of The New-York Historical Society, neg. 220.

Opdyke refused to approve this consultation or any
requests payments, insisting that the supervisors accept
his appointment.[35]

The commissioners were becoming desperate for
funding so that work could move ahead more quickly.
The approved funds had been spent long ago, and
$60,000 in claims for labor and materials remained
unpaid. The vendors were becoming hard pressed: for
instance, in October the Phoenix Iron Company still had
not been paid for the 15-inch wrought-iron beams that
they had invoiced in June and August. With war raging in
the South, the commissioners asked all workers to take an
"oath of allegiance to the Government of the United
States." Several construction workers had already volun-
teered for service in the Union Army.[36]

In December 1862 the courthouse situation was
described as an "entangled state of affairs." The Board of
Supervisors still refused to confirm the mayor's choice for
the third commissioner; the mayor maintained that the
commission was acting illegally by not having its full number; the cost of building materials had escalated in the
wartime economy; and vendors who had accepted scrip

rather than cash were being forced to sell at a substantial
discount. Construction had been "greatly delayed and
embarrassed," and by mid-December work was completely suspended. The supervisors decided to rescind their
November 1861 decision to hand the work over to the
commissioners and instead re-directed their own Special
Committee on the New Court House to proceed with the
construction "with all possible dispatch." With backing
from the corporation counsel, Mayor Opdyke, true to
form, refused to approve these resolutions.[37]

But in January 1863, under Supervisor Tweed's spon-
sorship, the board decided to override the mayor's vetoes.
All outstanding claims were to be paid, and construction
was to resume. The work would be done under contracts
or by day labor, whatever the supervisors preferred.
Throughout the spring of 1863 the iron and marble contractors and the architect submitted vouchers for substantial amounts. The supervisors confidently overrode the
mayor's vetoes for payments to vendors and for the weekly payroll. Still, some payments were delayed, and during
the summer of 1863 three construction workers, writing
on behalf of their colleagues, petitioned the supervisors

quarry at Sheffield, where, it was said, plain rocks had, like precious metals, "furnished a fortune as dazzling as any recorded in the history of Pike's Peak or Oil City." The paper predicted that its "present generation of readers" would have passed away before the building was complete. It published a lengthy report comparing its cost to that of the new courthouse in Brooklyn. The *Times* exaggeratedly wrote that the $3.6 million spent on the Manhattan courthouse had "thus far produced a great deal of quarreling, fighting, grumbling, wondering and *construction*; but as yet, with the exception of one poor little corner set apart for the Court of Appeals, there is no more of a County Court-house than there was in 1858, when the original appropriation of $250,000 was made."[56]

A few months later the paper argued that while it was unquestionably true that the courthouse was "solid" and would "last for ages," it could have been made equally enduring "without such enormous outlay of material." The massive iron components, for example, appeared "to have been constructed without the slightest idea of the strength of materials, and the strain of parts, but solely with the view of getting as much iron into the building as possible." Furthermore, the paper argued, the "marvelous pilasters and friezes, and cornices, and dentils, and architectural moldings," all made of iron, should really have been made of marble. The door surrounds had been painted white, to imitate marble; a building of this cost, the paper stated, "ought to have all its parts in fact what they purport to be."[57]

By the end of 1868 the lower floors of the courthouse were occupied: the sheriff had moved into the northwest corner of the building, overlooking Broadway and Chambers Street; the county clerk was in the northeast corner; and the surrogate's offices were in the southeast corner, facing City Hall. Each official had a suite of three rooms, "all fitted up with elegant black-walnut furniture." The east side of the second floor was given over to the supreme court, while the city chamberlain and the county treasurer were elegantly accommodated in a large room overlooking Broadway. The two rooms at the northwest corner were expected to be used as courtrooms.[58]

Now that construction was further along, the *Times* readily agreed that there was "no doubt that the materials used and the work done are of the first quality." The outside doors were of iron, and on the inside the doors were of solid black walnut. The hallway floors were laid with marble; the concrete floors of the chambers were covered with yellow pine and then finished with Georgia pine. The outside walls were four to five feet thick. The Chambers Street portico and stoop, then nearing completion, would be the "finest piece of work" of its kind in America. At this point even the *Times* was ready to con-

"The Broken Door through Which the Robbery of Vouchers from the Comptroller's Office Was Effected," showing the etched glass and paneling of the interior doorways in the courthouse. The vouchers disappeared as charges of corruption were being investigated. From Frank Leslie's *Illustrated Newspaper*, October 13, 1871. Collection of The New-York Historical Society, image 45887.

cede that all of the building would at last be finished, except for the "costly and ornate cupola."

In mid-December 1868 it was projected that the interior would be ready for occupants on the first day of the New Year, and it might take another year to finish the exterior. But this schedule was not met, and bills kept piling up during 1869, for amounts even greater than before. In just one session in July, for example, the Board of Supervisors approved payments to E. V. Haughwout and Co. for $36,142.68, to the Eastchester Quarry Company for $67,961.75, to J. B. and W. W. Cornell and Co. for $65,599.18, and to John Kellum for $26,669.30.[59]

Considerable progress was made on the building during 1870. By the early spring of 1871 the Broadway facade was finished, and stoops were being built on the south side, facing City Hall. The quarters for the surrogate and the county clerk, as well as courtrooms, had been painted and decorated with frescoes. The vault for the safekeep-

The courthouse when it was still under construction in 1871. Only the lowest portions of the columns of the Chambers Street portico are in *place. From Harper's Weekly, September 9, 1871.* From *New York in the Nineteenth Century* (New York: Dover Publications, 1977).

ing of the county clerk's records was in place, and the sheriff had use of a new private office and more space for his deputies. Nevertheless, major elements remained unfinished. The Chambers Street portico still lacked its marble columns, and the massive dome, a very expensive undertaking, had not yet been built. As a result there was still no permanent roof over the center of the building.[60]

Charges of Corruption and Tweed's Trials

In 1870 Tweed forced through the legislature in Albany a new charter for New York City that significantly enhanced the power of the Tweed Ring. It increased the power of the mayor, abolished the old Board of Supervisors and created a new one, made modifications to the Board of Aldermen, and established a Board of Apportionment to oversee city spending. To clear up the county's existing financial commitments, Supervisor Tweed and his

cohorts Mayor A. Oakey Hall and Comptroller Richard Connolly were charged with the responsibility to pay the county's debts and "audit all submitted claims."[61]

At the same time charges of corruption were brewing. Some of Tweed's supporters had floated a proposal to erect a statue of him to commemorate his many contributions to the city. His detractors responded that the courthouse would be a better monument to the city, for it would illustrate "in all its parts, from the foundation-stone upward, the various stages in [his] rise, progress, and prosperous career." The *New York Times* charged in May 1871 that it was at the courthouse that Tweed had secured the "foundation of his fortunes, both pecuniary and political, it was there that he learned the true value of money, and its intimate connection with his own advancement." He was credited with securing the annual appropriations that now totaled an astounding $6.45 million. "Just imagine," the paper editorialized, "the untiring industry, the wear and tear of muscle, the anxiety of mind, the weary days and the sleepless nights, that it must have cost the 'Boss' to procure all these sums of money, and superintend their outlay."[62] The newspaper's pointed suggestion that the courthouse be Tweed's monument came to pass, for the building has long been popularly known as Tweed Courthouse.

Years earlier Tweed had used his affiliation with a new volunteer fire company, Americus Engine Company No. 6, established in 1848, as a stepping-stone to political power, and the symbol on the fire engine, the head of a Bengal tiger, would become the symbol of Tammany Hall, Tweed's infamous political machine. Although he had won a seat in Congress in 1852, Tweed favored local politics. Elected an alderman in 1851 and a supervisor in 1856, he filled key city and county posts with his Tammany pals. In 1860 he became chairman of the New York County Democratic Committee, and, as head of Tammany's general committee, he controlled nominations for mayor, governor, and other top posts. Tammany's power not only rested on the services that it

"Design for a Proposed Monumental Fountain in the City Hall Park," a political cartoon depicting William M. Tweed in the foreground, flanked by his associates Peter Sweeny and Richard B. Connolly. From *Harper's Weekly*, October 7, 1871. Courtesy of New York Public Library, Mid-Manhattan Library, Picture Collection.

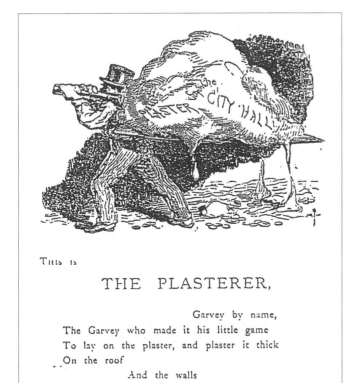

THIS IS

THE PLASTERER,

Garvey by name,
The Garvey who made it his little game
To lay on the plaster, and plaster it thick
On the roof
And the walls
And the wood
And the brick
Of the wonderful House
That TWEED built.

"This Is the Plasterer," cartoon and poem about Andrew Garvey, who was charged with submitting fraudulent bills for work at the court-house. From *The House That Tweed Built*, 1871.

On July 8, 1871, the *New York Times* unleashed evidence of a "chapter of Municipal rascality" that pointed to the "accumulated mass of official corruption which is being piled up against the Tammany Ring" and predicted that it soon would "descend like an avalanche upon their heads and crush them beneath its weight." The paper's exposé started with accusations that spaces for city armories and drill rooms had been rented and outfitted at exorbitant prices or never even occupied. Investigators had secured copies of the financial accounts and, based on that evidence, called Mayor Hall and Comptroller Connolly "thieves and swindlers," along with one of Tweed's business partners, James H. Ingersoll. Connolly and Hall, the paper alleged, approved the warrants authorizing payment of the sums stated and then handed warrants over to Ingersoll, who drew the funds from the Tweed Ring's own bank and divided the cash among Tweed, Hall, Connolly and Peter Sweeny, another Tammany operative. One would suppose, the paper continued, that contractor G. S. Miller was "the prince of carpenters": the accounts showed that he had billed $431,064.31 for work done for armories in only nine months. However, only a fraction of that sum fell to him; the rest went to Hall and Connolly. In another case, three or four tables and about forty chairs had cost taxpayers $170,729.60.[64] The system worked thus, the newspaper charged:

> A man does some work for the City authorities and charges $5,000 for it. When he presents his bill, one of Connolly's agents says to him, "We can't pay this, but make the amount $55,000 and you shall have your money at once." A warrant is drawn for $55,000, and endorsed by the presenter of the bill over to J. H. Ingersoll. He then receives five $1,000 bills, and the Ring pockets the $50,000. This is done every day, and done on a scale which will startle the most listless and indifferent.[65]

Some officials involved in the fraud had become so careless that they had assigned to some $636,000 of warrants a date that fell on a Sunday, when the offices would have been closed. Comptroller Connolly, it was said, now had armed men guarding his books.[66]

Each day brought more charges of corruption. Accounts showed that $565,731.34 had been spent on carpeting—enough, it was calculated, to spread three layers over the eight acres of all of City Hall Park. A visit to the courthouse, however, revealed that many floors were bare. Between 1868 and 1870 more than $2.8 million in warrants had been posted to the account of Andrew J. Garvey for plastering and materials and also for alterations and repairs at county buildings, including the courthouse, which was not even complete, let alone in need of repair.

provided to immigrants and the poor—work, food, and medical care for those in need—and the votes it then demanded of them; its power also relied on dishonest elections, where voters cast ballots more than once and illegal naturalizations, false registrations, and cheating were overlooked. During the 1860s Tweed's interests in a company in New York that printed city documents and the quarry in Massachusetts that supplied marble for the courthouse enriched him and afforded his family a comfortable life. However, despite his shortcomings, Tweed also provided important leadership during a time of frenzied, exponential growth in the city. He helped establish the city's professional fire and police departments; supported better almshouses, orphanages, public baths, and parochial schools; and argued that the site of the Metropolitan Museum of Art should be retained in Central Park. His public-works projects improved the city's streets, water supplies, and sewers, and he secured from the state more home rule for the city.[63]

"Who Stole the People's Money? 'Twas him," a political cartoon by Thomas
Nast depicting William M. Tweed at left, encircled by the courthouse
contractors and his Tammany cohorts. From *Harper's Weekly*, August 19, 1871.

Unfavorable comparisons were drawn to the Brooklyn
courthouse built in 1861–65: more had been charged for
the marble alone for Tweed's courthouse than it had cost
to build the entire Brooklyn courthouse. Thomas Nast's
cartoons skewering Tweed, the contractors, and the Tweed
Ring filled the pages of *Harper's Weekly*.[67]

The *Times* called for the defeat of Tammany candidates
in the next election and for criminal charges to be brought
against Hall and Connolly. It warned that if the public did
not soon come to the same conclusion, "then facts have lost
power to convince, and public spirit must be regarded as
dead." *Harper's Weekly* joined in, saluting the *Times* for its
"relentless and crushing exposures" of the ring and calling
the paper's investigations "a national service."[68]

Mayor Hall admitted that the vendors' charges had
been exorbitant but claimed that his role and the comptroller's were simply "ministerial" once the bills had been
approved by the Board of Supervisors. It was Tweed,
Harper's reminded its readers, who was the "head of the

Ring, the chairman of the Supervisors' committee upon
the Court-house, the chief sachem of Tammany, the head
of the city Department of Public Works by the appointment of the Mayor, and who, without any profession but
politics, has become notoriously rich."[69]

Political, business, and religious groups called for the
money to be returned and for the perpetrators of the
frauds to be prosecuted. Samuel Tilden, a Democrat who
disliked Tammany but had nevertheless befriended its
leaders, attacked Tweed and Tammany with a strategy that
promoted new Democratic leadership and propelled him
to the governorship. At the end of August 1871 a Joint
Special Committee of the Board of Supervisors and the
Board of Aldermen and the Associated Citizens set about
investigating the charges of theft and corruption, hiring
multiple accountants and contractors to evaluate the
work done. A civic group sought injunctions against the
mayor, the comptroller, the aldermen, the supervisors,
and Tweed that would prevent further expenditures and

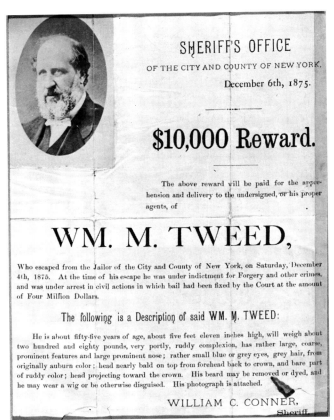

SHERIFF'S OFFICE
OF THE CITY AND COUNTY OF NEW YORK.
December 6th, 1875.

$10,000 Reward.

The above reward will be paid for the apprehension and delivery to the undersigned, or his proper agents, of

WM. M. TWEED,

Who escaped from the Jailor of the City and County of New York, on Saturday, December 4th, 1875. At the time of his escape he was under indictment for Forgery and other crimes, and was under arrest in civil actions in which bail had been fixed by the Court at the amount of Four Million Dollars.

The following is a Description of said WM. M. TWEED:

He is about fifty-five years of age, about five feet eleven inches high, will weigh about two hundred and eighty pounds, very portly, ruddy complexion, has rather large, coarse, prominent features and large prominent nose; rather small blue or grey eyes, grey hair, from originally auburn color; head nearly bald on top from forehead back to crown, and bare part of ruddy color; head projecting toward the crown. His beard may be removed or dyed, and he may wear a wig or be otherwise disguised. His photograph is attached.

WILLIAM C. CONNER,
Sheriff

Sheriff's poster offering a reward for the capture of William M. Tweed following his escape on December 4, 1875. Collection of The New-York Historical Society, image 31106.

prevent them from raising or collecting real-estate taxes. Tweed and the other officials denied any wrongdoing. The judge granted a permanent injunction and identified the comptroller as the "official mainly responsible." Connolly, the comptroller, refused to resign. At a rally in September Tweed accepted the nomination to serve again in the state Senate, but he spent the next years in court and, ultimately, in jail.[70]

In October 1871 a grand jury began hearing charges against Mayor Hall, claiming that he had failed to audit bills according to the 1870 city charter, but witnesses were evasive and Hall was acquitted. The State of New York filed a summons in state supreme court demanding that Tweed, Elbert A. Woodward (a clerk to the Board of Supervisors), and contractors Ingersoll and Garvey return $6 million in payments that had not been audited properly and charging collusion among them. Tweed was arrested but released when he raised $1 million in bail. Some of his co-defendants, including Woodward, Ingersoll, and Garvey, skipped town. Meanwhile, officials determined that the cost of constructing and furnishing the court-

house now totaled $11 to $12 million. The reform-minded Republicans handily won all the Assembly races in the November elections, but not Tweed's state Senate seat. Connolly resigned and was arrested. In mid-December Tweed was arrested again, this time on criminal charges of felony, grand larceny, and forgery; Tammany stripped him of his power, and his chair in the state Senate remained empty. More indictments followed. Plumber Garvey and John H. Keyser turned state's witness. Mayor Hall was found innocent.[71]

Tweed was tried on a 220-count indictment dated October 23, 1872. He appeared before the court of oyer and terminer, a state criminal court, which convened in the new courthouse; he was charged not with outright theft but with failing to audit claims properly. Jury selection began on January 8, 1873. Garvey appeared as a witness, stating that he had received a check for more than $1 million; however, before cashing it he wrote his own check for 65 percent of that amount, which was then deposited in Tweed's bank account. Keyser appeared again as a state's witness. On January 31 the jurors concluded their deliberations without agreeing on a verdict. A new trial began the following November, and this time the jury found Tweed guilty of 204 counts. The sheriff took him into custody, leading him down the west stairs of the courthouse and out to Chambers Street. The *Times* announced the conviction with the headline "Justice at Last," as the news "flew through the City with electric rapidity."[72]

On November 19, 1873, Tweed was given a thirteen-year sentence and taken to the prison on Blackwell's Island. After the Court of Appeals determined that holding him for more than one year was illegal, he was released in June 1875 but immediately arrested again on civil charges. This time he was put in the Ludlow Street jail. He could not raise the $3 million bail, but he did take advantage of privileges extended to certain prisoners that allowed them to leave jail occasionally. On December 4, 1875, Tweed did not return to his cell after his day out; he fled to Florida, Cuba, and in September 1876 to Spain, where authorities arrested him as soon as he landed. By late November 1876 Tweed was back at the Ludlow Street jail, depressed and in poor health. Other suits had been brought against him while he was away, and in March a jury determined that the state was owed more than $6.5 million in stolen funds. Tweed now offered to testify and surrender his remaining property, but he was rebuffed. His confession, published in the New York newspapers, included details on the kick-backs to the Board of Supervisors and implicated J. B. and W. W. Cornell and Co., but it did not win Tweed his freedom; he remained in jail. By 1878 judgments against him amounted to $25 million.[73]

In 1877 the Board of Aldermen had joined the fray, holding its own hearings on the Tweed Ring's alleged

that Eidlitz's "new style of architecture," while perhaps suitable for a "fashionable church on Fifth Avenue, or a highly decorated lager beer brewery at Yorkville," was "cheap and tawdry in comparison with the elaborate finishing and classic exterior of the present structure." The *American Architect and Building News* also denounced the new construction (but misread Kellum's cast iron as stone): "Of course no attention was paid to the design of the existing building and within and without a rank Romanesque runs cheek by jowl with the old Italian, one bald, and the other florid; cream-colored brick and buff sandstone come in juxtaposition to white marble."[84]

Threats, Neglect, and Redemption

During the twentieth century the courthouse survived several threats of demolition, but underwent some minor changes and one major alteration. A 1910 plan for new

municipal buildings proposed that the courthouse be demolished, but it continued to serve as the county courthouse until a new courthouse, located at 60 Centre Street, was completed in 1929. By 1908 the walls of the rotunda had been painted gray, obliterating Eidlitz's polychrome brickwork. In 1910 work was under way to install two ornate, open-cage electric elevators with corrugated-iron covered penthouses housing the elevator machinery on the roof. A third elevator was built in 1913 for the justices of the supreme court.[85]

Special revenue bonds in the amount of $211,000 were authorized in 1927 for alterations to convert the county courthouse into city courts. The largest projected costs were for general construction and new equipment; other expenditures were for plumbing, electrical, and heating work; window shades; and floor coverings.[86] Revolving doors were installed at the ground and upper entrances, and another set of doors was added at the entrances to rooms on the first through third floors.

Opposite: Second story of the rotunda, showing the juxtaposition of the ornamental cast-iron elements designed by John Kellem as part of the original construction of the courthouse and the polychrome-brick archway designed by Leopold Eidlitz during the 1880s, photograph by Walter Smalling, 1979. Library of Congress, Prints and Photographs Division, Historic American Buildings Survey, No. NY-5688-12.

View along Chambers Street, showing the original main entrance with the broad flight of stairs leading up to the portico, photograph by George P. Hall, early 20th century. Collection of The New-York Historical Society, neg. 69046.

The north façade after the stairway was removed to accommodate the widening of Chambers Street, photograph by Walter Smalling, 1979.

Library of Congress, Prints and Photographs Division, Historic American Buildings Survey, No. NY-5688-1.

A major change occurred in 1941, when the lower flight of granite stairs leading up to the portico was removed to accommodate the widening of Chambers Street. A parapet wall was built across the base of the truncated stairway, and a small vestibule at ground level under the portico became the primary entrance. This work was begun in April 1942 as a Works Progress Administration project and completed four months later.[87] During the war the skylight over the rotunda was covered over, and the stained-glass laylight was removed.

In March 1961 the city courts moved to new quarters at 111 Centre Street, and the family court, municipal archives, and various other city offices occupied the courthouse. Maintenance was neglected, and the building's polychrome masonry and cast-iron interiors were covered with layers of "mud-colored municipal paint."[88] With the stairs to its primary facade removed, Tweed Courthouse received even less attention from passers-by.

Boss Tweed's shadow continued to haunt the courthouse. Even in the 1970s, a century after Tweed's trial, the building was still such a powerful symbol of municipal corruption that its designation as a city landmark was considered too controversial. In 1974 the Manhattan Civic Center Task Force, organized by Mayor Abraham Beame, proposed that the courthouse be demolished to make room for an executive office annex to City Hall. The task force's report described the courthouse as one million cubic feet of "unusable space," cited its "extreme physical deterioration," and recommended that it be replaced with what was called a "sort of gas station modern" annex.[89]

The Municipal Art Society, the Victorian Society, the New York Chapter of the American Institute of Architects, and the Fine Arts Federation called for designating the courthouse as a city landmark. *New York Times* architecture critic Ada Louise Huxtable cited recent changes in public attitudes, which, she said, were moving away from the

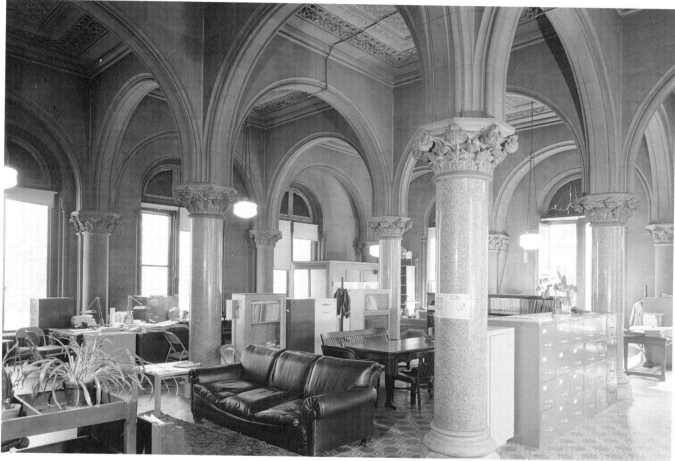

City government offices on the second-floor room of the south wing, photograph by Walter Smalling, 1979. Library of Congress, Prints and Photographs Division, Historic American Buildings Survey, No. NY-5688-24.

"conventional wisdom that the building is nothing but a shoddy piece of graft" and toward an understanding that it was a "legitimate New York landmark on every level from architectural to political history, and as a handsome period building as well." Paul O'Dwyer, city council president and co-chair of a "Save the Tweed" committee, enthusiastically endorsed its August 1974 listing in the National Register of Historic Places; two years later he moved his staff into the building. Ultimately, the city's fiscal crisis, erupting in 1975, precluded its demolition.[90]

In 1978 another task force, appointed by Mayor Edward Koch, worked to save the building, which had been designated a National Historic Landmark in 1976. Two years later, with the leadership of the New York Landmarks Conservancy and under the direction of architect Giorgio Cavaglieri, the original corrugated-iron roofing was replaced with asphalt roofing to help curtail further damage to the building. In 1980 the New

York City Department of General Services commissioned the engineering firm of Amman and Whitney, assisted by Beyer Blinder Belle Architects, to prepare a preliminary study of the condition of the building and its potential for reuse. Later, measured drawings were prepared. Preservation of the building was significantly advanced in 1984, when its exterior and certain elements of its interior—the rotunda, the courtroom in the south wing, and circulation spaces—were designated as landmarks by the New York City Landmarks Preservation Commission, which earlier had prepared a historic structure report for the building. Meanwhile, the interior was featured in several films, including *Kramer vs. Kramer*, *Dressed to Kill*, and *The Verdict*, and in the television series *Law and Order*.

With the architectural and historical significance of the courthouse now publicly and officially established, comprehensive planning for its restoration began under the auspices of the Department of General Services in 1989. At the direction of Mayor Rudolph W. Giuliani, the restoration program was begun in earnest in 1999 by the New York City Economic Development Corporation (EDC) with John G. Waite Associates, Architects. The fabled landmark was ready for a new life.

Finding a New Use for the Courthouse

Tweed Courthouse has had a long history of changing uses, dating back to its original construction, when it was to be the new City Hall. When Boss William Tweed assumed control of the construction, its intended use was changed to the county courthouse. Over the years the building housed city courts, family court, and finally various city government offices.

In December 1998 the Museum of the City of New York recommended to Mayor Rudolph Giuliani that Tweed Courthouse be restored as a multi-use cultural attraction and learning resource facility that would supplement the museum's exciting landmark headquarters at Fifth Avenue and 103rd Street. The new use would celebrate the history of New York City and utilize the grand spaces of the building appropriately. The initial project planning was done by Ralph Applebaum Associates, exhibit-design consultants to the museum. When the New York City Economic Development Corporation assumed responsibility for the restoration of the building in 1999, this concept, called "Gateway New York," was refined in a feasibility report issued by John G. Waite Associates, Architects working with Ralph Applebaum Associates. The restored building was to accommodate visitors' welcome center, restaurant, café, museum store, and galleries on the ground floor. The restored courtrooms on the main floor of the original building would house galleries and a digital theater.

It was expected that the Museum of the City of New York would have overall responsibility for the building and for three permanent galleries. Five changing exhibit galleries would be used by other museums located throughout the five boroughs of New York City. In the theme of "Gateway New York," visitors could sample what other museums had to offer, so that by coming to one location, they could decide which ones they wished to visit. These galleries could also accommodate traveling exhibitions from municipal museums around the world.

The former courtroom created in 1881 was to be restored for ceremonial receptions and city-sponsored social events. The third floor was to be reserved for the Mayor's Office. The west half was to house press and broadcast facilities, a briefing room for the mayor, and the east half would serve as a conference center. Offices for this facility, and museum operations, would be located on the fourth floor.

The "Gateway New York" plan provided for both cultural and government uses, which for the most part, were compatible with the historic character of Tweed Courthouse. The special configurations of the courtrooms would be preserved. Overall, the proposed program was sensitive to the special character and significance of the building. This reuse program was tentatively accepted by the City, and EDC was authorized to proceed with the restoration of the entire building in March 1999.

However, beginning in late 2000, the city implemented a major change in direction for the courthouse and the museum. In his State of the City address in January 2001, Mayor Giuliani announced a new agreement: rather than using the building as supplemental space, the museum would move its entire operation to Tweed Courthouse and would vacate its Fifth Avenue building.

Meanwhile, EDC continued with design and construction, with work now scheduled to be completed by December 2001, except for the painting and carpeting. It was anticipated that EDC would then turn over the restored building to the Museum of the City of New York by January 1, 2001, for fitting-out as a museum facility.

The museum selected an architect whose previous museum experience was primarily planning new buildings, and it soon became apparent that the museum's program was more appropriate for a purpose-built, new museum facility rather than the monumental historic spaces in the courthouse. Proposed modifications to meet the requirements of the program included raising the roof and constructing new spaces above the original roofline, removing floors and walls to accommodate a large auditorium, removing bearing walls between courtrooms to create larger gallery spaces, filling in courtroom windows to provide new "black box" galleries, and installing additional public restrooms in some of the courtrooms.

Had this program been carried out, it would have seriously changed the historic character of the building. The removal of interior partitions would have required the installation of new HVAC and electrical systems and resulted in the undoing of work recently completed at a cost of millions of dollars. Friction developed between the museum and EDC, which had worked very hard over the previous two years to design and construct a restoration program that respected the landmark quality of the building while providing high-standard museum-quality HVAC and electrical systems that would allow the building to be used for multiple functions.

As the museum's plans for changing the interior of the building became public, the historic-preservation

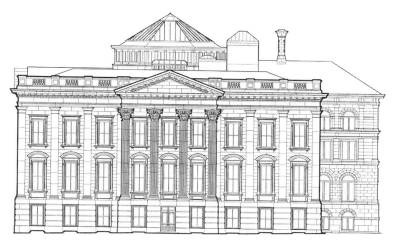

West elevation facing Broadway before restoration.

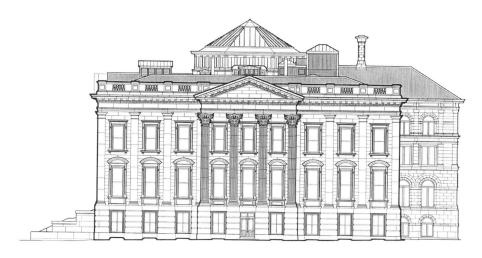

West elevation facing Broadway after restoration.

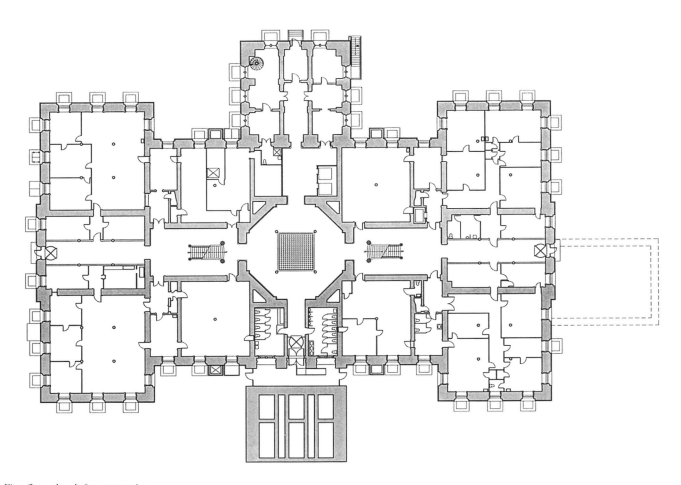

First-floor plan before restoration.

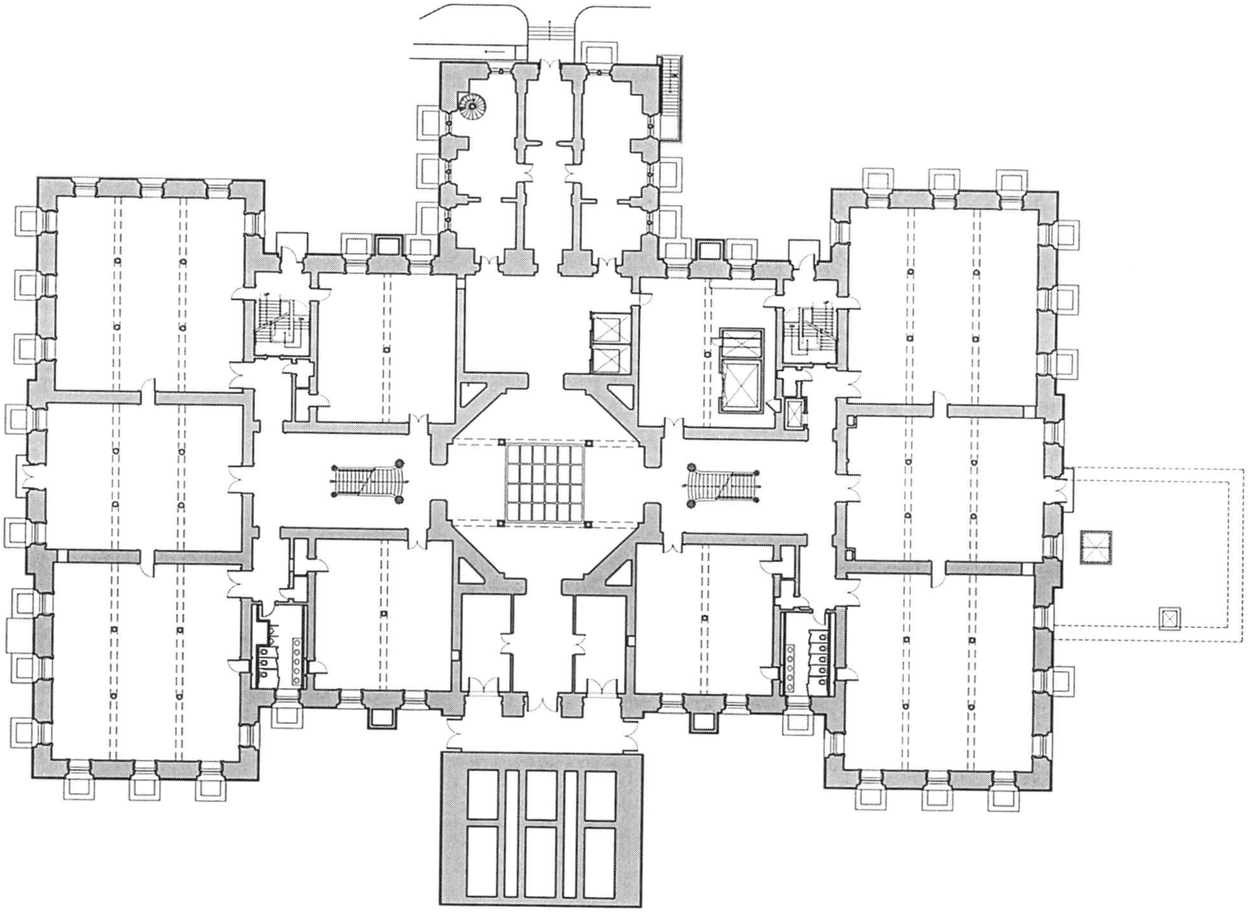

First-floor plan after restoration. The major spaces have been restored to their original volumes.

Intro-21 Second-floor plan before restoration. The original main entrance hall has been divided into public restrooms and a narrow hallway.

Second-floor plan after restoration. The main entrance hall has been returned to its original form and the Chambers Street stair rebuilt. New fire stairs and public restrooms were inserted in former service rooms.

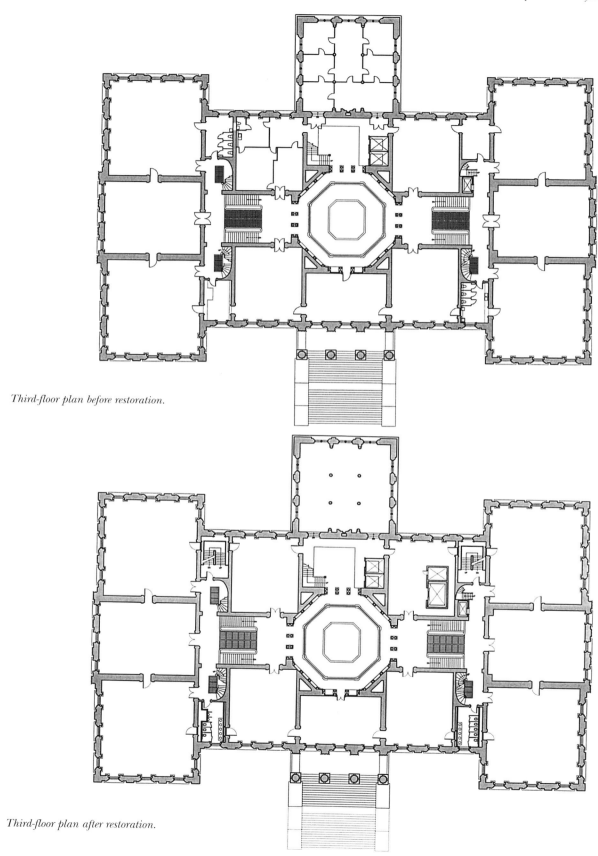

Third-floor plan before restoration.

Third-floor plan after restoration.

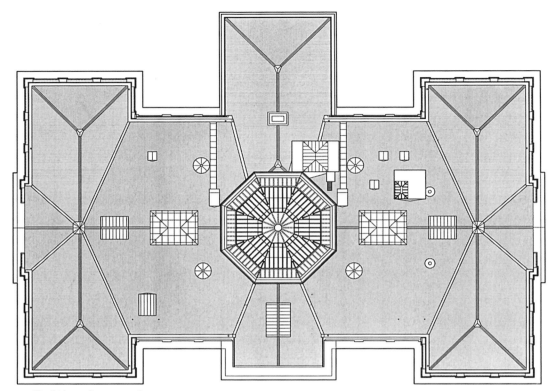

Roof plan after restoration.

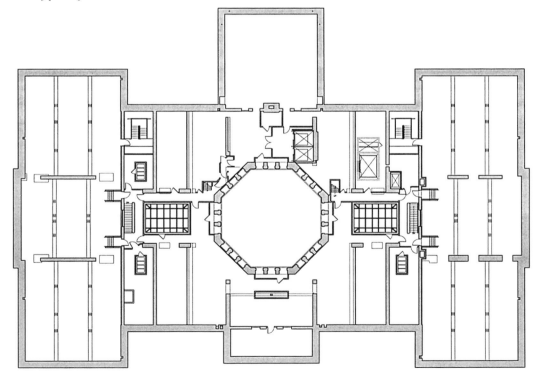

Attic plan after restoration. Because of its limited headroom and lack of natural light, the attic houses mechanical equipment.

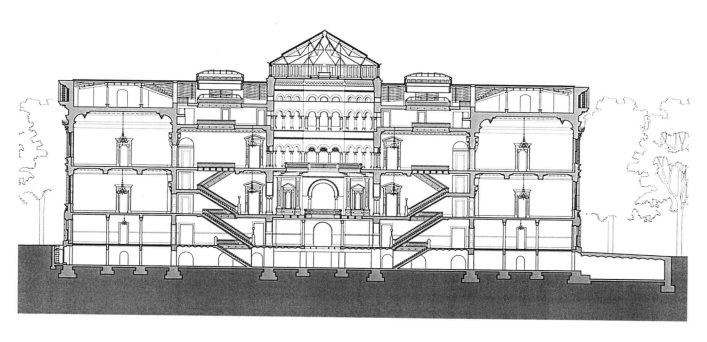

Cross section looking south after restoration.

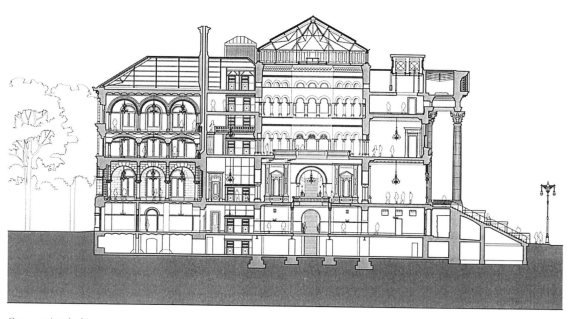

Cross section looking west after restoration.

CHAPTER TWO

Developing a Restoration Plan

In 1988 the City of New York decided to repair and restore Tweed Courthouse. The Department of General Services (DGS), the agency then responsible for the design and construction of municipally owned buildings, was charged with this task.

In the fall of 1988 DGS initiated a process to select a team of architects/engineers to oversee the restoration of the courthouse by issuing a request for qualifications. Several architectural firms responded, and four, all with considerable historic-preservation experience, were short-listed by a panel made up of DGS staff with advisors from the Landmarks Preservation Commission. The team assembled by Mesick•Cohen•Waite Architects, the predecessor firm to John G. Waite Associates, Architects, was selected for the project. The firm had been responsible for many significant restoration projects, including H. H. Richardson's Senate Chamber in the New York State Capitol in Albany; Blair House, the President's Guest House Complex in Washington, D.C.; and many historic courthouses and city halls throughout New York State, particularly the Ontario County Court House in Canandaigua and Kingston City Hall.

The John G. Waite Associates, Architects team had been carefully assembled in order to secure all the requisite professional skills, and most of the consultants had previously worked with the architects on comparable restoration projects. Key members of the Mesick•Cohen•Waite team included Robert Silman Associates, structural engineers; Goldman Copeland Batlan, P. C., mechanical, electrical, and plumbing engineers; and Norman R. Weiss, masonry consultant.

The Department of General Services staff who worked with the architectural and engineering team, included Adrienne Bresnan, deputy commissioner; Sarelle T. Weisberg, program manager, Public Works Unit; and Anne Khouri, project director, Tweed Courthouse. Other DGS staff members who later joined the project team included architects James Zethraus and David Holowka, both of whom made significant contributions to the project.

Planning for the restoration work began early in 1989 with an initial examination of the building to determine its condition and major problems. The development of the scope of work for a comprehensive feasibility study was undertaken jointly by DGS and the architects. The

purpose of the study was to examine the fabric of the building in detail and present a comprehensive approach for the treatment of the building that would include detailed recommendations. The feasibility study report was completed in 1991. It was the essential first step in planning the project, and it had enduring value: recommendations it made were still valid at the end of the project, and dog-eared copies of the report were still being used in the construction trailer when the final finish work was being completed over a decade later.

The format for the feasibility report, developed specifically for Tweed Courthouse, proved to be very effective as a model for other large historic public buildings, when modified to take into account individual conditions. The report for Tweed Courthouse was based on sound documentary research and a thorough investigation of the building fabric, from the monumental cast ironwork to the routing of the smallest ventilation chase in the stone walls and the condition of each window. The report contained the following chapters:

1. Exterior, which dealt with masonry, windows, doors, roofs, and bird-proofing. Detailed analyses of the stone and windows were included in the appendices.

2. Interior, which included an overall evaluation of the organization of spaces in the building and the circulation systems. Each floor was evaluated individually, from the basement to the attic, with separate sections on the rotunda, stair halls, and elevators. It included preliminary analyses of decorative finishes, historic lighting, and the rotunda's stained-glass laylight.

3. Utility Systems, which included heating, ventilation, and air conditioning; and electrical, plumbing, and fire-protection systems.

4. Site, which dealt with landscaping, fencing, street furniture, paving, and archaeology.

As the feasibility study evolved, it became apparent that dealing with the exterior masonry was the key to the survival of the building. A comprehensive examination revealed major structural problems with the stone, especially at the cornice level. DGS immediately authorized the architects to direct a program for cleaning the stone and erecting scaffolding around the entire building so that a detailed examination of each stone could be undertaken. Temporary shoring was installed to protect pedestrians from falling stone fragments.

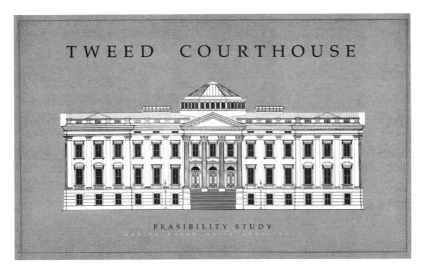

1991 Feasibility Study.

As part of the analysis of the exterior masonry, each stone was numbered and its level of deterioration recorded on drawings. This information was then incorporated into contract documents that identified which stones were to receive various repair treatments and which stones were to be replaced. Below is a diagram of the north portico, facing Chambers Street. Drawing by Mesick•Cohen•Waite Architects.

Opposite: A chart that summarizes the condition of each stone and provides recommendations for treatments.

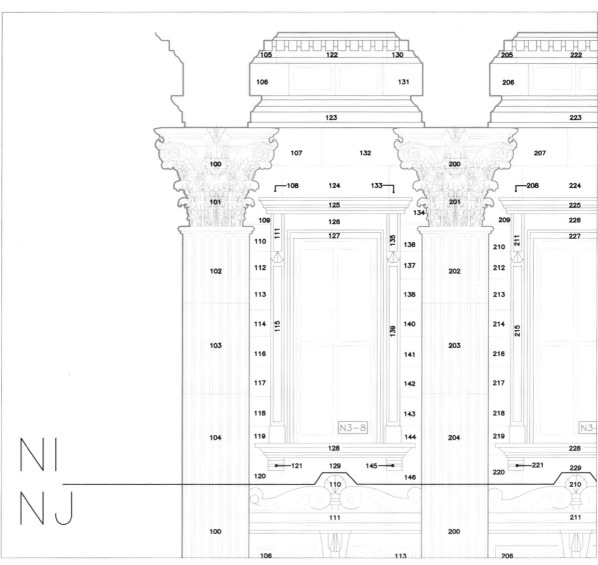

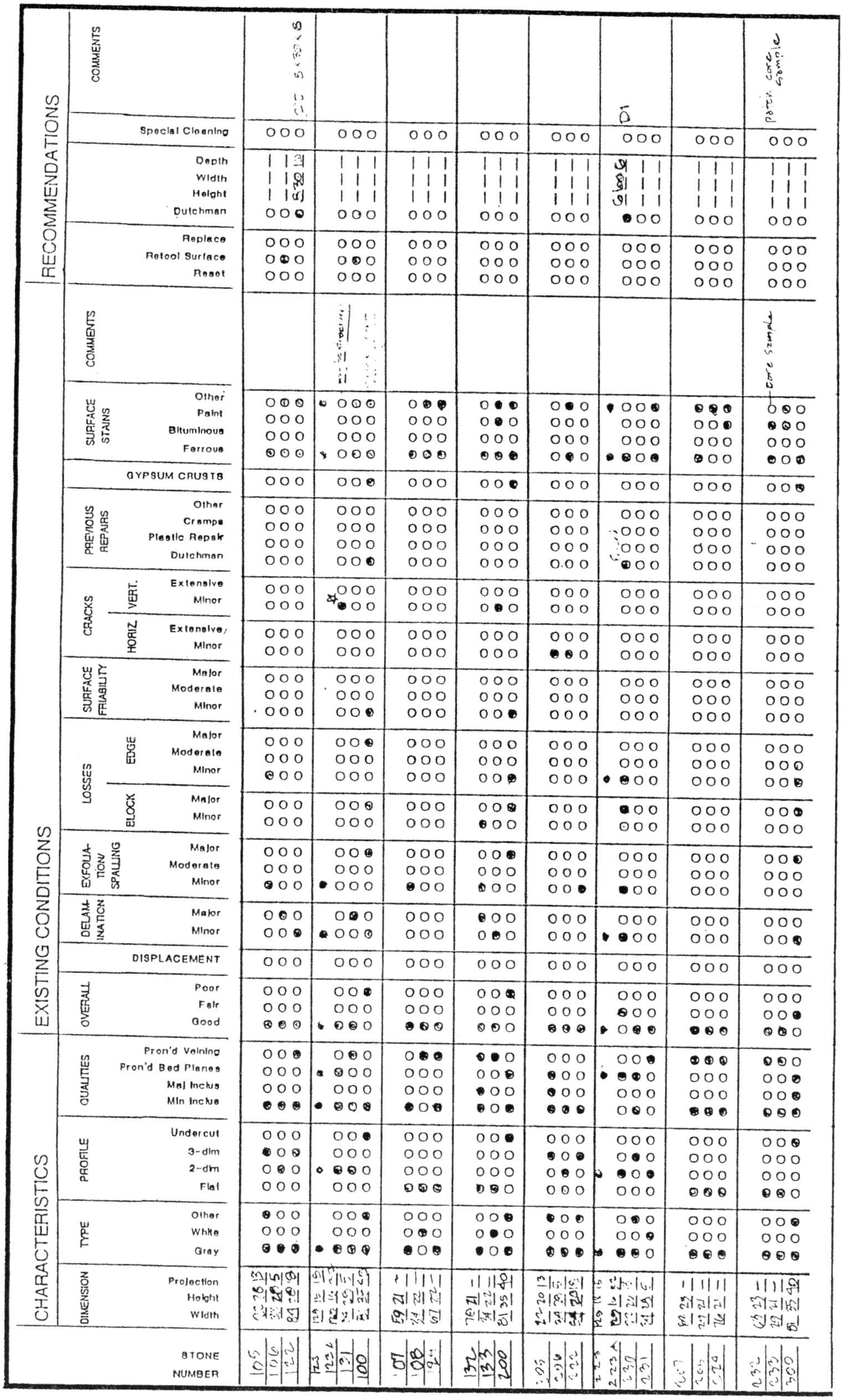

			COMMENTS	RECOMMENDATIONS

A condition survey chart organized into two major sections: **CHARACTERISTICS / EXISTING CONDITIONS** (left) and **RECOMMENDATIONS** (right). Each stone is recorded in a column with O / filled-circle markings indicating degree.

Row categories (top to bottom):

RECOMMENDATIONS
- COMMENTS
- Special Cleaning
- Depth
- Width
- Height
- Dutchman
- Replace
- Retool Surface
- Reset

EXISTING CONDITIONS
- COMMENTS
- SURFACE STAINS: Other, Paint, Bituminous, Ferrous
- GYPSUM CRUSTS
- PREVIOUS REPAIRS: Other, Cramps, Plastic Repair, Dutchman
- CRACKS — VERT.: Extensive, Minor
- CRACKS — HORIZ.: Extensive, Minor
- SURFACE FRIABILITY: Major, Moderate, Minor
- LOSSES — EDGE: Major, Moderate, Minor
- LOSSES — BLOCK: Major, Minor
- EXFOLIATION / SPALLING: Major, Moderate, Minor
- DELAMINATION: Major, Minor
- DISPLACEMENT
- OVERALL: Poor, Fair, Good

CHARACTERISTICS
- QUALITIES: Pron'd Veining, Pron'd Bed Planes, Maj Inclus, Min Inclus
- PROFILE: Undercut, 3-dim, 2-dim, Flat
- TYPE: Other, White, Gray
- DIMENSION: Projection, Height, Width
- STONE NUMBER

In addition, the preparation of the feasibility study established the protocol for working with the various city agencies having regulatory authority over the project, particularly the New York City Landmarks Preservation Commission (LPC), the New York City Department of Buildings (DOB), and the New York City Fire Department (FDNY). The relationships established with these agencies during the preparation of the study lasted throughout the entire restoration and were critical to its ultimate success. These agencies became in effect partners in planning the project. The LPC staff members were strong advocates throughout the process. LPC staff member Donald Plotts served as a very effective advisor to DGS during the architect selection process and the feasibility study phase. Kim Hoyt represented the LPC during the 1999–2001 restoration, attending the weekly project meetings. The support of the LPC staff was instrumental in encouraging the city to adhere to the highest preservation practices.

Corridor of ground floor used as makeshift storage area before restoration.

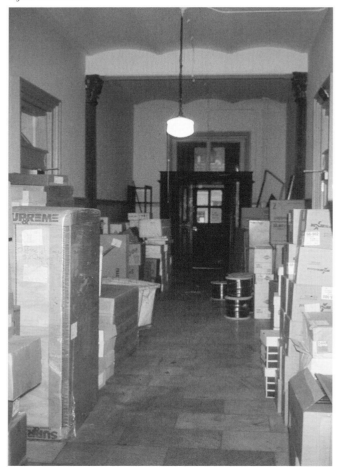

The feasibility study was completed in 1991; it was fully endorsed by DGS, LPC, and other city agencies. Funding, although limited to design fees and construction costs for the upgrading of the elevators, was allocated to the project, and major appropriations were scheduled for what were called "the outer years," usually three to six years in the future. The city's financial condition and the lack of a single, strong occupant for the building caused this schedule to slip. During the feasibility study phase, it was proposed that several small agencies occupy the building rather than one large single department.

During the administration of Mayor David Dinkins (1990–94) there were several proposals for the use of the courthouse, but none came to fruition. However, in 1993 it was decided to upgrade the three existing elevators—one of the last remaining manned attendant-operated open-cage cab elevators in a city building. The elevators would be converted to automatic operation and the historic open-cage cabs restored.

Because the Department of Buildings had participated in the development of the initial fire-management study and agreed with its general approach for code compliance, it was possible to proceed immediately with design and preparation of contract documents for the elevator project. Michael Curcio and Robert A. Petito Jr., both associates of Mesick•Cohen•Waite Architects, were project managers and John G. Waite was principal-in-charge. City responsibility for the project was handled by James Zethraus, Anne Khouri, and David Holowka. The architectural firm was reorganized as John G. Waite Associates, Architects in 1995. Michael Curcio, Robert Petito, and Douglas Bucher, formerly associates, became principals of the new firm and were actively involved in various aspects of the courthouse project.

Elevator construction work began in February 1993 and was carried out using the city's standard construction-procurement practices, including adherence to New York State's Wicks Law. After contract documents were prepared by the architects and approved by the city, the work was publicly advertised to prospective contractors. The Wicks Law was passed by the New York State legislature early in the twentieth century and requires that general construction, HVAC, electrical, and plumbing work for all state and local government projects be bid separately and that separate contracts be awarded for public construction projects. Thus the mechanical and electrical contractors are all prime contractors, rather than subcontractors to the general contractor. Intended to prevent abuses to small subcontractors, the Wicks Law makes it difficult for government agencies and design teams to coordinate large construction projects, especially those involving restoration work, because there is no single entity responsible for coordinating the construction work among the contractors. Despite strong efforts over the past several decades to repeal it because of the additional costs for public construction projects, the Wicks Law is still in effect. Although there were delays during the construction period, the elevator renovation project was finally completed in May 1999. Close cooperation between DGS, the architects, and LPC eventually resulted in a successful project.

During the first years of the administration of Mayor Giuliani, there were several proposals for the restoration and use of the courthouse. However, none advanced beyond the discussion stage until February 1999, when the mayor announced that Tweed Courthouse would be completely restored by the end of his administration in December of 2001. This allowed about two and a half years for design and construction, a seemingly impossible task. To oversee the project, the mayor turned to the New York City Economic Development Corporation, a public-benefit corporation established by the city to carry out large and complex construction projects. Although not normally used for historic-preservation purposes, EDC, under the leadership of President Michael Carey and Executive Vice President Melvin Glickman, turned out to be the ideal agency for carrying out the project. Mel Glickman, who had more than four decades of public-sector construction experience, provided the day-to-day leadership and direction for the project and was instrumental

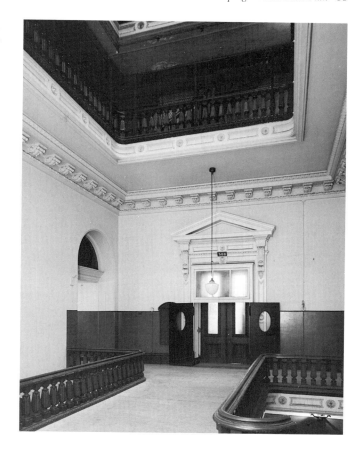

The east stair hall at the third floor before restoration. The skylights have been covered over and a plywood floor installed over the original glass tile flooring. Photograph by Walter Smalling, 1979. Library of Congress, Prints and Photographs Division, Historica Building Survey, NY-5688-19.

Original second-floor courtroom before restoration showing typical conditions of deterioration and marginal use of spaces as indicated by the peeling paint, makeshift electrical wiring, motley collection of furnishings, and inadequate lighting. Photograph by Walter Smalling, 1979. Library of Congress, Prints and Photographs Division, Historica Building Survey, NY-5688-33.

Original third-floor courtroom designed by
John Kellum and used as offices before the restoration.

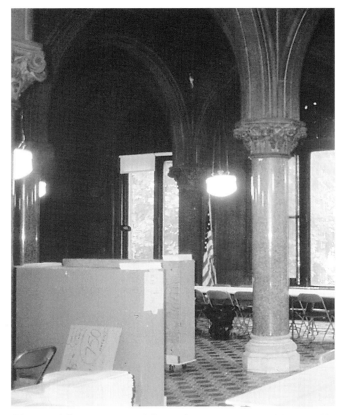

The second-floor courtroom of the south wing was designed by Leopold
Eidlitz. Before the restoration it was used as a meeting and work space.

in seeing it through to a successful conclusion. Presiding over the weekly job meetings, he followed each component of the complex project and made sure that they stayed on schedule and within budget and that decisions were made in a timely and definitive manner.

Because of EDC's involvement, the project could be carried out using a construction manager who held all the subcontracts and coordinated the work of the subcontractors, thus avoiding many Wicks Law problems. A selection process for the construction manager was developed by EDC, and Bovis Lend Lease (formerly Lehrer McGovern Bovis) was chosen for the project in March 1999. Bovis had also served as the construction manager for the Grand Central Terminal restoration project. The Bovis team was led by Joan Gerner, Donald Curtis, and Bill Hickman.

Once the construction manager was under contract, the architects, under the direction of John Waite and Robert Petito, and the Bovis field staff developed a detailed project schedule and budget that subdivided the job into smaller components that could be carried out in a logical sequence so that the final deadline could be met. Priorities were established, and items requiring long lead

times, such as the replacement stone for the facade and mechanical equipment, were identified. This procedure enabled those items to be ordered, even before the subcontractor who would install them was selected. Eventually more than one hundred separate construction contracts and dozens of individual contractors were utilized to complete the project. The preparatory work, which began in 1989, enabled the architects to issue contract documents for the initial phases of the project quickly in 1999, including those for the restoration of the exterior stonework.

In order to meet the mayor's very demanding schedule and to provide close monitoring of the complexities of the project, the architects established an office on site, located initially within the building and then, after work began, in construction trailers one level above the street on scaffolding. The bulk of the architectural working drawings for the project was produced in this field office. This integrated approach was critical to completing the project on schedule and within budget. However, the onsite office had a disadvantage: the architects were at times too accessible to the construction manager and the contractors and thus were often involved in solving many problems that otherwise would have been handled by the construction team.

The site office was directed by Nancy A. Rankin, an associate in the firm of John G. Waite Associates, Architects who had previously worked on the restoration of other large public buildings such as the Armory-Gymnasium at the University of Wisconsin–Madison and the Harry S. Truman Library in Independence, Missouri. Joining her in the office were Nicholas Cates and Andrew Sniderman, two recent graduates of the University of Cincinnati; John Chester, who had worked on rehabilitation projects with several New York City architectural firms; and Lee Pinckney, who had worked on the earlier feasibility study. Each member of the architectural team was assigned responsibility for defined areas of the design and construction. Working with the team were various principals and associates from the Albany office, including John Waite, Robert Petito, Douglas Bucher, Michael Curcio, and William Palmer. Specifications for the entire project were prepared by Dede Nash.

The consulting engineering team consisted of ARUP (mechanical, electrical, and fire engineering), led by Imtiaz Mulla, who had worked on the feasibility study while employed by Goldman, Copeland, and Batlan engineers; Robert Silman Associates (structural engineers) led by Robert Silman; Fisher Marantz Stone (lighting); Van Deusen Associates (vertical transportation); JAM Consultants (building code expediters); Langan Engineering and Environmental Services (civil engineer-

ing); and NASCO Construction Services (cost estimators). The historical research consultant was Mount Ida Press, and the archaeologist for the project was Hartgen Archaeological Services. Many of these consultants, particularly the mechanical/electrical and structural engineers and Mount Ida Press, had previously worked with John G. Waite Associates, Architects on the restoration of monumental historic buildings.

As in the feasibility study, historical research was essential for understanding the existing conditions of the building and the deterioration of the historic building materials. Because major restoration work was to be carried out in the building, it was decided to undertake new historical research to supplement the historic structure report. It was important to continue expanding the research begun in 1989, particularly focusing on the construction history of the building and not just its political and social history. As part of the restoration, all of the original construction records were reviewed, the first time that they were examined in a comprehensive manner since the trial of Boss Tweed over a century earlier. Located in several repositories in New York City, these records provided insight into how the building came into being and how the Tweed Ring actually functioned.

Good communication was crucial in a complex construction project with such a compressed schedule. In addition to daily interactions among the architects, construction managers, and contractors, the weekly meetings presided over by Mel Glickman were attended by the

Originally a single large courtroom space, the third floor of the south wing had been divided during the twentieth century into a dozen smaller spaces, which were used as offices.

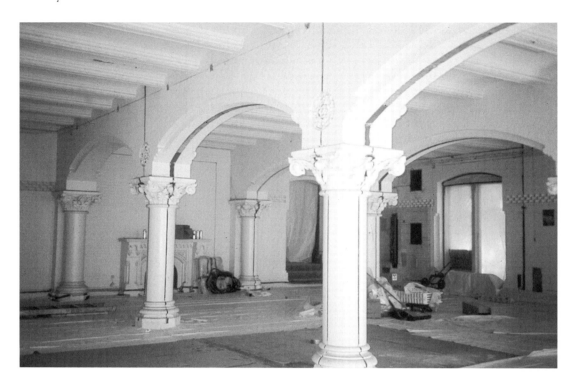

The third floor of the south wing during restoration after the later partitions had been removed, but before the paint had been stripped from the polychromed brick and stone masonry.

architects, engineers, specialized consultants, construction manager, contractors (as needed), and members from city agencies, including Terri Bahr from the Economic Development Corporation; James Zethraus from the Department of Citywide Administrative Services, successor to the Department of General Services; Kim Hoyt from the Landmarks Preservation Commission; and Jean Ross from the mayor's office. These meetings were very effective in keeping the project on track because all of the parties involved were fully informed and involved during the construction phase.

Design Approach

The basic approach to the treatment of the interior spaces of the courthouse had been developed in the 1991 feasibility study. A detailed investigation of the existing conditions and a review of the available historical information provided the architects with a good understanding of the building's historical development along with the current problems of repair and structural defects. Although the easiest approach would have been to remove the existing interiors and insert entirely new construction, it was clear that the historic interiors were of extraordinary significance and that the responsible architectural approach was to preserve the major original

spaces in their historic forms. The courtrooms, corridors, and rotunda would be restored to their historic conditions, which would involve repairing decorative plasterwork and flooring, reintroducing historic paint colors, restoring other historic finishes, and installing period light fixtures. Areas of the building that had always been unfinished, particularly the attic and subbasement, would house mechanical equipment and other service functions. New elements, such as fire stairs and public restrooms, would be located in former service rooms whenever possible, not in the major spaces. Modern utility systems—heating, ventilation, and air conditioning (HVAC), as well as electrical and communications systems—were wired into existing wall chases and service closets. This approach respected the designation of the rotunda and the public corridors as interior landmarks, a relatively rare distinction: most city landmark designations encompass the exteriors, and only a few publicly accessible significant interiors have been designated.

This approach was reaffirmed by the Economic Development Corporation when it assumed control of the project in 1999. Because Tweed Courthouse has had a history of changing uses since its original construction, it was decided to minimize permanent new construction so that the building would have maximum flexibility to accommodate changing uses in the future. One of the key elements in this approach was the insertion of new HVAC systems that would not intrude into the historic spaces or limit their flexibility in the future. It had been found in preparing the feasibility study that the original heating and ventilating chases built into the masonry bearing walls could be utilized by a new forced-air HVAC system. The new HVAC systems could provide stringent temperature and humidity controls suitable for museum use, as well as for less demanding uses such as public assembly spaces and offices. Similarly, an electrical and communications system grid would be needed within the subfloors of the former courtrooms. The concrete subfloors would also serve as a base for wood or carpet finish floors appropriate to the new use.

The unfinished attic and subbasement areas would house the equipment needed for the new mechanical and electrical systems. These areas, as in the past, would not be accessible to the public or to most users of the building. The fourth floor, which historically had been mini-

As part of the restoration work, the 1920s partitions and surfaces were removed and the original space was restored to serve again as the main entrance hall for the building.

mally finished with few decorative features, was to be renovated as support office space with modern lighting.

Throughout the building, the decorative finishes of the major spaces were to be conserved and restored as required. The original marble, tile, and cast-iron illuminating-tile floors were to be preserved and repaired in the circulation spaces and the south wing rooms. In the courtrooms in the main part of the building, the concrete subfloor would remain in place until the exact use of each room was determined. It was anticipated that carpeting would be installed, as it had been originally used in the building.

Despite various proposals for the use of the building made during the construction period, this flexible approach was carried through to the completion of the work. The complete exterior restoration and the basic interior restoration, except for final painting and carpeting, was accomplished in time for the dedication of the building on December 21, 2001, by Mayor Giuliani.

Code/Life-Safety Issues

Tweed Courthouse was constructed long before the City of New York established a comprehensive building code. Nevertheless, those responsible for its construction recognized the hazards of combustible building materials in a dense urban setting and built in a manner befitting a major civic monument in a prosperous and rapidly growing city. The courthouse is an early example of entirely fire-resistant construction, which utilized iron in place of traditional timber framing. The structure of the building consists entirely of wrought- and cast-iron beams with load-bearing masonry walls. Even the lath is made of iron, as are the concealed brackets supporting the decorative plaster cornices. Virtually all of the decorative elements in the public spaces are cast iron; the only exception is the ornate plasterwork of the ceilings.

Construction techniques have changed substantially since the courthouse was built, and building codes have reflected those changes. Today building codes establish a minimum level of safety, particularly with respect to fire, that must be provided for a structure and its occupants. All too often the treatment of historic buildings is adversely affected by a rigorous and inflexible interpretation of codes that were developed to regulate the construction of modern buildings. In order to protect the historic integrity of a building while making it safe for its users, it is essential that codes be applied in a flexible manner that addresses the intent of the code rather than its prescriptive regulations.

Planning for the restoration and reuse of Tweed Courthouse began in 1989 with an analysis of its compliance with the current Building Code of the City of New

This cross section looking south shows how the central rotunda is open to the main corridors and monumental staircases. By using the rotunda as a smoke reservoir, the historic, open character of the space was preserved. The four large fans, which extract smoke and gases from the rotunda, are located in the attic and are not visible from the rotunda or connecting public spaces. The fans, one of which is redundant and on standby in case of equipment failure, are controlled by the building management system and are activated by the new fire-detection and alarm systems.

York. While some deficiencies—such as the lack of fire-detection and emergency-lighting systems, standpipes, sprinklers, and a fire-command station—could be corrected easily, other code violations were not as easy to address. Many building features could not be brought into compliance with the code without completely reconfiguring the interior, which would have resulted in the loss of the building's historic integrity. The monumental cast-iron stairways, for example, were not enclosed; the central rotunda was open to the main corridors and stairways; the open-cage elevators were not in enclosed shafts; the elevator lobbies opened on to the rotunda; and unprotected cast- and rolled-iron floor and roof framing members were exposed in most spaces. The building did not even have an adequate amount of code-compliant egress from each floor or exits to the exterior.

The code analysis revealed that the key to an effective fire-management program for the building, regardless of its eventual use or occupancy, would be a strategy focused on the central rotunda. A conventional fire-safety approach would be to separate the rotunda from the rest of the building by filling in the openings that connected it with hallways and the open staircases. This approach would have seriously altered the historic arrangement of the interior and compromised the rotunda, the major interior architectural feature of the building.

Instead, the large central space of the rotunda was treated as an advantage in managing the effects of a fire.

By using the volume of space above and below the laylight, the upper portion of the rotunda would act as a smoke reservoir, collecting and exhausting smoke and combustion gases. Central to the success of this approach was the installation of four large fans at the attic level that would extract smoke from the rotunda. These fans are not visible from any level of the rotunda or occupied floors, only from within the attic. The fans are ducted to air plenums located above the monumental staircases, and smoke is ejected through dampered vents surrounding the base of two large skylights over the staircases. Connected with a new detection system and emergency generators located in the basement, the fans are controlled by a computer that activates them automatically when a fire is detected. Firefighters can control the system manually, once they have assessed smoke and building conditions.

In order to make the upper section of the rotunda an effective collector of smoke, the arched masonry openings on the fourth floor were filled in with glass panels and most of the laylight was fabricated from heat-resistant, tempered, laminated glass. By extracting smoke and dangerous gases into the upper levels of the rotunda, the connecting corridors and other major spaces were made safer in the event of a fire. These circulation spaces could then be used as additional exits from the building.

The basic concept of the fire-management program, developed early in the project by the architects and engineers, was approved by the New York City Department of

Buildings in 1990. The historic open-cage passenger elevators, which were scheduled for restoration as the first phase of the larger comprehensive project, did not meet modern code requirements. The DOB approval allowed the restoration of the elevators to proceed alongside planning for the restoration and reuse of the rest of the building.

In 2000 the fire strategy for the entire building that had been developed in 1990 was tested by ARUP, a fire-engineering consultant to the architect, using computer-simulation studies. These tests analyzed various fire scenarios with different building-user populations, combustion locations, fire intensities, and fuel loads. The computers were used to model the development, size, and behavior of smoke plumes, as well as to show graphically the exiting patterns and times required for people to evacuate the building, given each hypothetical fire situation. Mixtures of age, mobility, and number of occupants were formulated to provide the most comprehensive analysis possible. Carried out with participation of the DOB and FDNY, these timed-egress studies were among the first done for a historic building in New York City. Because they can model, measure, and quantify the performance and effectiveness of alternate solutions to the prescriptive requirements of conventional codes, these studies hold a great deal of promise in restoring and rehabilitating historic structures so that they can be made safe without destroying their distinctive character.

The fire-management program included, and integrated into a coherent whole, all aspects of the building relat-

Fire-simulation and computer-simulation studies analyzed different scenarios with varying building-user populations, combustion locations, fire intensities, and fuel loads. The studies graphically depicted the development, size, and behavior of smoke plumes and heat, as well as the exiting patterns and time required for people of different ages and levels of mobility to exit the building. These plans show how people dispersed throughout the building proceed to exit within 10, 30, and 120 seconds. The plans also show the performance of one of the new fire stairs as part of the exiting process. These studies helped to confirm the concept of using the rotunda as a smoke reservoir.
Drawings by ARUP for John G. Waite Associates, Architects.

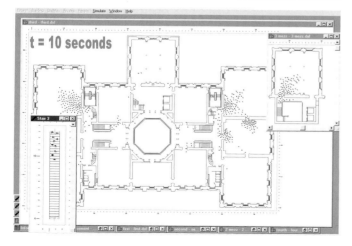

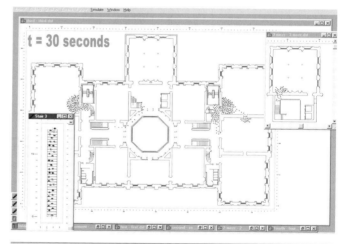

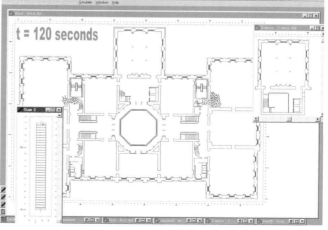

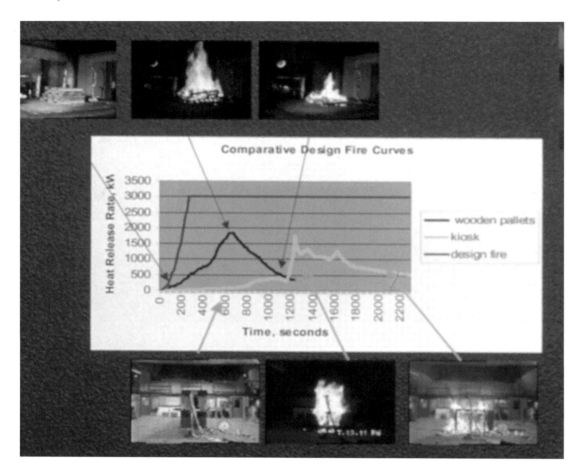

Various types of fire hazards in various locations throughout the building were investigated and assessed as part of the computer-simulation studies. This graph indicates the amount of heat released versus time in seconds for simulated test fires involving wood pallets. Drawing by ARUP for John G. Waite Associates, Architects.

ing to fire and life safety. As part of this program, a sophisticated, interconnected, smoke- and fire-detection and alarm system was installed throughout the building. The installation of some detectors required innovative techniques so that they were effective yet inconspicuous within the historic spaces. Monitored at the central security command center within the building and off site by the fire department, the system provides early detection of heat or smoke conditions related to a fire. In most of the spaces traditional smoke and ionization detectors were installed in the ceilings with the conduits buried in the new concrete floor slab above. In the rotunda, infrared beams are used for early smoke detection; this system minimizes the visual impact. In the large interconnected spaces of the south wing, an air-sampling system was installed; it continually monitors air to detect smoke and other products of combustion. Flexible plastic tube piping for the system was laid underneath the new tile flooring and connected to monitoring tanks located in the basement and attic. The small intakes were incorporated into reproduction chandeliers within the spaces and are virtually unnoticeable.

In 1999, prior to detailed discussions with the fire department, acoustical tests were conducted within the central rotunda, major corridors, and large rooms. These tests measured the acoustic performance of the various spatial configurations; the plaster, marble, and cast-iron surfaces; and their respective audibility and sound-intelligibility levels. The tests were critical in determining the type, quantity, and placement of horns and strobe alarms. The acoustic demonstrations, especially within the open four-story rotunda space, also supported the fire department's decision to approve a fire-alarm system for the courthouse that notifies all occupants simultaneously, instead of only those in certain zones, as the code stipulates for modern high-rise buildings.

Another analysis that tested the performance of structural members when exposed to fire indicated that sprinklers were not required in the historic courtrooms, corridors, or other public spaces. However, sprinklers were installed throughout spaces in the basement, first floor, and fourth floor and in confined areas of the attic that were not connected with the rotunda smoke reservoir. Most of these areas had low ceilings and were thus more likely to contain combustible materials because of their potential uses and projected occupancies. Standpipe risers were installed within the new fire-stair enclosures as well as in the passenger elevator lobby adjacent to the central rotunda. Outside the building fire department Siamese connections for the standpipe risers were installed in three locations; they stand clear of the granite base of the marble facade. The building's location is within a public park; thus the entire perimeter is accessible to fire trucks, and firefighters have more options for fire suppression and management.

The standpipe and sprinkler systems were planned to accommodate future expansion and distribution capabilities within the courthouse. A fire pump was installed in anticipation of extending the system to provide protection inside the wood-framed attic of City Hall, less than 100 feet away. In order to provide adequate water pressure for both of these systems, a ruptured eighteenth-century water main that had been abandoned by the city was restored and reconnected in front of the courthouse at Chambers Street. This repair, which required careful monitoring because of the archaeological sensitivity of downtown Manhattan, restored the local integrity of the underground water-supply grid in the area while also pro-

viding two independent sources of water for the fire-suppression system within the building. In addition, a new fire hydrant was installed at the relocated curb edge of Chambers Street.

The original, unprotected, metal framing of the building—consisting of cast-iron columns, bottom flanges of rolled-iron floor beams, and rolled-iron trusses—was also analyzed. Rather than encasing the iron members in conventional concrete or plaster fireproofing, selected cast-iron columns and other critical structural members were protected with intumescent paint, which expands to form a protective layer when subjected to high temperatures. In other areas, the beam flanges were already protected by the original plaster on corrugated-iron lath ceilings.

The structural performance of the roof-framing members, many of which were fabricated from both wrought- and cast-iron components, was also studied. The analysis focused on the major support elements that, if compromised by fire, would trigger larger structural failures; these elements were also protected with intumescent paint. The new corrugated metal roof assembly incorporated a fire-retardant underlayment installed over metal decking, which further protects critical structural members of the roof.

As part of the computer-simulation studies, the need for sprinklers was evaluated. Based on these studies, it was determined that only the basement, ground floor, fourth floor, and attic spaces needed to have sprinklers in order to be safe for the building's new uses. Most of these areas are not directly connected with the central rotunda. Drawing by ARUP for John G. Waite Associates, Architects.

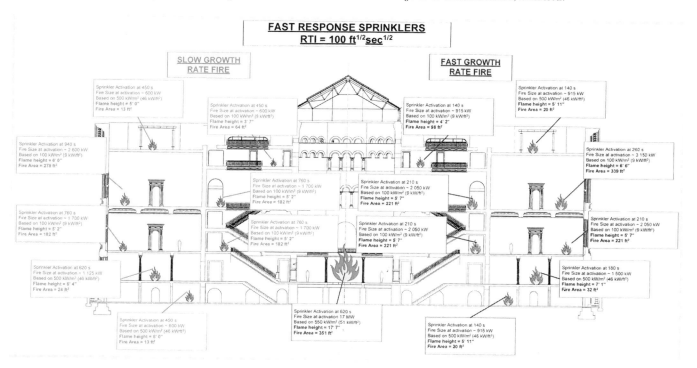

South entrance, facing City Hall, during restoration. Over the years the finished grade of City Hall Park had been raised several feet requiring a stairway to the ground floor of the building.

A new emergency-lighting system was installed throughout the building. Instead of visually intrusive battery-pack emergency lights, many historic gasoliers and wall brackets were wired to emergency panels. The emergency panels are energized in the event of a fire by two diesel generators in the basement that power all life-safety systems in the building as well as in City Hall. Because these generators were in service on September 11, 2001, even though construction on the building was still under way, Tweed Courthouse and City Hall were among the few buildings south of Canal Street that had power and could be used by emergency workers and government officials.

Another critical component of the fire-safety strategy was providing sufficient exits from the building to the exterior. The installation of the smoke-management system made it possible to restore the two original cast-iron stairways adjacent to the rotunda and leave them open to the corridors and the rotunda without fire-rated enclosures. New steel-and-concrete fire stairs were constructed at each end of the building in spaces previously occupied by service rooms. Fully enclosed, these 5-foot-wide stairs exceed the code-mandated width of 3 feet, 8 inches; they serve all floors including the attic and basement and exit directly to the exterior. The stairs, made of steel with concrete pan treads, are sus-

pended by steel rods from the roof framing and do not touch the 2-foot-thick masonry bearing walls, thus allowing the preservation of the original plaster wall finishes and cast-iron architectural trim. In the future, the rooms can be restored to their original conditions if the stairs are removed and new floors inserted.

The key to providing additional exits was to rebuild the original Chambers Street staircase. As a result of increased vehicular traffic and the reduced use of the courthouse, the staircase at the Chambers Street entrance had been truncated in the 1940s, and the remaining stairway was covered over. In 2000 the city approved plans to narrow Chambers Street by removing a lane of traffic and reorganizing the flow of traffic. These changes allowed the courthouse's primary entrance to be reconstructed. The monumental entrance staircase was rebuilt, and the front entrance lobby and the three original double doorways at the main-floor level were restored. These improvements provided additional exits that exceeded the code requirements. The reconstructed staircase was also critical in reestablishing the original character of the building.

Most building materials within the courthouse—stone, brick, and iron—have an intrinsic fire resistance that greatly enhances the containment of smoke or fire within a given space. As part of the fire-safety strategy, especially with regard to smoke management, the historic courtrooms needed to be separated with fire-rated construction from the circulation spaces and the rotunda. This compartmentalization was inherent in the plan of the building and its bearing walls, but it could be compromised at the doors to each room. Computer modeling simulations that demonstrated smoke and heat development were conducted to examine the behavior of various fire scenarios contained in a typical room; results showed that smoke would most likely vent through the large windows rather than through doors. To add an extra level of safety, the wood doors were restored; magnetic door hold-open catches connected to the fire-alarm system were installed (which would release in the event of a fire, allowing the door to close); and the original etched-glass panels were replaced with a technically advanced ceramic that duplicated exactly the appearance of the etched glass but could withstand temperatures of 1,200 degrees Fahrenheit. This material had been developed for use in the space program and has only recently been made available for architectural installations. The use of the material provided the door assemblies with a performance fire rating equivalent to one hour, as required by the code.

The custom fire-management program for Tweed Courthouse demonstrates that a building can be made safe without compromising its historic integrity if the fire risks, and resulting building performance, are carefully analyzed and a comprehensive strategy is developed to address those risks. This approach requires the utilization of state-of-the-art technology and procedures as well as the cooperation of code and fire-service officials.

Accessibility

Multistory, nineteenth-century, public buildings were never fully accessible to disabled people when they were first constructed. Often the main story was elevated above grade and reached by a flight of stairs. Access to the upper floors was also gained using flights of stairs. The original configurations of public restrooms typically did not meet modern accessibility requirements.

Today, when dealing with the restoration of historic public buildings, there is always the issue of balancing historic-preservation goals with the need to meet modern accessibility standards, as defined by the Americans with Disabilities Act (ADA) and various state laws. Certain buildings listed on the National Register of Historic Places have been exempt from full compliance with ADA requirements because their historic integrity would have been compromised. However, it is essential that public buildings be fully accessible to all, including people with physical disabilities.

At Tweed Courthouse, the rehabilitation of the historic elevators using new ADA-compliant control panels greatly improved the building's accessibility. However, additional measures were required to make the building fully accessible. The first-floor entrance from Chambers Street was of particular concern. A change in grade level required several steps between the elevation of the existing concrete sidewalk and the higher grade of the building. This problem was greatly alleviated when Chambers Street was narrowed, the city sidewalk was widened, and the Chambers Street stairs were reconstructed. Since the sidewalk was wider, it was possible to have it slope gently upward from the curb to the entrance underneath the stairs. This modest grade change, less than one in twenty, complied with the ADA requirements and eliminated the need for exterior steps, a separate ramp, or even a handrail. This design concept was also followed at the

New accessible entrance to the front of the building from Chambers Street. After the main entrance staircase was removed in 1942, this entrance, as well as one on the other side of the former stairs, became the public entrance to the building. As part of the restoration work, several concrete stairs were removed and the bluestone sidewalk was sloped up to the ground floor of the building to provide full accessibility. This entrance connects with a small hallway that opens directly to the ground-floor rotunda area and the passenger elevators which service all floors.

South entrance after restoration with new ramp alongside the building. The ramp was constructed of the same granite and bluestone that was used in the restored City Hall Park paving.

east entrance to the building, where the paved pathways within City Hall Park adjacent to the building were changed to accommodate minor adjustments to the grade level.

The south entrance to the building, which is used most often by people coming from City Hall, required a different strategy. While the street level on the north side of the courthouse had been lowered slightly since its original construction, the grade levels within City Hall Park had been raised significantly. Thus the pathway between the two buildings was almost three feet higher than the ground floor of the courthouse. The solution combined the restoration of the existing small retaining walls and stone steps at the courthouse with the construction of a new short ramp and a power-assisted opening device for the exterior wood doors. Granite and bluestone identical to other landscape elements used in City Hall Park were chosen to integrate the exterior ramp with the recent restoration work in the park and to minimize its visual impact on the courthouse.

Most importantly, new functions and spaces within the building, such as public restrooms, were planned to meet ADA guidelines for required clearances, heights, and features within the existing construction. The accessibility standards for these new spaces were integrated seamlessly

into the new construction and respected adjacent restored areas. The result is a building that provides ample accommodations for individuals with disabilities through the reuse of existing elements that provide accessibility, such as the elevators, and the introduction of new elements that do not compromise the historic or architectural integrity of the building.

Insertion of New Elements

In nearly all preservation projects new elements must be inserted into existing spaces to satisfy modern building codes and functional requirements. There are two basic approaches to the insertion of these elements. The first treats the elements as obviously modern insertions; the second attempts to disguise them as historic features that have always been in the building. A more moderate approach, somewhere between the two, is to design elements in an understated, contemporary manner using details based on historic precedents.

Inserting new fire stairs in historic spaces often poses difficult and sometimes controversial design problems. At Tweed Courthouse new code-compliant fire stairs and accessible restrooms were especially important because of the building's intended public use. In order to preserve the integrity of as many of the former courtrooms as possible, small, lower-ceiling rooms that had originally been constructed as service areas were modified for use as fire stairs and restrooms. There were only a few such spaces on each floor. Because of the building's symmetrical and axial arrangement, the floor plan divided naturally into four quadrants, with the northeast and northwest quadrants facing Chambers Street and the southeast quadrants and southwest ones facing City Hall. Reflecting this arrangement, new restrooms were placed along the north sides of the building, and new fire stairs on the south.

These locations were chosen in response to specific concerns: while using existing rooms as restrooms did not necessitate extensive modifications to the spaces or the building facades, the insertion of fire stairs might require changes to the exterior walls and the replacement of existing windows with new grade-level doors. The city's fire and building departments agreed that locating the fire stairs on the south sides of the building was preferable, because occupants would exit to the safer area of City Hall Park and away from the vehicular and pedestrian traffic on Chambers Street, where emergency personnel and equipment would most likely be stationed.

At the beginning of the design phase the Economic Development Corporation had directed that the architects and engineers plan for the largest possible building-occupant load, thereby providing flexibility for future building uses. Using those guidelines, a generous number of restrooms were planned, and two sets of wide fire stairs were designed to accommodate a large number of people. The public restrooms were located in two of the four small rooms available on each public floor, with the women's rooms stacked on the west side and the men's rooms on the east. This vertical arrangement of fixtures—including toilets, lavatories, janitor's mop closets, floor drains, and water fountains—allowed for the consolidation of plumbing piping and venting through only two minor areas of the building and avoided the removal of the iron-beam and brick-vault floor construction. Additionally, the space and proposed fixture configurations within these rooms were sufficient to allow walls containing plumbing to be furred out from the original walls, thereby avoiding costly cutting and patching and leaving most of the original plaster wall surfaces and cast-iron trim intact.

Modern, energy-efficient plumbing and lighting fixtures were specified for the restrooms, which were located adjacent to the landmarked rotunda space. Modern finishes compatible with those used historically in the building were selected for the restrooms. Ceramic tile was installed on the walls and waterproofed floors, and a horizontal band of decorative wall tile, reflecting the building's historic interior brick colors and patterns, was chosen for each restroom. A suspended, perforated-metal panel ceiling was installed in each restroom to allow access for maintenance.

The need to insert a different kind of new element was encountered in the restoration of the second-floor courtroom of the south wing, the grand courtroom designed by Leopold Eidlitz. A significant feature in that room is the large sandstone fireplace mantel, which fills the center bay of the north wall. Over the mantel is a semicircular recess with a rough plaster finish, where Eidlitz intended to incorporate an ornament of unknown design. However, the ornament was never installed; a 1908 photograph of the room shows the empty recess in the otherwise finished space.

About the same time that the courtroom in New York was being built, Eidlitz designed similar mantels for three rooms at the New York State Capitol in Albany. The mantel for the Court of Appeals chamber had a clock with a

The new public restrooms were inserted in two of the four former service rooms on each public floor. Because the restrooms were stacked one above the other, plumbing pipes and vents were consolidated behind new walls furred out from the original surfaces. This approach resulted in a reversible condition that allowed the preservation of the original cast iron and plaster surfaces so that the rooms could be restored to their historic form in the future.

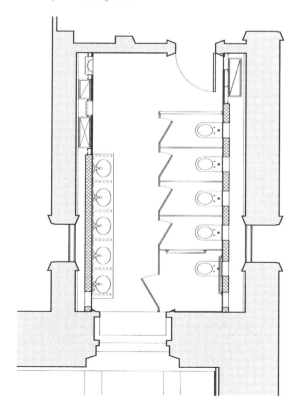

stone face integrated into the recess. The mantel in the assembly chamber initially remained empty, but a massive stone carving of the state seal soon filled the overmantel. In the assembly parlor it took longer to complete the mantel: a bronze bas-relief depicting Henry Hudson was installed between 1900 and 1911.

In June 2001 EDC concurred with the architects' recommendation for the completion of the overmantel in the courthouse. The architects' familiarity with the mantels at the New York State Capitol suggested various possibilities, including the insertion of a stone sculpture, a metal plaque, or even an elaborate clock. The architects and EDC were concerned that the carved stone and clock options would compete with the historic features created by Eidlitz. However, the insertion of a carefully designed, cast-bronze relief panel would provide a subtle contrast with the surrounding stone and would meld comfortably with the historic surroundings.

After considerable discussion, the architects proposed a design that featured a large centrally positioned representation of the current seal of the city flanked by smaller images of the city's seals from the Dutch and English eras. The current city seal, based on the English seal and adopted in 1784, includes figures of an American Indian and a mariner beside a shield emblazoned with the four sails of a windmill surrounded by two beavers and two flour barrels, all representing the trade and commerce of

New York. Above the shield a semi-globe surmounted by a soaring eagle replaced the crown that had been found on the English seal. Below the seal is written the year 1625 (in recognition of the Dutch origins of the city) and the Latin inscription "Sigillum Civitatis Novi Eboraci" (Seal of the City of New York).

The contract for the production of the bronze plaque, including the creation of the artwork, making the mold, casting the bronze, finishing, and installation, was awarded to the Johnson Atelier of Mercerville, New Jersey. This firm had fabricated some of the carved stonework for the exterior restoration of the courthouse. The Johnson Atelier recommended that a full-size model for the plaque be produced based on the architects' original drawing. Using computer technology, the image was refined for depth of detail, eventually resulting in a three-dimensional surface. The evolving design could be reviewed on the computer screen from various angles as a fully developed three-dimensional object. The next step was the production of a full-size model of the plaque mechanically "carved" from high-density foam.

A latex mold was made from the approved model, and in turn a wax model was made to create a final ceramic mold to cast the finished bronze plaque. The rough bronze casting was cleaned, hand polished, and installed in the mantel to complete the Eidlitz courtroom.

Model for the new bronze overmantel in the grand courtroom in the south wing designed by Leopold Eidlitz. The design of the overmantel featured the current seal of the City of New York flanked by smaller images of the city's seals from the Dutch and English colonial periods. After being sculpted using computer technology and carved mechanically from high-density foam, the model was used to form a latex mold. A wax model was then made and augmented with clay to create a ceramic mold, which was used to cast the finished bronze plaque.

Opposite: After casting, the rough bronze plaque was cleaned, polished, and installed in the stone mantel over the fireplace. This mantel is similar to those designed by Leopold Eidlitz for the New York State Capitol in Albany.

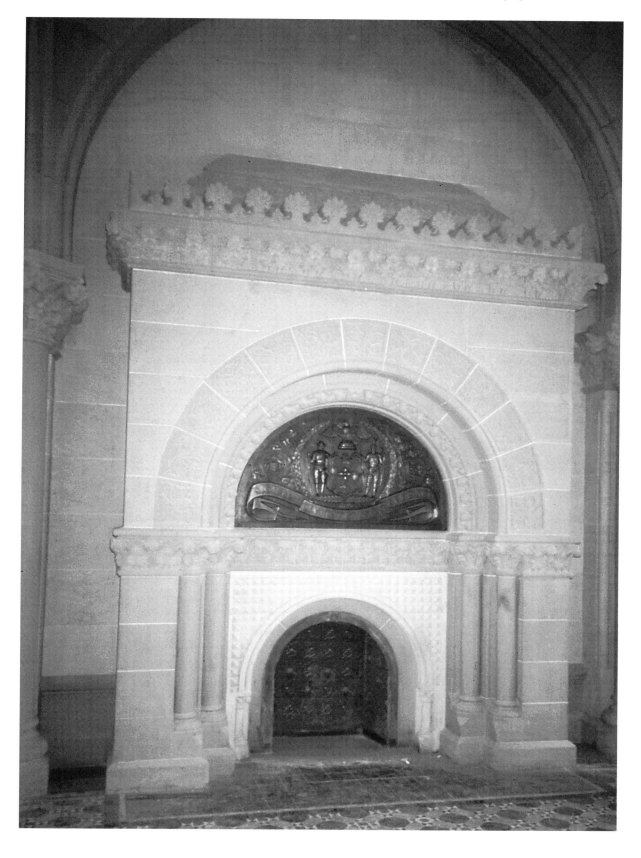

CHAPTER THREE

Interior Restoration

Decorative Masonry

The contrast between the original Tweed Courthouse, designed largely by John Kellum, and Leopold Eidlitz's south wing is most dramatic on the second floor of the rotunda. Kellum intended the octagonal rotunda and the flanking stair halls to work together as one continuous space. His rotunda design had four diagonal walls, each with a pedimented niche framed by paneled pilasters constructed entirely of cast iron. The east and west sides of the octagon opened to the stair halls, and the north and south sides opened to the entrance lobbies. Above each pilaster was a pair of large consoles supporting the cast-iron balcony; the soffit was elaborately paneled in cast iron.

When Eidlitz began work in 1874, the walls of the rotunda were completed only up to the top of the piano nobile, or second-floor level. Eidlitz displayed his distaste for Kellum's work by enclosing the north, south, east, and west sides of the octagon with Romanesque arches made of polychrome brick and having a course of dogtooth

bricks acting as an archivolt. These arches were supported by pairs of sandstone columns. Eidlitz then completed the upper floors of the rotunda using polychromatic brickwork semicircular arches.

Once the work was finished, criticism was directed toward Eidlitz's design and its relation to Kellum's cast-iron construction. The Board of Aldermen referred to "brick obstructions to the passageway leading to and from the large open space beneath the dome." Eidlitz could not understand the criticism, asking "is it possible for anybody to fail to see that this performs a function, and that [Kellum's] does not?" It indeed proved possible to misunderstand Eidlitz's intentions, and by 1908 the entire rotunda was painted a uniform gray, nullifying, in architecture critic Montgomery Schuyler's words, its "pristine force." The rotunda remained painted through 1999, although the color was changed to maroon and beige with marbleized columns.

Eidlitz's addition also used polychrome brickwork as the predominant interior building material on the first floor, the third floor, and the third-floor mezzanine. By

1999 all of the decorative masonry in these areas had been painted white, and the large rooms were divided with partitions.

The most elaborate room of the addition, the second-floor courtroom, like most of Eidlitz's major rooms in other buildings, is predominantly stone. Four polished granite columns with white marble capitals and bases support sandstone arches that divide the room into nine bays. The arches are supported at the walls by engaged columns, also of sandstone. Other features, such as the doors and windows, are framed by smaller engaged stone colonettes. The stone slabs in each bay of the ceiling and the massive stone fireplace are intricately carved. Blackened from years of exposure to dirt, smoke, and atmospheric pollutants, the various stones were virtually indistinguishable from one another.

To restore Eidlitz's stone and brick masonry to its original splendor, it was essential to strip away the layers of paint and dirt and once again expose the patterns of the brickwork and the details of the stonework.

During the summer of 1990, as part of the feasibility study, paint was removed above a second- and third-floor arch in the rotunda, revealing patterned walls of cream, red, and black brickwork. At the same time, tests were performed in the second-floor courtroom to determine the best method of cleaning the soot, grime, and smoke residue from the stone surfaces.

As the first step in the 1999 decorative masonry restoration process, an extreme cleaning campaign was undertaken to remove all of the paint from the rotunda and the south wing. A chemical paint remover was used on the brickwork. Areas were isolated, the alkaline gel product was thickly applied and left for at least twenty-four hours, and the paste was removed. The exposed brick surface was washed completely, neutralized, and then thoroughly cleaned. The third-floor mezzanine level of the south wing was the first room to undergo paint removal, and it took several applications of the paint remover to achieve the desired result. By the end of the cleaning process the complex patterns of polychrome brick were exposed throughout the building.

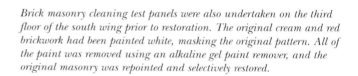

When the deteriorated plaster was removed from the south wall of the rotunda at the main-floor level, the second pair of original entrance arches designed by John Kellum was exposed. When the south wing was constructed beginning in 1876, these arches were filled in and plastered over.

As part of the investigations carried out during the feasibility study, paint removal test panels were undertaken in the rotunda to determine the most effective paint removal agents, as well as the patterns of the original multicolored masonry. On the basis of this investigation, it was decided to remove all of the paint and expose the original colors and patterns of the polychromed masonry surface throughout the building. Photograph by Lily Wang.

Brick masonry cleaning test panels were also undertaken on the third floor of the south wing prior to restoration. The original cream and red brickwork had been painted white, masking the original pattern. All of the paint was removed using an alkaline gel paint remover, and the original masonry was repointed and selectively restored.

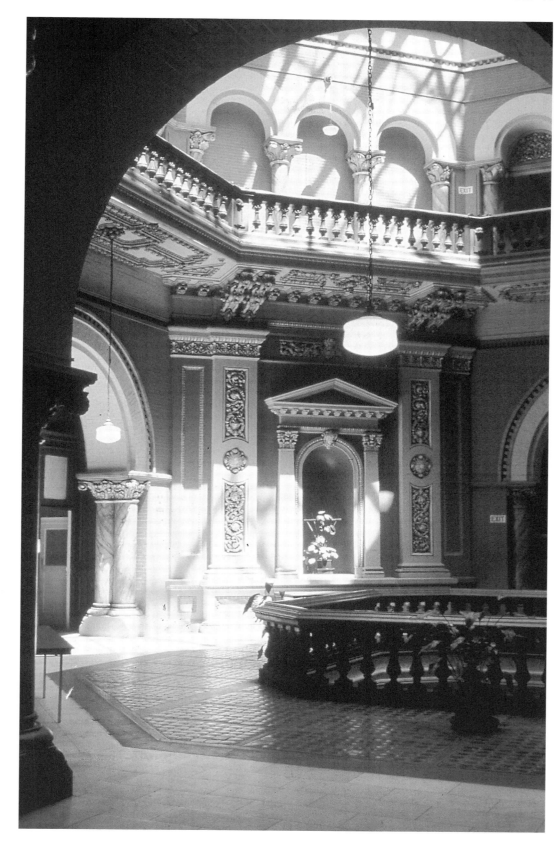

The rotunda at the second floor before restoration. The decorative cast iron-work was designed by John Kellum and the masonry was added by Leopold Eidlitz. The original polychrome masonry had been painted so that its character was dramatically changed.

Although never painted, the polished granite columns, white marble capitals and bases, and brown sandstone arches and walls of the south wing main courtroom had become a monochromatic dark gray because of decades of exposure to dirt, smoke, and atmospheric pollutants. The stone was cleaned with alkaline gel cleaning agents specifically formulated for each type of stone. After repeated applications, the original splendor of the room was restored.

For the second-floor courtroom additional testing was done since new alkaline gel cleaning products had become available since the testing that was carried out in 1990. For the final cleaning two different cleaning agents were used to remove the buildup of more than one hundred years of dirt and stains. Each product was selected to correspond to the type of stone needing to be cleaned, one for the sandstone and another for the granite and marble. After each application the surfaces were thoroughly rinsed with water, often several times. The cleaning revealed a spectacular room with richly colored sandstone and subtle changes in the color of the stone trim.

Once cleaned, interior masonry construction documents could be prepared. Throughout the building mortar joints had been damaged or mortar was missing. Every surface needed to be repainted to some degree, but the location of the damaged joints within each wall appeared to be random. Sections of brick were also damaged or missing. Typically, these areas corresponded to the previous locations of walls, partitions, or mechanical-system components that were not part of the original building.

Measured drawings recording the elevation of each masonry surface throughout the building were created. A visual survey identified mortar joints requiring repointing and areas of masonry needing replacement or repair. The survey information was recorded on the measured drawings, creating a detailed set of construction documents that were then used for bidding purposes.

Samples of the existing mortar were tested to determine its original composition, and several mortar colors were identified. This information was used to specify compatible new mortar mixes. Original bricks, salvaged from areas of demolition, were earmarked for reuse and stacked and stored in the building.

Once a contractor was chosen, the final steps of the restoration process began. Samples of different mortar types were made for various masonry conditions. The contractor prepared several rounds of samples until the proper color and texture was achieved to provide a seamless match with the original mortar. Beige bricks, salvaged from walls removed at the ground-floor entrance, were used as replacements because they provided the best color match. New red bricks were made to match the existing ones. With the drawings and materials, the contractor could move meticulously through the building to restore each area of decorative masonry.

Some portions of the brick that had been painted, once exposed to the air, started showing a buildup of salt deposits on their surface. Known as efflorescence, the deposits were a result of the leaching and crystallization of soluble salts from within the brick. These deposits were easily removed with a brush and water, and the process ended when a new HVAC system with adequate temperature and humidity controls was installed in the building.

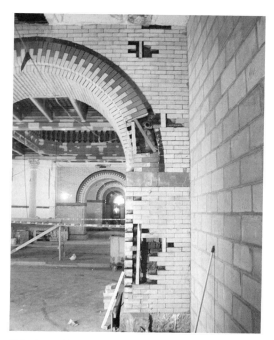

Selective replacements of decorative brick masonry units.

Masonry repointing where joints were deteriorated at the attic level of the rotunda, below the building's central skylight.

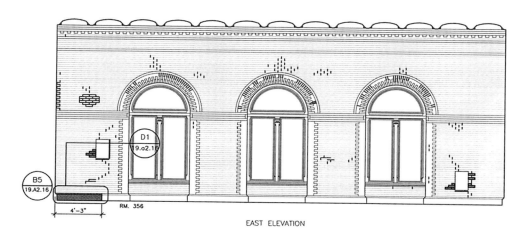

EAST ELEVATION

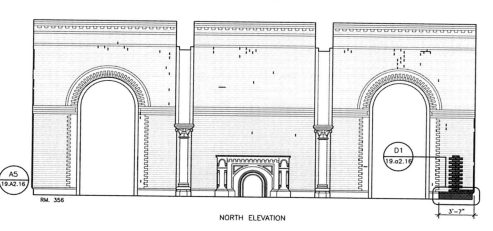

NORTH ELEVATION

Contract documents prepared for interior masonry restoration of former courtroom on the third-floor mezzanine of the south wing.

Third floor rotunda arches after restoration. Many layers of paints have been chemically removed, uncovering Leopold Eidlitz's original design of sandstone columns and cream, red, and black brick.

Cast Iron

The abundant cast-iron structural and decorative elements throughout Tweed Courthouse are among the most impressive in any American public building. From the monumental staircases to the structural Corinthian columns to the hundreds of smaller ornamental castings, cast iron plays a significant role in almost every aspect of the building's interior. Cast iron was used for its fire resistance, its strength in compression, and its manufacturing process, which made elaborate shapes easily repeatable.

A limited visual survey of the cast iron was carried out in 1990 as part of the feasibility study. That survey showed that after years of service most of the cast iron remained in remarkably good condition, largely because of its inherent strength and hardness. Interior iron elements were sheltered from exposure to a damp atmosphere, thus protecting them from oxidization. Furthermore, the heavy weight of the cast-iron members used in the courthouse contributed to their durability. J. B. and W. W. Cornell and Co., the iron founders, were paid for their work by the pound; given the demands for kickbacks to the Tweed Ring, it is not surprising that the castings are significantly thicker than normal, ranging from ½-inch to ¾-inch.

Despite its good condition, the cast iron needed a significant amount of work to ensure its continued performance and to restore it to its original visual beauty. The pre-

liminary 1990 survey was supplemented with a more comprehensive survey done as part of the restoration campaign. First the paint had to be removed from all cast-iron surfaces. Cracked and peeling paint would hinder the survey process; also, historic cast iron often has air holes and inclusions that can weaken its structural integrity and the paint could obscure the evidence of this condition. In addition, the numerous layers of paint obscured the original detail of the cast iron.

Several methods were tested to verify the safest and most effective means of removing the paint. Tests with a chemical paint remover showed that several applications would be needed, and the additional time for each application would impede construction. Moreover, the chemical remover left the surface of the cast iron quite smooth, casting doubt on the adhesion of new paint. Tests with sponge blasting (pressure application of small sponge fragments) proved unsuccessful: it did not remove all of the paint, and it left a residue containing lead paint. Ultimately, a needle-gun method was selected. In this process a hand-held pneumatic gun causes a series of small, needle-like rods to vibrate across the surface of the cast iron, abrasively removing the layers of paint. Although harsher than sponge blasting, the robustness of the cast iron used in the courthouse made this method possible. Because lead in the old paint was released as airborne particles, the mechanics wore respirators and each area was isolated from the rest of the building.

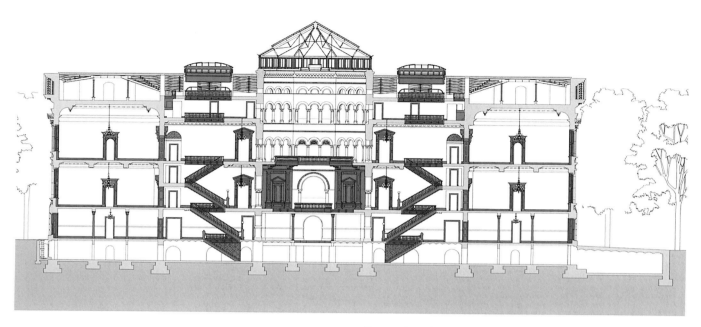

Cross section of building with cast-iron structural and decorative elements highlighted. Tweed Courthouse contains some of the most impressive cast ironwork of any nineteenth-century public building constructed in the United States. All of these elements were repaired or conserved as part of the restoration.

Immediately after the paint removal, a corrosion-inhibiting primer was applied. This step was very important because it retarded the formation of rust, which could prevent proper bonding between the cast iron and the paint.

Once the built-up paint had been removed, the visual survey was carried out to identify any damaged or missing portions of the cast iron (elements that had to come off during the paint removal, such as small portions of trim or individual floral castings, were carefully marked and cataloged so that they could be returned to their original locations). The information gathered during the survey was organized into a set of construction documents that provided exact locations for reattaching the original elements and for installing new cast replacement elements, and cast baseboards—for example, the Corinthian capitals of the building's thirty-two columns each had thirty-six separate cast-iron pieces, including rosettes, flowers, large and small volutes, and acanthus leaves. The construction documents diagramed each capital, showing the location of every missing element and listing the type and quantity of missing pieces.

The construction documents also provided detailed drawings for several larger cast-iron elements. Profiles of the three types of cast-iron baseboard used throughout the courthouse were carefully drawn and keyed to the floor plans. A plan, elevations, and details were drawn for a missing railing that once protected the opening to the

Cleaning test of cast-iron shutter and window entablature to remove many layers of paint. After considerable testing, it was determined that using a pneumatic needle gun was more effective than either chemical paint removers or sponge blasting. Immediately after cleaning, corrosion-inhibiting primer paint was applied to the metal to retard rusting.

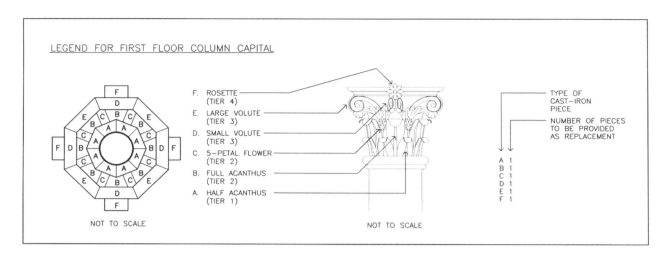

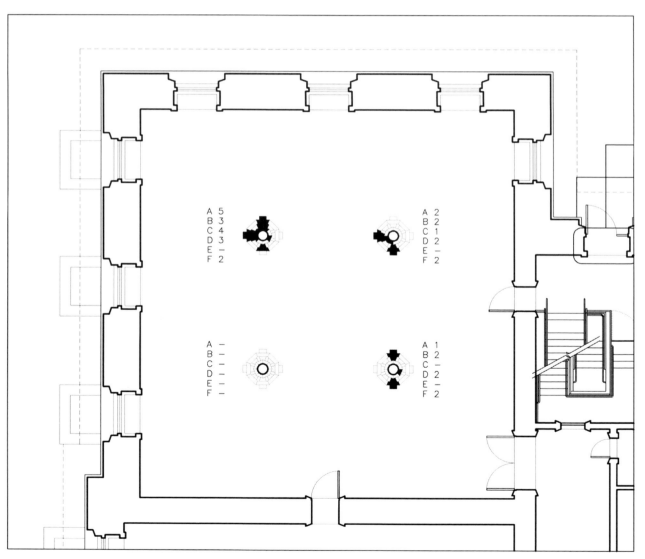

Opposite: *Typical restoration drawings indicating where cast-iron elements were to be replicated because they were either missing or badly damaged. These drawings illustrate column capitals located in the southeast quadrant of the first floor.*

Decorative cast-iron treads of the main stairway during restoration. In the twentieth century, the decorative treads were coated with concrete in an effort to reduce maintenance. The concrete was removed and the original tread surfaces were restored.

Structural cast-iron and glass flooring panel during restoration. The cast glass blocks were removed so that the iron could be cleaned and repaired.

small cast-iron spiral stairway to the first floor from the second-floor courtroom in the south wing. Measured drawings, both elevations and sections, also recorded the elaborate detail of the three missing door surrounds in the courtroom on the west side of the second floor.

The newly exposed cast iron revealed the original screw holes and fasteners that still secured the various elements. In order to prepare the surfaces for painting and to ensure a smooth finish, it was decided to patch over these fasteners. At the same time and using the same material, the holes and imperfections in the surface of the cast iron, inherent from the original casting process and, to a lesser extent, caused by the needle-gun process, could be smoothed out. A steel-based epoxy filler with a high content of steel fibers was used as the patching compound.

The various sizes and shapes of the elements to be replicated ultimately determined the process and material used. Missing portions of baseboards were replicated in cast iron. A structural cast-iron and glass floor panel, missing at the northwest corner of the second floor, was also replicated. Precisely matching the size, profile, and detail of the existing floor panel was extremely important as the

new panel was to be placed in an existing opening and was to receive new cast glass blocks. In order to help guarantee a successful fit, the contractor supplied to the architect shop drawings that indicated the exact tolerances of each piece being fabricated. Molds of several details were made from the existing floor panels, modified to compensate for the amount of wear to the original surface, and incorporated into the final production. Following a similar process, the new railing for the second-floor courtroom was fabricated to match exactly the existing portion of railing wrapping around the spiral stair. The original cast-iron newel post, which had been found behind one of the radiators in 1990, was reinstalled alongside the new railing.

The numerous floral castings were replicated using a plastic-steel product, the same material used as the patching compound in order to meet the construction schedule. A series of mock-ups, with original pieces as models, indicated that this alternate product could meet the exact standards of quality needed. The replicated elements, along with the salvaged original cast-iron pieces, were secured in place at the original fastener locations wherever possible and with flat-head screws to match the original conditions.

Various cast-iron elements including heating grilles, column capital components, and moldings that have been removed for examination and repair before being restored.

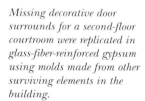

Missing decorative door surrounds for a second-floor courtroom were replicated in glass-fiber-reinforced gypsum using molds made from other surviving elements in the building.

The missing decorative door surrounds in the second-floor courtroom, because of their size, were replicated using a third product, glass-fiber-reinforced gypsum, and involved a contractor who specialized in its use. Full-scale rubber molds were made based on existing door surrounds in the east side of the courthouse. The molds transferred accurately all of the intricacies in the original cast-iron ornamentation, including even the screw holes, to a solid unit of glass-fiber-reinforced gypsum. These units, significantly lighter than their cast-iron alternatives, were produced on site. Once cured, the reproductions were removed from their molds and slowly raised into place over the lower portion of the existing door surrounds. With a framework already in place against the masonry wall, the elaborate castings could be anchored securely, providing a virtually seamless fit.

After intense research and planning, months of work, and a final painting, the cast iron once again serves as one of the premier features of the restored courthouse.

Left: Replica door surround after the glass-fiber-reinforced gypsum has cured, prior to installation.

Below: Underside of the cast-iron spiral stairway to the second-floor courtroom in the south wing. The metal has been cleaned and prime-painted. The missing railing at the second floor level was also replicated and new cast-iron elements were installed.

Bottom: Structural cast-iron and glass flooring at the second-floor level in the rotunda. The use of the iron-and-glass flooring system allowed light from the central skylight to penetrate to the ground floor. A missing section in the northwest quadrant of the building was replicated in cast iron.

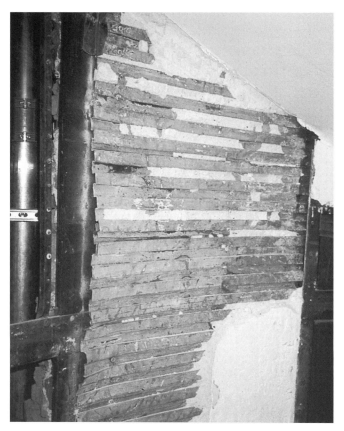

Original corrugated iron lath exposed in one of the third-floor courtrooms during restoration.

Deteriorated plaster has been removed from the ceiling of a third-floor courtroom, exposing the original corrugated iron lath and furring strips.

Plaster

The original plasterwork in Tweed Courthouse was done by Andrew Garvey, who was dubbed the "prince of plasterers" after his astronomically high bills and kickbacks to the Tweed Ring were revealed. Nevertheless, Garvey and his crew provided a high-quality product. A three-coat flat plaster finish, typical for the period, was applied to nearly all the interior walls by one of two methods. Corrugated iron lath was attached to the masonry walls of the building's perimeter using iron furring strips, with an air space between the masonry and the plaster. This system helped prevent the accumulation of condensation on the interior face of the masonry (caused by differences in temperature and humidity between the air inside and outside the structure) from being trapped and damaging the plaster. On interior walls, where condensation was not a concern, plaster was applied directly onto the brick masonry.

Plaster was applied directly to the curved undersides of the brick-vaulted ceilings of the first and fourth floors, while flat plaster on iron lath and iron furring strips was used in the second- and third-floor courtrooms and hallways. Decorative plaster wainscoting was used throughout the halls and courtrooms. On the second and third floors large-scale plaster cornices were decorated with brackets and egg-and-dart moldings. Ornate plaster medallions, some as large as ten feet in diameter, were centered on the ceilings in courtrooms and large public hallways; large chandeliers originally hung from the center of these medallions. The chandeliers were replicated as part of the restoration work.

Most of the plaster in the building still remained sound in 1999, but a few problems were found consistently throughout the interior. Various degrees of cracking were apparent on the walls and ceilings; some areas of plaster had become loosened from the lath or brick backup material. This condition was especially prevalent in areas where the plaster had been patched after alterations were made to mechanical or electrical systems concealed in the walls and ceilings. Most of the decorative plasterwork was in remarkably good condition as restoration began. A few areas of the cornices in the courtrooms were damaged when steam heating was installed earlier in the century; the pipes were run vertically between floors, typically directly through cornice moldings. The ceiling medallions were generally in excellent condition; only a few small ones were missing, and most of the others had only minor damage, usually at the center where light fixtures had once been located.

Because most of the plaster in the courthouse was original, the approach was to keep as much of it intact as was practical. The architects made a visual inspection of the

One of the third-floor courtrooms, designed by John Kellum, during restoration. The original plastering of this room was done by Andrew Garvey, the 'prince of plasterers.' Deteriorated plaster has been removed from the walls and ceilings, leaving areas of sound plaster to be retained. New plaster matching the composition of the original was installed to provide smooth finished surfaces.

Plasterers using a scissor-lift to repair wall plaster in a former court-room. The decorative cornices are plaster, but the door and window trim, as well as baseboards, are cast iron.

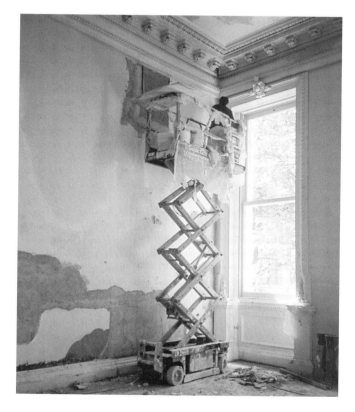

conditions in order to understand the general scope of the repairs needed; then it became the responsibility of the plaster contractor to identify and remove areas of plaster that would require replacement. The damage to the decorative plaster elements was easier to identify than the condition of the flat plaster. Damaged or missing elements were noted by the architects on a reflected ceiling plan of each floor. Large amounts of flat plaster were removed because extensive infrastructure improvements were being made within the walls, and the removal process itself often loosened neighboring surfaces that were once only tenuously attached, invisible from the floor level.

Skilled plaster craftsmen casting a new ceiling medallion using an intact original element as a model. The casting occurred in one of the courtrooms, which was used as a temporary studio.

Areas that were exposed after the plaster was removed often revealed interesting aspects of the building's history. For example, in a third-floor courtroom two niches flanking the center window were revealed; they may have once housed sculptures behind the judge's bench. On the second floor marble arches were uncovered within the brick wall that separates the south wing from the elevator lobby. This provided the only glimpse of the original rear facade, which had been concealed when the south wing was added.

The restoration of the flat plasterwork consisted of three coats of traditional plaster blended into the remaining original plaster to match its thickness of approximately one inch. On the perimeter walls modern steel lath replaced missing corrugated iron lath, and new plaster was applied. On interior walls a bonding agent was brushed onto the exposed brick, and the new plaster was applied directly to that surface. After the plastering was complete, wall cloth was attached, much like wallpaper, over the entire wall surface. The wall cloth was intended to help stabilize the original plaster and tie the old and new plaster together. It would help prevent future cracks in the plaster from telegraphing through to the wall surface. The walls were then prime-painted.

In order to restore the ornamental plaster, highly skilled plasterers were brought on site to make molds from existing intact examples. After curing, the rubber molds were removed and one of the courtrooms became a temporary studio for casting the new plaster pieces. Damaged cornices were rebuilt to match the adjacent surfaces, and the new elements—rosettes, leaves, flowers, and often entire brackets—were applied. In a few cases, entire ceiling medallions were replicated and reinstalled.

The restored walls, ceilings, and ornamental work had such a uniform appearance that it was virtually impossible to distinguish which portions of plaster had been original and which had been repaired or replaced.

Paint

Finishing restored spaces in public buildings for adaptive uses always raises the question of paint colors. As the restoration of historic buildings became more widespread during the 1960s and 1970s, their interiors were often painted white, with no reference to their original color schemes. Today, with the growing sophistication of the historic-preservation movement and the development of scientific paint-analysis techniques, there is increasing recognition that using accurate historic color schemes can greatly enhance the restoration work. This approach is usually encouraged by local, state, and national historic-preservation agencies that have design-review responsibility for projects.

During its one hundred and thirty years of occupancy Tweed Courthouse underwent numerous changes in its decorative schemes. On some surfaces as many as eighteen layers of paint were uncovered, revealing the broad spectrum of color schemes that had been used. These color schemes ranged from exposed cream-white primer coats to completely rendered, stenciled, and decorated surfaces, some with faux finishes that imitated expensive materials. Other early finishes consisted of a single color used on the walls of a room.

Throughout the building the paint was cracked and peeling. This deterioration was caused by the dirt buildup and improper preparation before painting and the use of different types of paints (oil-base, water-base, and alkyd), which have different and often incompatible physical and chemical properties. In the rotunda, layers of paint hid the originally exposed brick and stone surfaces. The buildup of paint on cast-iron surfaces obscured the detail of the original castings.

The restoration of the rotunda and other public spaces provided the opportunity to re-create the historic paint colors. The detective work for determining and reconstructing these decorative schemes was closely linked with the other building investigations and the historical research undertaken to guide the restoration work.

The scarcity of contemporary detailed documentation concerning the decoration of the courthouse made the restoration challenging; only a few published references and illustrations have been located. An article published in the *New York Times* on April 22, 1868, states that "none of the apartments are as yet painted or decorated in any way." However, an 1871 account notes that "the rooms occupied by the Surrogate and County Clerk . . . have been painted and frescoed." Only a few illustrations of the interior of the courthouse have been found.

A woodcut from the December 1, 1877 issue of Frank Leslie's *Illustrated Newspaper* (see page 84) illustrates the completed Surrogate's Courtroom, which was one of the painted and frescoed rooms; and investigations carried out in 1999–2000 by Evergreen Painting Studios confirmed that the room had been elaborately decorated as recorded in the illustration. The décor consisted of elaborate patterns and painted panels on the plaster wall and ceiling surfaces. Small areas of the historic decorative schemes such as this that were exposed during the paint investigations of 2000 remain exposed in various rooms.

A colored lithograph of the Board of Supervisors chamber, located on the second floor, was published in the *Manual of the Corporation of the City of New York* in 1868 (see front section with color illustration). The walls, door, and window trim are shown in a monochromatic cream or white color. It is possible that the plaster walls, cornice, and ceiling in this room remained unpainted, an accepted treatment in the mid-nineteenth century for both public and domestic interiors. However, once the surfaces became soiled, particularly from the combustion of illuminating gas, they were painted, often in elaborate polychrome schemes.

These two historic illustrations represent two aspects of the original interiors, a completed room on the first floor and an occupied but not completely decorated space on the second floor. Later in the nineteenth century many of

An investigation of the historic paint schemes of cast-iron elements within the rotunda was undertaken as part of the feasibility study work in 1990. This research indicated that the early multicolored schemes were very different from the recent monochromatic paint finishes of the rotunda.

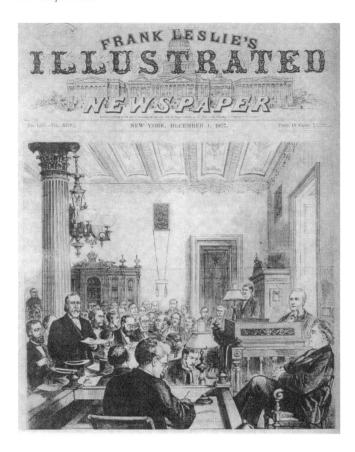

FRANK LESLIE'S
ILLUSTRATED
NEWSPAPER
NEW YORK, DECEMBER 1, 1877.

the courtrooms would be lavishly decorated in polychrome and faux-painted finishes.

The unusually long duration of the original construction of the building, which spanned more than two decades, and the involvement of two architects with widely diverging views on the decorative treatment of interiors made the reconstruction of the original painting schemes complex. John Kellum and Leopold Eidlitz were from different generations and had different training. Kellum favored exuberant detailing and rich finishes, as represented in the extraordinary cast-iron trim, vibrant polychroming, painted and stenciled decorations, and faux finishes imitating expensive materials. Eidlitz, who wrote extensively about his architectural philosophy, favored using building materials in an honest, straightforward manner, similar to the principles of the arts-and-crafts movement emerging at the time. His use of color was also very direct, relying on saturated colors of paint, gold leaf, natural stone, and polychrome tiles and brickwork.

In order to understand the work of these two architects better, their other buildings were studied, particularly those designed or constructed at the same time as the courthouse. Contemporary photographs of Kellum's interiors of the A. T. Stewart residence in Manhattan, designed in 1864 and completed in 1869, revealed that their architectural character mirrored that of the courthouse. The richly painted decor of the residence provided clues to

Surrogate's Courtroom in 1877. Illustration by Frank Leslie for the *Illustrated Newspaper.*

An investigation of original decorative ceiling and wall paint was conducted in the original Surrogate's Courtroom, prior to plaster restoration work on the first floor. This evidence confirmed historical documentation, including an 1877 woodcut, that the room had been elaborately decorated. The historic paint was documented and stabilized by Evergreen Painting Studios and left exposed in situ.

Kellum's treatment of the courthouse. Eidlitz's involvement in the courthouse began in 1876 and coincided with his work in Albany at the New York State Capitol. The character of his designs for these two buildings is very similar in terms of materials, detailing, color, and decorative finishes.

By the time of his death in 1871 Kellum had determined the character of the interior of the courthouse, although few of the spaces had received their intended decorative finishes. The plaster walls were either primed with cream or white paint or remained unpainted. The cast-iron elements had been primed with a rust-inhibiting coating, red lead, before they were installed; once in place they were painted a light gray.

Determining the decorative program for the restoration began with the microscopic examination of hundreds of small samples of paint taken from various surfaces throughout the interior of the building. With every sample, each layer of paint was exposed by scraping with a scalpel. The exposed layer, and in some cases the accumulated dirt layers sandwiched between the paint, was examined under a microscope. This seriation analysis was compiled into a chart showing a chronological layer-by-layer listing of colors, arranged by rooms. These colors were matched to pure colors of the Munsell color-notation system. This information was used to determine the historic paint schemes. The earliest schemes were fully analyzed so that the colors used by Eidlitz when the building was completed in 1881 could be restored and then matched to modern commercial paints.

The paint schemes to be restored were then outlined on presentation boards for review by the Economic Development Corporation and the Landmarks Preservation Commission. The boards included samples of each color to be used and schedules listing the appropriate coatings for every surface of the building. Drawings on the boards delineated the exact locations and boundaries of each color, and specifications provided detailed descriptions of each coating of paint to be used, including its type (alkyd, acrylic, or epoxy), its sheen (flat, eggshell, or semi-gloss), the appropriate primer, and techniques for paint application. Each type of paint was selected for its surface compatibility, overall appearance, and historical appropriateness.

In addition, contract documents for the removal of the old paint were developed. Because the old paint on the cast iron and the rotunda masonry contained lead, a hazardous material, it was removed in compliance with stringent governmental regulations that required that those areas be sealed off from the rest of the building while the paint was being removed and that workers wear respirators and protective clothing.

Before repainting began, test panels or mock-ups were prepared to demonstrate the restoration color schemes.

Investigation of original hallway wall with trompe l'oeil painting surface to give the appearance of three-dimensional moldings. The main surface of the wall was faux-painted to resemble marble. This decorative approach to the building was typical of the post-Eidlitz era.

One test panel consisted of an entire wall in a second-floor hallway, including a door frame, baseboard, and cornice. The proposed color scheme for the public areas was reviewed and approved by representatives of the Economic Development Corporation and the Landmarks Preservation Commission in 2001. One painting contractor undertook surface preparation and painting of the flat wall and ceiling areas. A second contractor did the decorative painting, including the marbleized columns, gold-leaf column capitals, and faux-painted brick walls of the first floor.

The original paint schemes for the public spaces indicated that Eidlitz favored a limited palette of colors for the courthouse. The cast-iron trim, including the door and window architraves, was painted a light buff color that related to the color of the cream brick used in the rotunda and other spaces. In some instances, the trim was highlighted by a subtle, pale yellow-white tone. The iron baseboards were painted a warm gray color that matched the sandstone selected by Eidlitz for details in the rotun-

Left: The ground-floor walls of the rotunda were originally plastered and then faux-painted to duplicate the appearance of the brickwork used on the upper floors. This appearance was recreated as part of the restoration.

Above: When the Department of Education took over the building, the former courtrooms, which were to be used as offices, were painted in a palette of colors that had originally been selected by Leopold Eidlitz for these public spaces. Sample panels of these colors were painted in the courtrooms so that it could be determined which of the historic colors would be used in which room.

da. The paint scheme that Eidlitz developed for the rotunda was particularly successful in uniting his brick and stone masonry with Kellum's cast iron.

The walls of the former courtrooms were painted following a palette of colors that had been originally selected by Eidlitz for the courthouse. The location of these colors was determined after the building was assigned to the Department of Education in 2002.

Tile Floors

The floors in the south wing of the courthouse, designed by Eidlitz, were finished with colorful unglazed ceramic tiles, much like those used in other major nineteenth-century public buildings, including the Houses of Parliament in London, the U.S. Capitol, and the New York State Capitol. Two types of tiles were used, encaustic and geometric, both manufactured in England by Minton & Co. The encaustic tiles, which had patterns made from two or more colors of clay, were used as borders in rooms on all four floors of the wing. The geometric tiles, which were solid colored and made in different shapes, were installed in the fields within the border tiles. The tiles were laid in nine different patterns to complement the polychrome masonry of the wing.

When the restoration project began in 1999, portions of tiles were missing on each floor, and years of accumulated dirt and wax dulled the surfaces of all the tiles. The tile of the entire third floor was obscured by layers of vinyl flooring and office partitions.

During the restoration of the New York State Capitol, the architects had worked with H. & R. Johnson, the manufacturer of the Minton Hollins brand tile based in Stoke-on-Trent, England. For the restoration of the Smithsonian Institution's Arts and Industry Building during the Bicentennial, the company had reintroduced the production of unglazed tiles in standard shapes and colors common during the mid-nineteenth century. H. & R. Johnson assured the architects that they would be able to supply all the geometric tiles needed for the courthouse from their line of standard tiles; the firm would also manufacture all the replicas of the encaustic tile. This capability helped ensure that the restoration of the tile floors would be possible.

The architects made measured drawings of each floor of the south wing, showing every tile and its various color patterns. Other drawings indicated the various encaustic border tiles on that floor. Each floor was then surveyed tile by tile to determine the number of broken or missing tiles, each of which was marked on the drawings. Once the extent of damaged tiles was known, the drawings were reviewed to determine the best approach for restoration.

The colorful tile floors were a major character-defining element of the south wing, and since the majority of the original tiles remained in each space, it was important to retain as much of this original flooring as possible. Only missing, loose, or badly broken tiles would be replaced. Tiles with small surface imperfections, or short or thin cracks, would remain in place as long as they were still securely fixed and did not pose a threat to the safety of visitors. Because it was very important that the replacement tiles matched the color of the original tiles, a replacement strategy was developed for each floor: some original tiles would be used to patch small areas of damaged tiles, while newly made tiles would be used for large areas needing replacement. Two sets of plans were drawn for each floor. The first set indicated damaged tiles to be removed as well as large areas of sound tiles that would be carefully removed, salvaged, and reused as replacements for small areas of patching. The second set of drawings indicated the small areas or individual tiles that would be replaced with the sound original tiles; these drawings also showed large areas where new tiles would be installed. This method would help ensure an even overall appearance to the floors.

Meanwhile, a sample of each original tile was sent to the factory in England for the purpose of matching exactly the color, shape, and pattern of the tiles. Subsequently, samples of reproduction tiles were submitted to the architects for approval.

Damaged or loose tiles were removed on each floor as indicated on the drawings. Often during this process adjacent tiles became loose as well, increasing the number of tiles to be reset. On the first floor an entire room of original tiles, more than 1,000 in all, was removed to provide enough material to patch damaged areas elsewhere on the first floor and on the third-floor mezzanine. On the second floor approximately 3,500 tiles were removed to provide enough replacements for other sections of the floor. On the third floor all of the original tiles were removed to provide access for the installation of new lighting and fire-protection equipment to the second floor below. All of the conduits for the second-floor ceiling fixtures and third-floor power circuits were laid on this floor, thereby allowing the decorative stone ceiling of the second floor to remain free of unsightly exposed conduits.

After the removals were complete, salvaged tiles were used to replace nearly all the small areas of missing or damaged tiles. New tiles made to match each type were installed in some locations on every floor. For example, on the third floor, salvaged encaustic border tiles were reinstalled along with new border tiles; new geometric tiles were then installed over the conduits as a red field to match the historic appearance. The combination of using salvaged and new tiles proved to be a successful strategy.

Damage to original encaustic and geometric tile floor in the second-floor courtroom of the south wing designed by Leopold Eidlitz. The damage was caused first by the installation of piping for a non-original steam heating system that utilized radiators, and later by the pipes leaking.

Restoration drawing for the floor of the second-floor courtroom showing the color and pattern of the finished floor. Other drawings showed every tile that was to be replaced and indicated which tiles would be salvaged for reuse.

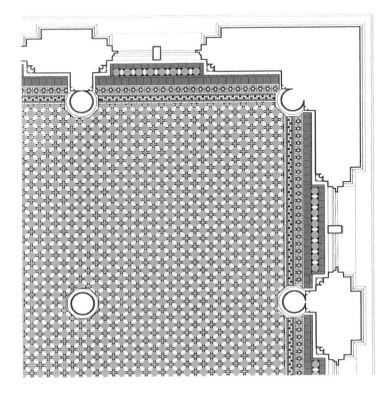

Installation of new and salvaged original tiles to exactly duplicate the original pattern. Replacement tiles were manufactured in Stoke-on-Trent, England, by the successor to the company that made the original tiles.

Completed tile floor restoration at the first floor of the south wing. Different encaustic tile patters were matched on each floor.

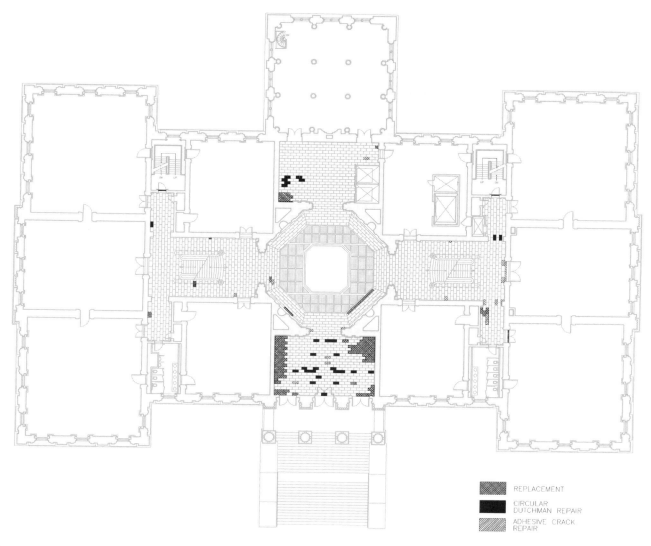

REPLACEMENT

CIRCULAR
DUTCHMAN REPAIR

ADHESIVE CRACK
REPAIR

Restoration drawing of the main floor indicating where the marble flooring was to be replaced or repaired. Where the paving stones were cracked or damaged to the extent that they were unsafe, they were replaced with recycled material or new stone.

After the floors were cleaned and sealed with chemicals specially chosen to be compatible with unglazed tiles, the floors exhibited a highly consistent appearance.

Not all steps in the process went as planned, however. On the second floor more than sixty new encaustic tiles, each with a pattern of four colors, were needed to complete the border. When these tiles could not be delivered in time for Mayor Giuliani's press conference, decorative painters who were completing work on the first floor's faux brick and marble successfully stenciled the original patterns onto the temporary concrete infill. A few months later, the trompe l'oeil work was replaced with proper tiles, and the floor restoration was finally complete.

Stone Floors

In most monumental public buildings the use of a durable and handsome flooring material is an important character-defining element of the interior spaces. At Tweed Courthouse, John Kellum used Tuckahoe marble tiles on all floors throughout the public spaces. Each stone tile was approximately 1¾ inch thick; most measured 1 foot in width and 2 feet in length, and most were finished with a honed surface. This type of marble paving was also used at the U.S. Capitol and other major American public buildings. At Tweed Courthouse, the tiles were well maintained, with constant cleaning and waxing, up through 1999. However, daily use for more than one hundred and thirty years had caused wear in some areas of the floor. Many tiles were cracked or broken, while others had been removed during various alterations.

Beginning with the first feasibility studies, plans called for retaining as much of the original marble flooring as possible, since most of it remained in excellent condition. During the restoration work, the architects created a plan of each floor showing each tile and door threshold. Next, a visual survey was undertaken to record the condition of each tile and to determine whether it could remain as is, had small cracks that needed minor repairs, or was badly cracked, damaged, or missing and required replacement. Only damaged stones that were unsafe were marked for replacement. Stones with patterns of wear from years of foot traffic would be kept in place since the wear represented the building's years of service and had become part of its historic character.

Replacement stone from the Tuckahoe and Sheffield quarries that was used in the original construction of the courthouse and would have matched exactly the color and veining of the existing floor was not available for the restoration. Another solution had to be found for replacing single tiles or small areas of damaged or missing tiles or large areas that were highly visible and where matching was critical. Since stone tiles already in place provided the best match, areas in two rooms on the first floor became a "sacrificial quarry" of material. Located just inside the east and west entry doors, these two rooms retained only

a center swath of stone; the rest had been removed during a previous alteration. These stone tiles were carefully removed and stockpiled, then recut where necessary and reset. For example, many tiles were missing in the second-floor entry vestibule where new restrooms had been added during the late nineteenth century. Recycled stones were used to patch this entire area, thereby creating a uniform field of flooring in a space that would now become the building's main entrance.

However, the number of tiles removed from the first floor did not provide sufficient replacements. New tiles, made of white Georgia marble, were quarried and cut to match the size of the originals. These stones were lighter in color than the existing marble, so they were used for all new door thresholds and for areas where large numbers of tiles were missing; in large areas they blended together much better than if they were used for single replacements that would create a spotted appearance. This method worked well on the first floor where the original marble had been removed at the judges' elevator and replaced with wood and also where a restroom with a ceramic tile floor had been installed in the main elevator lobby near the south wing. In the third-floor elevator lobby of the south wing, most of the marble tiles were slightly darker and had more prominent veining than those in the main part of the building. This floor was one of the last to be replaced, and by that time the stock of recycled flooring had been depleted. The new Georgia marble was too light in color. However, some marble restroom partitions, removed and salvaged early in the project, provided an

Resetting marble floor tiles. New electrical conduits were installed within the setting bed beneath the stone flooring.

The original portion of the courthouse was constructed with one-over-one double-hung wood windows with cast-iron frames and entablatures. In the 1930s, the wood sash were replaced with new two-over-two double-hung sash which substantially changed the appearance of the window and the building's facades. As part of the restoration work, these sash were replaced with wood sash that duplicated the appearance of the original windows. Prior to the restoration, many of these windows also had portable air conditioners with later radiators in front of the decorative cast-iron panels beneath the windows. The new HVAC system allowed these later additions to be removed.

Original cast-iron sash after removal from south wing window originally designed by Leopold Eidlitz. Several of the original sash had been replaced with wood windows at various times and the remaining cast-iron sash were warped, corroded, or damaged.

excellent match, so that marble was cut into tiles and set in place.

Stones that were only slightly damaged and still firmly set in place were repaired with epoxy. Cracks and small holes were cleaned of dirt and debris, filled with custom-colored epoxy resin, and tooled flush with the surface of the stones; open joints between pavers were grouted. This process helped create a smoother, safer walking surface that could be easily maintained. Finally, all of the marble flooring was cleaned and rehoned, removing the top 1/32 inch from the surface to give the floor a uniform finish not apparent since the building's original construction.

Wood and Cast-Iron Windows

Originally, two main window types existed when Tweed Courthouse was completed, reflecting the different tastes of its two architects. The original portion of the courthouse had wood two-over-two double-hung windows on the first floor, one-over-one double-hung windows on the second and third floors, and double, single-light wood casement windows on the fourth floor—all with durable, fire-resistant, cast-iron frames. During the late 1930s all of the original double-hung windows were replaced. Muntins were added in the center of the windows so that the one-over-one configuration on

the second and third floors was changed to a two-over-two, thereby considerably altering the appearance of the building.

All windows in the south wing, by contrast, had cast-iron frames and sash. Two windows were paired to form a single bay, with fixed arched windows, or lunettes, above the movable, paired windows on the first, second, and third mezzanine floors. Each movable marble cast-iron sash pivoted at the center.

During the initial analysis of the building, every window was surveyed to identify the condition of each component and make detailed recommendations for its restoration. In 1999 funding became available to replace the 1930s sash. Both the wood double-hung and the casement windows were replicated based on the original designs, fitted with insulated glass, and carefully sized to operate within the existing cast-iron frames, which were as large as 5 feet 6 inches wide by 14 feet tall on the second floor. Damaged or missing pieces of the

cast-iron frames were replaced, and displaced or warped elements were secured to the masonry openings. Many layers of paint were removed, and the frames were repainted.

Before this work began, however, a prototype window was installed, and controlled tests were performed to determine its weathertightness. Water was sprayed against the window from the outside while on the inside a partial vacuum was created to test the effectiveness of the weatherstripping against water infiltration. The first configuration did not meet the required standards, as the vacuum slowly allowed water to penetrate between the sash and the frame. The prototype was refitted with neoprene gaskets mortised into the perimeter of the sash, which sealed any irregularities along the existing cast-iron frames. The window passed the second test, and the weatherstripping configurations were recorded. The new windows, which were made of mahogany because of its resistance to rotting, were then installed along with new, heavier sash

Replacement wood windows and restored cast-iron frames replicated the original appearance of the building's fenestration.

Replica cast-iron sash being installed in south wing. Although steel and aluminum were investigated as substitute materials for cast iron, it was determined that the only way the original design could be replicated, while meeting the new energy code requirements, was to cast the sash in iron.

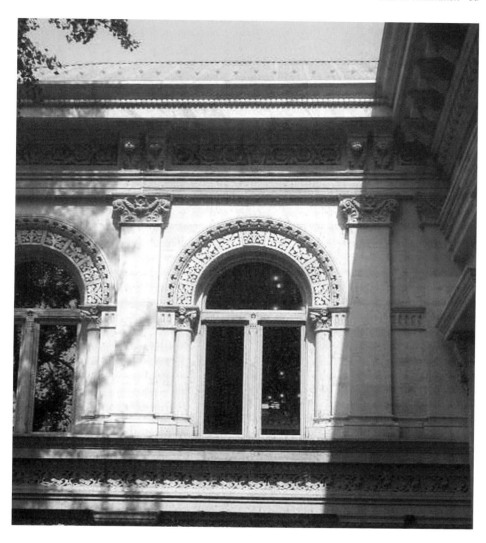

New cast-iron windows of the south wing after restoration. The dimensions and profiles of the casement sash and frames were replicated, weather stripping was added, and new insulated glazing was installed.

weights to counterbalance the added weight of the large panes of insulated glass.

In the south wing the sash as well as the window frames were replaced for several reasons. The original sash jamb and window stop did not permit the installation of the thicker insulated glass required by the design of the new HVAC system. Many of the original cast-iron sash were missing altogether, having been replaced at different times with wood sash. Because the center-pivoting sash and frame worked together as a unit, many of the frames were badly warped or damaged, thereby compromising their operability and weathertightness.

The new windows for the south wing were designed to replicate the originals as closely as possible. Materials such as aluminum and steel were considered, but cast iron was selected because of its long-term durability, resistance to corrosion, and strength needed for such

large windows (the largest sash measured 2 feet 8 inches by 9 feet 1 inch). Because cast iron is so strong, profiles of the frame and sash, including the thin muntins, could be replicated despite the added weight of insulated glazing in the pivoting sash.

The architects and contractors worked together to maintain historic details and finishes and to ensure that assembly tolerances would permit smooth operability yet provide a weather-tight seal. The sash were then inserted into the frames at the foundry in Alabama, shipped to New York, and installed as a unit into the masonry openings.

Reproducing the material, texture, and operating configuration of the historic sash in both parts of the building, while only very slightly modifying the profiles to allow for insulated glazing, resulted in high-quality windows whose appearance was identical to the originals.

Interior and Exterior Wood Doors

The main entrance doors of nineteenth-century public buildings were important character-defining features. Usually fabricated of mahogany, walnut, or oak, at Tweed Courthouse the doors were highly decorative and grandly scaled. The window sash and flooring were the only other wood architectural elements to be found in the courthouse.

The exterior of the building had entrances on each facade, and all of them had been altered by the time the restoration project began in 1999. The original main entry to the building on the second floor at the top of the partially removed monumental stairway facing Chambers Street had three identical pairs of large inward-swinging walnut doors that were 13 feet in height and surmounted by fixed lunette transoms. This entranceway was recessed within arched openings behind the north portico. The

doors had boldly detailed classical moldings inside and out, similar to the interior cast-iron trim.

Four of these doors had been fixed in place when the entry hall was subdivided to provide men's and women's restrooms in the late nineteenth century. A large portion of the center of each door was removed, and a double-hung window was installed to provide light and ventilation to each restroom. The two doors in the center bay survived intact and in excellent working condition; however, they were almost completely obscured from view inside by a wood vestibule and revolving doors. The entry doors on the first floor located under the monumental stair, and the original main entrance, had undergone similar alterations. The space outside these doors had become a vestibule when the iron gates under the east and west sides of the staircase were replaced with wood doors with glass lights. Over time the original doors at the other entrances had been replaced with smaller, single-leaf doors, and wood vestibules or revolving doors were added inside. All exteri-

Restoration drawing of ground floor entrance doors.

Interior doors with etched glass before restoration.
Photograph by Lily Wang.

Original wood interior door during restoration. The old finishes have been stripped and damaged areas repaired using new wood pieces fabricated to match the original.

Restored interior doors with replicated etched glass panels.

or doors had been painted black, covering the original stained and varnished finish. The alteration or replacement of the doors had resulted in substantial changes to the exterior character of the building at the locations where visitors first came in contact with the courthouse.

However, most of the original wood doors remained intact; the first floor was the only area with a substantial number of missing doors. On the first, second, and third floors, openings facing the rotunda or public stair halls contained paired or single doors with large glass panels etched with the municipal seal. Doors opening into service spaces or connecting courtrooms did not include glass panels, but single doors on the first floor originally had been stenciled.

Since the doors were such an important character-defining element of both the interior and the exterior, the design approach for the restoration was to reuse as many of the original doors as possible and to replace damaged or missing doors with reproductions of the originals. Because the original doors had been constructed of hardwood 2 to 3 inches thick, the Department of Buildings accepted them as the equivalent of modern fire-rated doors. The restoration of the original exterior entrances became a high priority, in order to provide a coherent appearance and a welcoming face to the public. The architects carried out a detailed survey of each door to document the existing conditions; thirty-one door types were identified. This information was used to prepare contract documents indicating the extent of repair needed for each door; the locations, types, and construc-

Restoration of the original walnut main entrance doors leading to the reconstructed Chambers Street staircase, prior to installation.

tion detailing of doors to be altered and new doors to be produced; and the hardware required for every door.

The first step in the restoration process involved carefully removing all the doors, numbering them according to the architectural drawings, and attaching a metal tag to the top edge. The doors were then crated individually and shipped to the door restoration subcontractor's facility, where they were cataloged and stored. Next, the doors were carefully stripped of built-up finishes to reveal the bare wood. They were then reevaluated because numerous layers of finish had sometimes hidden damage or inferior wood. Unlike doors on the lower floors, the fourth-floor doors were made of pine and had been painted numerous times; they most likely were replacements dating from the mid-twentieth century.

The field survey also had revealed that a closet door in one of the first-floor courtrooms still retained the original stenciling on its inside face. These panels were preserved and used as the model for the restored stain coloring and finish sheen to be applied to all existing and new doors. Meanwhile, the painted design was used to make a new stencil and served as a color sample for first-floor doors to be stenciled.

After the doors were stripped, several doors served as prototypes for the restoration work. Dutchman repairs were made to all damaged areas, and these doors were finished. The architects then examined the sample doors for the quality of repairs, the finish color and sheen on each type of wood, and the painted stenciling. Once approved, these doors provided the standard for matching the hundreds of new and restored doors.

The other doors underwent the same repair and finishing process. Meanwhile, new doors were being fabricated to match existing doors of the same type, but for some entries there was no evidence of the configuration of the original doors. At the east, west, and south, for example, entrances had to be based on the designs of existing doors. At these locations new paired doors were installed within a thin wood frame and stop in the existing openings and configured so that the doors would swing outward for ease of egress, as well as fire safety.

At the main Chambers Street entrance on the second floor, the two original doors were reinstalled in their central position, while four new flanking doors were made to replicate the center pair—because the originals had been removed when the public restrooms were constructed in the original entrance hall. These doors added to the building's egress capacity, and the swing of all three pairs of doors was also reversed so that they opened out, in the direction of traffic exiting the building. The interior wood-paneled walls beside these doors were restored and refinished to match the doors, and a modern bronze-framed interior glass door was installed behind the main center doors, so that the large wood doors could be held open during daytime hours. At the first-floor level, the wood doors under the main stair were removed and replaced with new all-glass doors recessed within the masonry opening where the iron gates once stood.

As the interior doors arrived on site, they were hung with reproduction bronze hinges in the original cast-iron frames. Modern door closers, latches, and locking hardware were installed to make the doors fully operable, and code compliant, but the installation of the reproduction hardware would have to wait until the project's completion so that they would not be damaged during construction.

Etched Glass

The large scale and the fine materials of the original interior doors of Tweed Courthouse—heavy moldings and cast-bronze hardware—made the doors an important design feature within the building. Etched-glass panels, or lights, were used in many of these doors, including the paired doors that opened into the public rooms on the first, second, and third floors. The etching allowed light to filter through the decorative motifs while maintaining visual privacy.

The glass panels varied in size (from approximately 9 inches to 2 feet in width and from 3 feet 6 inches to 6 feet 6 inches in height) depending on the size of the doors. The municipal seal was prominently located in the bottom portion of the light, usually at about chest height. The seal was surrounded by a border that varied according to the height of the glass; in tall panels the space within the border at the top was transparent, since it was located well above eye level. The seals and border motifs had been created through an acid-etching process in which differing exposures to acid were used to produce two distinct levels of translucency.

Most of the lights in the original doors were still intact in 1999 when the restoration began. The Department of Buildings had determined that the wood doors would provide an adequate fire rating between spaces, as had been suggested in the fire-strategy report prepared by the architects and the engineers. This decision was important, because it meant that the original glass could remain in place even though the sizes of the glazed openings were larger than the maximum permitted for fire-rated doors used in new construction. The plan was to remove the original glass panels as each door was being restored, thoroughly clean the glass, and then reinstall it. Any damaged or missing lights would be reproduced to match the existing patterns.

By mid-2001 the original glass had been removed from all the doors and fully cleaned. Reconstruction of the

doors was nearly complete, and the glass was about to be reinstalled. During a meeting with officials from the Department of Buildings to discuss requirements for the building's sprinkler system, the preservation of the original glass in the doors was questioned. The future use of the building was being clarified and sprinkler requirements could be more definitive. Since the architects wanted to keep the public spaces and courtrooms clear of sprinklers, the fire rating of the large doorways in the thick masonry walls separating the public halls from the courtrooms was critical. The Department of Buildings was concerned that the actual glass would not withstand the intense heat of a fire and could shatter and injure occupants as they passed through the doorways. Therefore, the Department of Buildings determined that, although the fire rating for the original wood doors would be acceptable, the glazing would be required to meet a forty-five-minute fire rating. The historic plate glass, fabricated a century earlier, could not meet that requirement, so a suitable substitute material was researched.

The material chosen was Fire-Lite Plus, a $\frac{5}{16}$-inch-thick laminated, tempered-ceramic, fire-rated glazing engi-

Etched glass before restoration.

New etched glazing panel. Instead of the original glass, a laminated, tempered-ceramic fire-rated glazing was used to meet code requirements. The design of each panel duplicates the original patterns of each existing door.

Replicated etched glass panel installed in restored interior wood doors.

neered in Germany. This highly advanced glass offered a sixty-minute fire rating, and it was thin enough to fit within the existing door moldings. In addition, the glass could be slightly sandblasted to replicate an etched finish and still maintain its overall rating. Sandblasting also avoided modern safety and environmental concerns associated with acid etching.

Once the replacement glass had been selected, the next step was to replicate the municipal seal and other design motifs. A sample of the seal and the borders was sandblasted onto a piece of the new glass in order to ascertain the contractor's ability to replicate the finest detail of the historic patterns and the two levels of translucency. The architects, contractor, and fabricator sorted through the scores of rubbings that had been made from the original glass, one for each light, numbered to identi-

fy the door from which it came. Existing glass would be copied exactly and reinstalled in the original doors; however, for new doors, mainly found on the first floor, new patterns were introduced based on the historic designs. One of three seals was chosen for each door, based on their locations on other floors, and in a few cases they were reduced in size to fit within the new pairs of narrow doors. Borders were designed to match the seals.

In order to replicate the two levels of translucency of the original glass, the sandblasting occurred in stages. A plastic resist was applied to the glass, and the areas of the design intended to be the most opaque were cut and peeled away first and then sandblasted. The next area of the resist was peeled away, and the previously sandblasted area was sandblasted again along with the newly exposed area. The resist was never removed from areas of the glass that were to remain completely transparent. This step-by-step process was used to create ninety-eight new lights, which were installed in the doors on site.

Hardware

The door hardware selected by Kellum for Tweed Courthouse illustrates a significant turning point in the manufacture of hardware in the United States. The first attempt to produce complex door hardware was carried out by Enoch Robinson of Boston in the 1860s. The elegantly detailed, beautifully crafted Robinson knobs, roses, escutcheons, and other fittings used at the courthouse were made of copper-clad cast lead. However, this combination soon proved impractical when the soft lead was subjected to heavy use.

The Metallic Compression Casting Company (MCCC) of Boston developed a manufacturing process for fine cast-bronze hardware, based on compression-molding technology commonly used in the glass industry, and on June 7, 1870, over forty hardware designs were patented by the company. In the early 1870s the Russell & Erwin (R&E) Manufacturing Company of New Britain, Connecticut, acquired the patents and the designs of the Metallic Compression Casting Company, for whom they initially acted as agents.

At the courthouse the copper-clad cast-lead fittings were used in the original building, and compression cast-bronze hardware was selected by Eidlitz for the south wing. All of this hardware was fashioned in various designs in the neo-Grec style popular at the time.

A few surviving original mortise locks illustrate another chapter in the development of hardware technology in America. Financial records of county expenditures for the courthouse dating from October 5, 1867, indicate that one hundred and thirty-eight rotary brass mortise locks were supplied by Johnson's Rotary Lock Company. Frank G. Johnson of Brooklyn had patented various forms of this unusual type of lock whose unique mechanism is operated by a key that features six projecting pins that enter the circular keyholes and depress the tumblers. The lock is stamped "Johnsons Rotary Lock Co. NY F.G. Johnsons Pat. Feb.5 1861." Physical evidence indicates that they were used on the closet doors, along with copper-clad cast-lead escutcheons and knobs. The unusual keyhole escutcheon featured an integral knob rose, a small plate at the base of the doorknob shaft. This element had been removed from the only surviving escutcheon in the building. Apparently the rotary locks proved impractical and were soon replaced throughout the building with conventionally keyed locks.

Rotary mortise lock supplied by Johnson's Rotary Lock Company in 1867. This lock type was originally used on closet doors.

This large double-keyed mortise lock was originally used on all of the primary doors. It has no manufacture's marks.

Original Robinson-type copper-clad cast-lead combined rose and keyhole escutcheon. The rose is missing.

Original Robinson-type copper-clad cast-lead keyhole escutcheon.

Original Robinson-type cast-bronze keyhole escutcheon.

Original Robinson-type copper-clad cast-lead knob rose.

By the time of the 1991 feasibility study, nearly all of the original door and window hardware had been replaced several times. Fortunately, a few examples of the original hardware remained in place in scattered locations. In the main portion of the building, extant original door hardware included one large and one small keyhole escutcheon, a 2-inch-diameter knob rose, and the damaged combined rose-escutcheon mentioned previously; however, no matching knobs remained. These fittings were all Robinson-type copper-clad cast-lead hardware dating to the late 1860s, but they bore no manufacturer's marks. A few original mortise locks remained in place, including the Johnson rotary locks and a large double-keyed lock that was unmarked. Originally, the doors with this hardware were hung on cast-iron pintle hinges; the pintle supports were screwed into the cast-iron door frames. Nearly all of these hinges had been replaced with large butt hinges, most likely because the pintle hinges proved inadequately sized for the heavy solid-walnut doors. Because the original windows had been removed and replaced in the 1930s, no original window hardware remained in the Kellum portion of the building.

More original door and window hardware survived in the south wing. One latch body with a rabbeted faceplate and several keyhole escutcheons, roses, and flush-bolt mechanisms complete with faceplates and knobs remained in use on the doors. Some of the large pivoting cast-iron window sash still had their original latching mechanisms, and one original cast-bronze window lever was found in situ. This door and window hardware was finely crafted of cast bronze. The knob roses were stamped with the number "952," and the keyhole escutcheons were marked "Pat. June 7, 1870," indicating that the escutcheon and possibly the other fittings were supplied by Russell & Erwin from a design originally patented by the Metallic Compression Casting Company. This hardware was not installed at the courthouse until 1877 or slightly later, when the south wing was nearing completion.

No original doorknobs survived in the south wing. It is possible that levers rather than knobs were used, since Eidlitz, the architect of the south wing, had used lever handles for windows and doors in work then under way at the New York State Capitol.

The window and door hardware was important in the overall design of the interior spaces, since it provided a point of physical contact for the building's users. Furthermore, the decorative nature of the hardware suggests that the original architects were concerned with its aesthetics. The goal of the restoration work was to re-create, as closely as possible, the historic appearance of the windows and doors while ensuring that they would meet modern security and code requirements. As a result, the windows and doors needed both replicated historic hardware and new, modern elements.

The architects began the investigation of the hardware by removing the few original pieces and cataloging them according to function, style, and door type or window from which they came. All of the doors were carefully examined for evidence of original hardware, and all later hardware was documented.

The few pieces of original hardware were taken to E. R. Butler & Co., in New York, a specialty hardware supplier and custom manufacturer that maintains a library of several thousand historic hardware trade catalogs as well as an important collection of period hardware.

The architects worked closely with E. R. Butler & Co. to select decorative hardware appropriate for the building. Illustrations in nineteenth-century hardware catalogs were compared to the surviving hardware to determine when the pieces were originally produced. This process also helped to identify possible matches for pieces that had been removed from the courthouse long ago. For example, a doorknob with a flanged shank to fit the Robinson-type cast-lead rose was selected from among the few cast-lead examples that were known to have been produced. The feasibility of replicating the hardware was discussed as well, and it was determined that exact copies could be made of all the pieces, cast in bronze for durability, and finished to match the surviving examples.

Each piece of hardware needed for every door in the building was then determined, based on its location, type, function, and code requirements. Several sets of reproduction hardware were defined; they included a knob or lever, rose, and keyhole escutcheon. The appropriate set was assigned to nearly every door on the first through fourth floors, again based on its location, type, and function, as well as on any evidence on the doors of what had historically existed. Each set was then combined with a set of modern hardware appropriate to the function of the particular door. There were more than twenty sets of modern hardware, which included such elements as automatic closers, magnetic hold-open devices, deadlocks, latch bodies, stops, and hinges, all fabricated with a dark bronze finish in order to blend with the reproduction hardware. This information was added to a revised door schedule (the doors had already been removed from the building and were undergoing restoration at the time). Specifications were drawn up and bids were requested.

The contract for hardware installation was awarded to Petersen, Geller, Spurge of New York, the same contractor responsible for the restoration and installation of the doors and windows throughout the building. The firm worked closely with the architects and manufacturer during the entire fabrication and installation process.

The replication of the historic hardware required a relatively long lead time and was very labor intensive, so work began on this phase first. The best representative

Original cast-bronze Eidlitz-type rose from south wing.

Original cast-bronze Eidlitz-type keyhole escutcheon from south wing. It is stamped, "Pat. June 7, 1870."

Eidlitz-type cast-bronze window lever handle from south wing.

Diagram of door hardware from main part of the building.
The knob, rose, and keyhole escutcheon were replicated.
Drawing by E.R. Butler & Co.

Replica knob and keyhole escutcheon on restored door
in main part of the building. The knob features the head
of a warrior and a Greek key motif.

example of each original piece was loaned to the contractor to be used as a model during production. Petersen, Geller, and Spurge subcontracted with E. R. Butler & Co. to produce the custom pieces. Rather than making a mold directly from the original hardware, each piece was scanned three-dimensionally. This information was used to produce a plastic model of each piece, which was then reworked by hand to refine surfaces and any details that had been worn by time on the original artifacts. Some models were made much larger than the original example in order to re-create more accurately the fine details that existed when the original hardware was new. The new knobs, which featured the head of a Roman soldier, a Greek key motif, and a raised, ribbed border, were modeled in this way. After tooling, the size of the enlarged models was reduced, and molds were made. The pieces were then cast in bronze, and an oil-rubbed finish was applied, resulting in a rich, dark color.

Meanwhile, the new wood windows and the new and restored wood doors were being installed throughout the building. Since no original hardware from the wood windows had survived, the new pulls, sash locks, pulleys, and chains were not custom made; instead, commercially available hardware that was traditional in design and made of bronze with an oil-rubbed finish to match the other hardware was used. The new cast-iron windows, located in the south wing, received new bronze latch bodies, custom made to match the appearance of the surviving example. However, they did not have a functional latch, for it would have been prohibitively expensive to re-create the functioning mechanism for windows that would rarely be opened. Instead, the latch bodies had fixed posts onto which the reproduced levers were installed in a stationary position.

The wood doors were hung in the original cast-iron openings using new bronze hinges and were fitted with the modern hardware. Some original hardware was also installed at this time, such as flush bolts in the inactive leaf of paired doors. Because the replicated historic hardware was so valuable, it was decided to install it only at the end of the restoration project, when the new occupant was ready to move in. In the meantime, less expensive, standard knobs were installed so the doors would be fully functional. New doors in the basement and the attic, which would not be seen from the public spaces and were not scheduled to receive any historic hardware, were fitted with good-quality, modern, stainless-steel hardware.

Finally, just before the Department of Education was ready to move in, the reproduction knobs and levers, roses, and escutcheons were installed on the doors on the second, third, and fourth floors, signaling the completion of the restoration work.

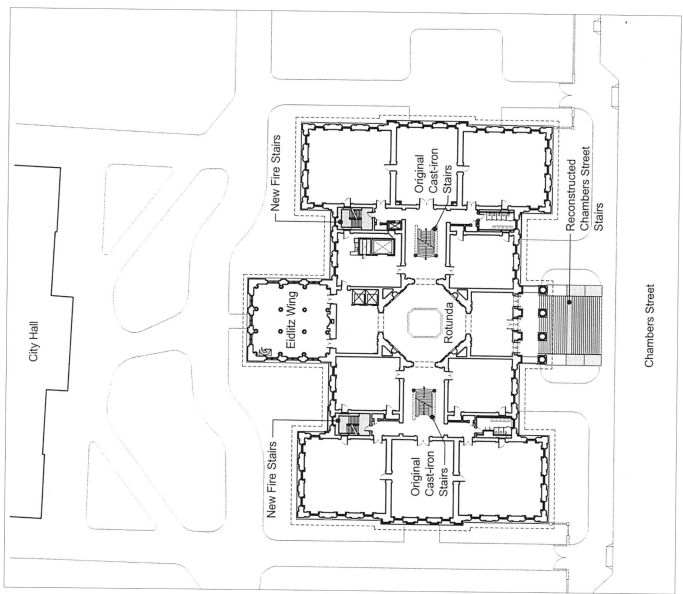

Floor plan with new, enclosed fire stairs located in former service areas. The construction of the two new code-compliant stairs allowed the orig- *inal monumental cast-iron stairs, which opened off the rotunda, to be restored to their original appearance.*

New Fire Stairs

Nineteenth-century public buildings were often constructed with monumental stairs that do not meet modern building codes for a number of reasons, including lack of separation from adjacent spaces, length of runs, and sufficient landings. Prior to its restoration and renovation, there were no code-compliant fire stairs in Tweed Courthouse. To increase the egress capacity of the build-

ing, two separate sets of enclosed fire stairs were added. These stairways connect all the floors of the building—including the basement and the attic—to an exit at grade level at the south side of the building. Initial planning and design for the vertical stairway shafts began in the preliminary stages of the project, when smaller rooms that had been constructed as service areas were identified as suitable locations. Combined with the smoke-management system in the rotunda and the increased exit capacity from the second floor to the restored Chambers Street

Shaft for new fire stairs created from former service areas, retaining original cast-iron door and window trim and baseboards.

Right: Section looking west through new fire stairs located in former service areas. The landings of the staircase are suspended by steel tension rods from a beam in the attic, allowing the stairway to appear to float within the space. The original wood door, cast-iron door and window trim, cast-iron and baseboards have been retained and restored.

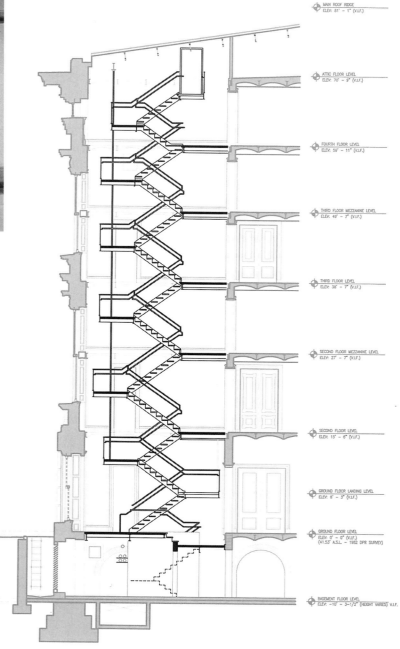

Original wood door with fire-rated etched glazing and panic hardware leading to new fire stairs.

New exterior doors at fire-stair exit at grade. The doors were fabricated to resemble the first-floor interior cast-iron shutters when closed.

stairway, these two new fire stairs were an integral part of the comprehensive fire strategy.

Several approaches for supporting the new stairs were evaluated. The adjacent bearing walls varied in their detailing from floor to floor. In addition, the vertical distance between the floors was irregular and varied greatly in different locations. Vertical chases were located within these masonry walls and were to be reused for the distribution of the new HVAC system. Therefore, the goal for the design of the new structural system was to design a stairway within the new shafts that would meet existing floor levels in the adjacent landmark spaces, to preserve existing window and door openings with their original trim, and to avoid conflicting with the existing ventilation chases.

Working closely with the structural engineers, the architects determined that the most efficient and cost-effective structural design for the new sets of stairs—as well as the most desirable from a historic standpoint—could not rely entirely on the bearing capacity of the shaft walls. The first proposed design was a fully cantilevered staircase, which was supported at each floor on a platform that spanned the width of the shaft. This scheme would alleviate the need for random bearing points otherwise

required at each floor level if a simple span stair was used. However, the cost of this construction would have been prohibitive because the structural connections would have to be fully welded on site within the shaft, which was 13 feet by 20 feet in plan and 80 feet tall; in addition, on-site welding can pose a significant fire hazard in a historic building. Other designs were investigated.

The design that was finally selected utilized two continuous steel tension rods that would be suspended to form a transfer beam at the attic level to support the stairs. In each stairway, these two rods would support the landings of each flight of stairs, allowing the stairway to appear to float within the shaft. This solution utilized bolted connections, which were much less expensive than on-site welding.

The use of tension rods would also avoid the introduction of randomly placed point loads from the cantilevered beams in the existing masonry walls. This proved important later when many original heating chases in the masonry walls were reused for the new HVAC system. In those sections of the walls containing the heating chases, there would be insufficient bearing to carry the loads of the cantilever beams. The tension rods would also allow

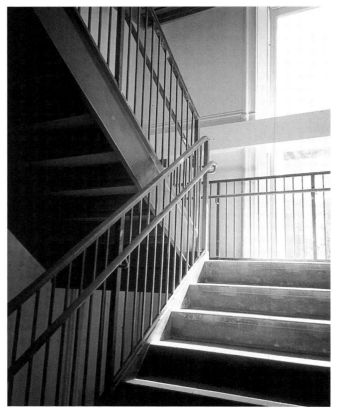

New fire stairs during construction. The landings do not touch the exterior wall, allowing the original window trim and baseboards to be preserved.

the flights of stairs to vary in length, thus accommodating the different floor-to-ceiling heights. This design allowed the exterior wall construction to remain intact, and the width of the stairs and the location of guardrails and handrails could be varied where required. At most locations the stairs could be 5 feet wide at each floor to accommodate the largest number of possible occupants. Concrete treads were poured as the final step in the construction process.

The original solid 2½-inch wood doors leading to the fire stair from the public spaces at each interior level were restored, and new fire-rated etched glazing, historic hinges, and operational hardware were installed. Door swings were reconfigured and new panic hardware was installed. Secondary doorways from adjacent spaces were infilled with a recessed fire-rated partition, providing a closet on the room side. The cast-iron baseboards and the cast-iron door and window trim at each level remained intact. Finally, new exits at grade level were provided at two existing first-floor window openings on the south facade facing City Hall. This concept, developed in coordination with the Landmarks Preservation Commission and the

Department of Parks and Recreation, provided for direct access from the building into City Hall. The new doors were detailed and finished to resemble the original cast-iron shutters of the first-floor window openings.

The obviously modern stairs addressed new requirements for the building, but their discrete location and understated design are very compatible with the historic character of the building. Because the fire stairs serve a strictly utilitarian purpose, the design of the steel and concrete stairs was simple in approach and the stair railings were not ornately detailed. The historic plaster walls and cast-iron trim have been restored; this approach preserves the original configuration of the former rooms and provides a design for the new stairs that is reversible. A fire standpipe runs exposed within each stairway shaft, and a gypsum-board soffit for electrical conduits is integrated at each floor level.

With a minimum amount of modification to the interior or exterior of the building, new, code-compliant, enclosed fire stairs were installed from the basement to the attic level, providing an additional measure of safety for occupants throughout the building.

Elevators

Public buildings in the nineteenth century were usually constructed without elevators. America's first hydraulic passenger elevator was installed in 1857 by the Otis Steam Elevator Company in the E. V. Haughwout & Company building at the corner of Broadway and Broome Street in New York City. However, it was not until 1887 that the first electric elevator was installed. The use of elevators in public buildings became widespread after 1903, when the Otis Elevator Company perfected the electric traction elevator system. Two Otis passenger elevators were installed in Tweed Courthouse in 1911, and a small elevator for judges was added in 1913.

Today the restoration of nineteenth-century public buildings demands that barrier-free access be provided throughout the entire building. Usually an elevator must be installed either within the historic volume of the building or in an addition or appendage outside the historic envelope. Both approaches present potential problems. If installed inside the structure, the elevator can be an intrusion in the historic spaces. If located outside the building, it can affect the integrity of the exterior form and massing. Therefore, the location of a new elevator must be considered carefully, so that it is located correctly and logically within the overall circulation system without compromising the building's historic character. The location of an elevator is often one of the greatest challenges in planning the restoration and reuse of a historic public building.

Detail of rendered building section from the 1991 feasibility study showing the proposed restoration of the 1911 passenger elevators.

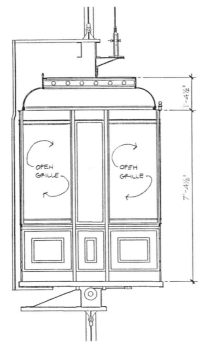

NORTH ELEVATION

EAST ELEVATION

Record drawing of 1911 passenger elevator cars.

EAST ELEVATION

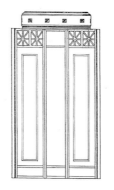

NORTH AND SOUTH ELEVATIONS

Record drawings of 1913 judges' elevator car.

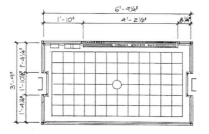

CAR FLOOR PLAN

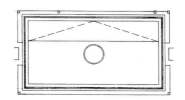

REFLECTED CEILING PLAN

Copper-clad judges' elevator car during restoration.

Fortunately, when the passenger elevators were installed in Tweed Courthouse in 1911, they were located in an area adjacent to the rotunda and connected with the building circulation system but did not intrude on its most significant spaces. The judges' elevator was discreetly located in the southwest quadrant of the building. By the time the restoration of the courthouse began, the two 1911 passenger elevators were considered historic in their own right: they were one of the last remaining city-owned, open-cage, manually operated elevators in New York City.

The restoration of the three elevators was established as a priority following the completion of the feasibility study in 1991. Contract documents were prepared, the Department of General Services selected a contractor, and work commenced in February 1993. The incoming electrical service was upgraded to bring the operational aspects of the elevators into compliance with the electric code. Additional minor code modifications were required to meet life-safety and accessibility regulations.

The judges' elevator was removed entirely from its shaft and taken off site for restoration. Meanwhile, excavation began for the new buried electrical conduits for the elevators. The conduits would run from the courthouse to the nearest public utility underground vault. Work was stopped when previously unknown burials were discovered directly beneath Chambers Street, in front of the building. The architects coordinated a redesign for the routing of the underground conduits with representatives from the Department of General Services, the Landmarks Preservation Commission, Con Edison, other city officials, and an archaeological team. Several months later, after an extensive archaeological research and sampling period, excavation began in a location within City Hall Park and proceeded without incident under the observation and documentation of the archaeologists.

Passenger elevators before restoration.

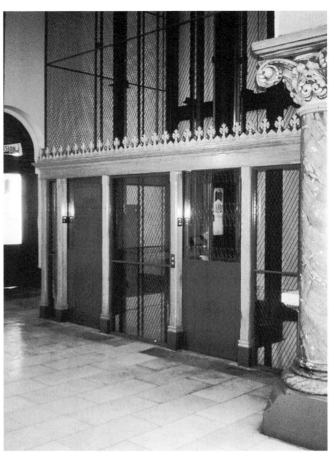

Passenger elevators after restoration. The historic metal cage shaft enclosure and iron gates were retained and restored.

The copper-clad panels of the judges' elevator cab were taken to a specialty contractor, where they were restored and replated in copper. The elevator shaft was reinforced, new elevator machinery was installed within the basement and the attic, and the roof penthouse for the elevator pulleys was restored. Following the car and cab reconstruction, the wall panels and gate were reinstalled, and new lobby and cab controls and indicators were added. In October 1994, with the judges' elevator again in working order, the two passenger elevators were taken out of service for restoration.

Neither the metal cages, which separated the lobbies from the passenger elevator shafts on each floor, nor their metal-and-glass cab, nor their manual controls had been modified since they were installed in the building in 1911. Because they had become significant historic and architectural elements of the public spaces surrounding the rotunda, it was important that upgrades to the open shafts and cabs not detract from their character-defining

attributes. A variance to the building code was obtained so that their significant historic features could be preserved. Working with the Department of Buildings, the architects designed a panelized glass wall and frame assembly to improve the safety and compartmentation of the shaft without compromising the predominant features of the elevators. Many of the original features, like the hand-operated controls and the mechanical equipment, were left intact, while modern equipment, such as self-operated controls and upgraded machinery, were installed to meet modern code requirements.

The two cabs were dismantled and taken to the restoration contractor's shop; the woven metal cage was stripped, reprimed, and repainted. The surrounding wood trim was repaired and refinished prior to the addition of the glass panels on the exterior surface of the cage structure. Modifications made to the roof penthouse included the installation of new elevator machinery, new skylights, and provisions for future smoke-control-system

Passenger elevator car after removal from hoistway, prior to restoration.

exhaust ventilation. The restored cabs, which had been reglazed and repainted off site, were installed with modernized controls and indicators. They resumed operation in February 1998.

In order to protect the elevators during the restoration of the rest of the building, the Economic Development Corporation decided to limit their use to only those people undertaking routine maintenance and safety checks. All construction personnel and materials used other means of vertical transportation including a construction elevator that was part of the scaffolding outside the building. As a result only minor repairs and operational adjustments were needed. Final acceptance by the Department of Buildings of the three restored historic elevators occurred in parallel with the two new service elevators completed in 2001. The service elevators were constructed in the rooms southwest of the Rotunda to accommodate large pieces of furniture and exhibition components when the building was programmed for museum use.

Lighting

Providing adequate lighting in restored public spaces that will still be used as a workplace can be a challenging design problem. Modern lighting levels, as moderated by current codes, usually far exceed the light provided by restored or replicated fixtures, particularly those originally designed to burn oil or illuminating gas. However, these historic fixtures were almost always important design features, and in order to maintain the historical and architectural integrity of the spaces they need to be retained or replicated. Therefore, the question remains, how can these fixtures be electrified without compromising their character, and how can they be supplemented with modern fixtures that are compatible but not imitative in order to achieve the required lighting levels? Too often this is done by the introduction of modern fixtures with some pseudo-historic components, or modern recessed fixtures and track lighting. All of these can intrude in the historic spaces and seriously compromise their integrity.

At Tweed Courthouse, because of the significance of the historic spaces, the architects developed a lighting program that called for the restoration of the handful of surviving historic gas-lighting fixtures along with the replication and electrification of those that were missing. In those areas slated for office use, modern task-lighting fixtures were incorporated into the office landscape furniture system. This approach allowed the monumental rooms to be restored to their historic forms, while providing adequate lighting levels to be provided on an as-needed basis as part of the furnishings, which would also be completely reversible. An exterior lighting design that illuminated the facade of the building and highlighted the front entrance stairs and portico was also developed and implemented.

The original sections of the courthouse, as well as the south wing, included a system of gas illumination that was fully integrated into the structure. The system featured a variety of gas fixtures ranging from simple, utilitarian wall brackets to complex, multitiered chandeliers. Late in the nineteenth century electricity was introduced into the courthouse, initially operating in conjunction with the gas-lighting system but ultimately replacing it. Analysis of the wall brackets in the corridors revealed that they were converted from gas to electricity sometime after April 1892, the patent date found on an insulator installed as part of the conversion.

By 1989, when the feasibility study was initiated, there were only a few nineteenth-entury lighting devices still in the building. These included several massive wall brackets in the main corridors, several simple combination gas-

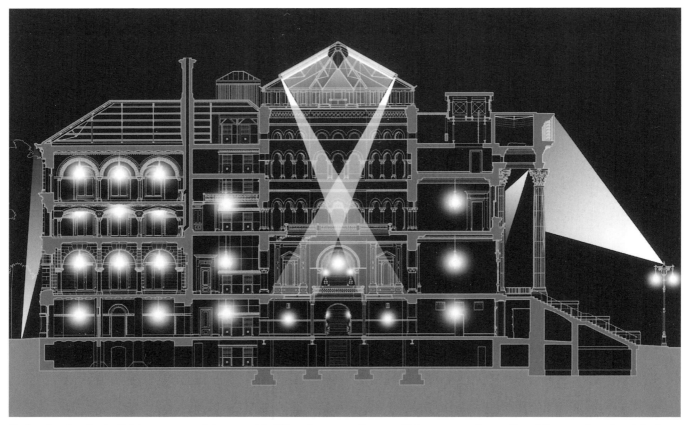

Design drawing for the lighting program of the restored building show-ing historic fixtures in the restored rooms and modern lighting above the laylight and on the exterior. The historic fixtures were either existing *fixtures which were restored or replicated fixtures where the originals were missing.*

electric wall brackets in the fourth-floor corridors, and pairs of light standards positioned on the newel posts of the main stairways on the first and second floors. The standards were old but were not part of the earliest light-ing scheme. None of the numerous original chandeliers survived, and no nineteenth-century photographs show-ing them were discovered.

A room-by-room survey documented later lighting, including many early twentieth-century suspended "schoolhouse"-type fixtures in the former courtrooms. Other areas had modern incandescent and fluorescent fixtures, often fed by a surface-mounted electrical con-duit and exposed piping that were historically inappropri-ate and unsightly. The illumination provided by the exist-ing light fixtures compromised the historic ambiance of the interior spaces and did not meet the practical needs of the new occupants; thus there was little doubt that a total restoration was necessary.

The process leading to the re-creation of the historic lighting fixtures involved a search for historic documents, drawings, and photographs and the analysis of physical evi-dence in the building, including surviving fixtures. Period lighting devices, located at other sites and in public and private collections, were also studied, as were fixtures used in other buildings designed by Kellum and Eidlitz. The records of county expenditures from 1867 provided important information about the original lighting, includ-ing fixture types (chandeliers, pendants, and standards), sizes (two, eight, and twenty-four lights), and shades (8-inch cut-glass globes), but no manufacturer was named.

The only known early interior photograph of the courthouse appeared in the October 1908 issue of *The Architectural Record*; it showed a corner of the courtroom in the south wing (second floor) and two electric chande-liers, which do not appear to be modified gas fixtures. The photograph revealed that five fixtures were used in the room, and this number was confirmed when the orig-inal gas piping was uncovered.

Four illuminations reproduced in the 1980 historic structure report—three woodcuts published in Frank Leslie's *Illustrated Newspaper* in the 1870s and a colored lithograph from the1868 *Manual of the Corporation of the*

Undated photograph of original courtroom used as office space before restoration. The incandescent "schoolhouse"-type light fixtures had been randomly suspended from the ceiling. Prior to the building's restoration, this lighting was typical in all of the historic rooms of the building. Photograph provided by the Department of Citywide Administrative Services

Original gas wall bracket before restoration alongside a twentieth-century incandescent fixture. The former gas fixture was converted to electricity sometime after 1892 and was powered by surface-mounted electrical conduit. Although the basic cast-bronze fixtures remained, various original fittings and glass shades were missing.

City of New York—provided important information about other missing chandeliers. The lithograph and two of the woodcuts illustrate an impressive multitiered scroll-type chandelier once located in the largest courtrooms. The other woodcut, a view of the surrogate's courtroom dated December 1, 1877, shows two handsome neo-Grec chandeliers.

The entire building was searched for evidence of the locations of lighting fixtures. In nearly every space the original positions of gas fixtures were indicated by the capped-off projecting gas pipes. In some spaces, including the corridors, the existing electrical wall brackets had been placed in the same location as the original gas fixtures. Elaborate plaster center medallions on the ceilings of second- and third-floor rooms indicated the original locations of chandeliers.

The inspection revealed the positions of approximately seventy chandeliers. Repeated probing of the surfaces of the central rotunda produced no evidence of gas lighting in that space. Apparently natural light from the skylight filled the entire upper portion of the rotunda, and

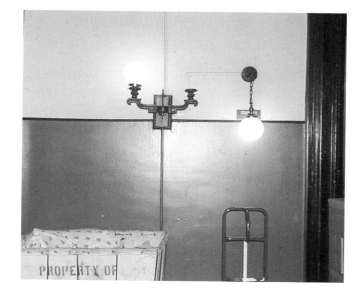

gas light from the chandeliers in the nearby corridors was the only source of illumination for this space.

Historically accurate lighting fixtures were placed in the corridors and primary spaces throughout the building, including the monumental courtrooms and smaller adjoining rooms. In some instances the fixture type to be replicated was obvious; in the corridors, for instance, the existing neo-Grec wall brackets would be restored and reproduced in cast bronze as needed. Because the utilitarian gas-electric brackets on the fourth floor were in very poor condition, exact copies were produced and installed in the original locations.

For the twelve large courtroom spaces on the second and third floors, the rococo scroll chandelier, seen in the 1868 and 1870s illustrations, was reproduced. With a diameter of 5 feet and with twenty-four globes arranged in three tiers, this large fixture fits comfortably in the monumentally scaled rooms. The illustrations documented a fixture similar to a chandelier made circa 1870 by Mitchell, Vance and Company of New York, which is now displayed in the parlor from the Jedediah Wilcox house at

Restoration drawing for original gas wall bracket. Missing elements, such as the torch handle below the urn and the shade supports, were replicated and installed on the restored fixtures.

Reproduction of the 5-foot-diameter, three-tiered chandelier used in the large second-and third-floor courtrooms. These fixtures were finished in a gold-toned polished brass with deeper patinated details.

Restoration drawing of two-tiered, twelve-arm chandelier used in smaller historic rooms on the principal floors. This fixture is similar to chandeliers manufactured by Archer and Pancoast in the 1870s and was finished with a dark bronze paint with metallic gold details.

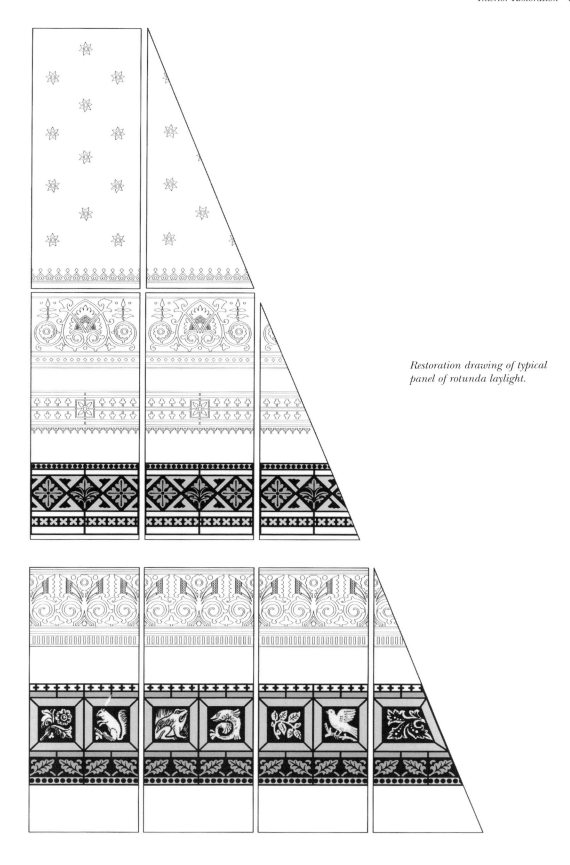

Restoration drawing of typical panel of rotunda laylight.

Original cast- and wrought-iron laylight frame system, prior to restoration.

tively textured or stained glass, laylights are often missing from historic public buildings because of deterioration resulting from a lack of maintenance. Furthermore, because nineteenth-century laylights do not meet modern building and safety codes, they are typically removed from public spaces. Changing tastes in architecture also contribute to decisions to remove them. Nevertheless, laylights are often important character-defining architectural elements in major public spaces. When dealing with laylights, it is necessary to assess their significance both as individual elements and as components of an overall architectural scheme. If historic laylights are to be conserved or replicated, extraordinary measures are often required to render them safe and code compliant.

Perhaps the most dramatic contribution made by Eidlitz to the interior of the Tweed Courthouse interior was the immense skylight at the top of the rotunda. The cast-iron dome that architect Kellum had intended to grace the courthouse was never constructed. In its place Eidltz inserted an octagonal skylight and a laylight set with large panels of etched glass that were overlaid with bands of leaded stained glass. The laylight thus served as the ceiling for the rotunda. This modification to Kellum's design was in part the result of budget demands, but also in part the result of Eidlitz's entirely different architectural sensibilities.

For security reasons during World War II the laylight glass was removed and stored in the attic. Although intended to be reinstalled in the future, most of the orig-

inal glass elements were broken, either during the removal process or while in storage. In 1978 the surviving glass was retrieved, cleaned, and cataloged by the Landmarks Preservation Commission and a group of students from Columbia University. In 1990, using this information as a starting point, architects and glass conservators conducted extensive research on the framework of the laylight and the remaining glass fragments as part of the feasibility study.

The laylight frame was constructed of 9-inch-deep cast-iron I-beams and T-bars. Nine-inch-wide I-beams divided the octagon into eight equal trapezoidal sections, which in turn were divided in half by 4-inch-wide members. The smaller T-bars provided intermediary support for the glass. The central square of the laylight frame was raised 2 feet 6 inches above the other parts of the iron frame; the sides of the raised frame were kept open for ventilation.

Originally, ½ inch-thick slabs of annealed clear glass (made by the Berkshire Glassworks, a company that went out of business in the early 1900s) rested in the iron frame, supporting bands of leaded stained glass. The texture of the glass indicated that it was originally poured and formed on a steel table and later sandblasted.

The surviving pieces of leaded glass had geometric or naturalistic motifs painted in black on red, blue, green, and amber stained glass. The glass was ⅛ inch thick, smooth, and regular, suggesting that it was manufactured rather than hand blown. The glass was set in narrow lead caming. Six different painted designs were identified in the 9-inch amber squares, including depictions of a squirrel, frog, fish, bird, flower, and leaf. On the smaller green squares, two motifs were found: a quatrefoil and a leaf. Fortunately, the long glass slabs retained marks left by the lead cames, which made it possible to determine the placement of the stained glass.

The ideal approach for restoring the laylights would have made use of the surviving original glass slabs and returned them to the iron framework, with new matching glass inserted where pieces were missing. However, for the 1999 restoration, this option was not feasible. The existing glass slabs did not meet current building-code requirements, which called for a minimum of ⅜-inch laminated safety glass for horizontal glazing in public areas. Therefore, it was determined that new heat-strengthened, laminated, safety-glass panels and new panels of leaded stained glass would be fabricated to replicate precisely the appearance of the originals.

After additional research, the architects and glass conservators developed a panel of laminated glass that met modern safety requirements and matched the texture, thickness, and decorative scheme of the original annealed glass. The new glass panels consisted of three layers: a heat-strengthened textured-glass float on top, a PVB (polyvinyl butyral) interlayer, and a heat-strengthened clear-glass float on the underside. The replication of the original patterns on the laminated glass was achieved through a sandblasting process that involved covering the clear glass with a thick resist, stenciling the artwork into that resist, and removing the decorative patterns. The resulting new glass panels were visually identical to the original glass.

Prior to the completion of the final drawings and specifications for the laylight, a presentation was made to the New York City Art Commission to gain their approval. The Art Commission must approve all works of art incorporated in city buildings. A sectional drawing of the rotunda showing the laylight was prepared, as were rendered plans of the proposed laylight and full-scale color plans of various stained-glass elements. In addition, the approach and technical information were compiled into a short paper, accompanied by samples of the proposed glass. The presentation was enthusiastically received and quickly approved, and a final bid package was finished soon afterward.

Given the highly specific nature of this part of the project, the customary bidding process required on public jobs was not required. Cummings Stained Glass Studios, Inc., received the commission and began fabrication in April 2000.

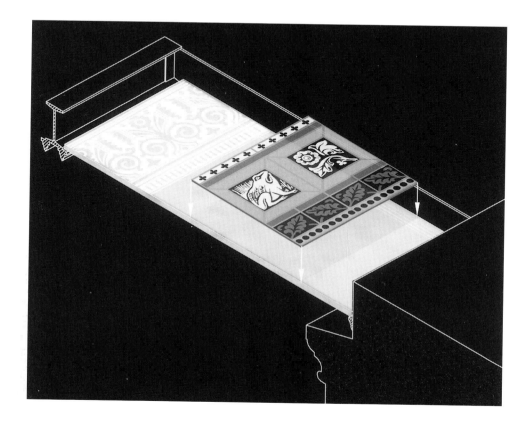

Restoration drawing for installation of rotunda laylight. Replica stained-glass panels were installed over clear laminated glass. The laminated glass panels were sandblasted to reproduce the original etched design.

*Fabrication of stained-glass
panels at Cummings
Stained Glass Studios.*

The new stained-glass sheets were produced by a factory in Germany that duplicated the original colored glass with pot glass (created by a process of mouth-blown cylinders that are then opened up into sheets). Then, at the Cummings studio, an eleven-step process was used to reproduce faithfully the various design motifs with the same quality and character found in the original hand-painted glass.

The existing iron framework of the laylight was thoroughly cleaned and coated with epoxy paint for a durable and long-lasting finish. The laminated-glass panels were then set into the framework using a combination of an elastomeric spacer and a structural silicone glazing sealant. These products provided ample adhesion to the cast-iron rabbet, as well as sufficient elasticity in the event of thermal movement. The silicone was selected to prevent any future delamination because it is compatible with the PVB.

After receiving the stained glass from Germany, Cummings silk-screened and assembled the stained-glass panels in their studios in Massachusetts. The clear patterned glass was purchased from AFG Industries, Inc., in Kingsport, Tennessee, and was then laminated and sandblasted. Glass conservators made wooden templates of each existing opening in the cast-iron framework to ensure a perfect fit upon final delivery to the building. Scaffolding to span the 50-foot-wide rotunda space was suspended just above the fourth-floor level, nearly 60 feet above the first floor. Each laminated panel was carried to the staging area and hoisted into place by glaziers. Working alongside the glaziers, glass conservators installed the new stained-glass panels above the laminated glass panels. The restoration was finished in June 2001. When the scaffolding was taken down in the following month, the rotunda was once again filled with daylight and colored shadows.

The laminated etched and patterned glass was set into the cast-iron frame prior to the installation of the stained-glass panels.

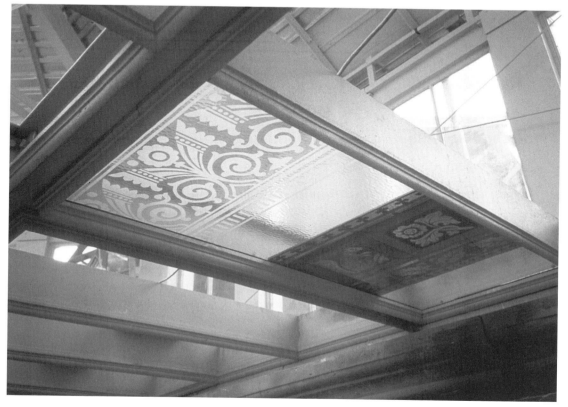

Test installation of first panel of replicated laylight. The new laylight duplicated exactly the appearance of the original while meeting modern code requirements.

Opposite: Briggs quarry, Sheffield, Massachusetts. This quarry, along with the Eastchester Marble Company, supplied all of the original marble for the building. Owned by John R. Briggs, one of Tweed's cohorts on the Board of Supervisors, the Sheffield quarry was closed when the Tweed ring was exposed.

CHAPTER FOUR

Exterior Restoration

Exterior Stone

The exterior masonry of a nineteenth-century public building is often one of the most complicated, costly, and critical components of a restoration project. The skill with which it is handled can make the difference between a successful project and a failure.

At the beginning of a project a thorough evaluation should be undertaken to deal with the following questions:

1. What types of stones are used in the building? What are their physical and chemical characteristics, and their susceptibility to various types of failures?

2. How extensive and serious is the deterioration of the masonry? What are the causes of this deterioration?

3. What are the options for treatment of the stone?

4. Is there a need to use chemical consolidantes to strengthen the stone?

5. What are the options for getting replacement stone from original quarries or other sources?

6. What is the feasibility and desirability of cleaning? Should the effects of age and wear be retained or should the building be restored to an "as-new" condition?

7. Has the soiling of the building resulted in a patina, or is there a coating of pollutants that continues to attack the stone?

8. What is the budget available for the project? Can the entire project be completed during one construction campaign, or does it need to be extended over several years?

To be most effective this evaluation should include historical research on the materials and their sources, laboratory investigations, and field-testing of proposed treatments.

The evaluation of the exterior masonry of Tweed Courthouse began with a thorough examination of the building. This investigation revealed that the building is constructed of two types of stone: the base of the building below the water table is granite, and the rest of the facade is marble. The blocks of the granite base are flat and smooth. The face of the marble blocks originally had a tooled finish. The more decorative elements—including column and pilaster bases, shafts, and capitals; windowsills and heads; entablature and cornices; and balustrades—are also marble.

Marbles are limestones metamorphosed, or formed under intense heat and pressure, resulting from the movement of the earth's crust. This crust causes the limestone to recrystallize as marble. Marbles are crystalline and compact forms of calcium carbonate ($CaCO_3$), sometimes combined with magnesium carbonate ($MgCO_3$), that are capable of taking a polish. Marbles containing less than five percent magnesium carbonate are classified as calcitic marbles; those with more than forty percent magnesium carbonate are dolomitic marbles. The limestones from which the marbles are formed are themselves created by the layering of calcareous remains of marine organisms deposited on the ocean floor and cemented together. The remains of the marine organisms contain other minerals, which become minor elements but often distinguishing characteristics of the stone. There is a wide range of characteristics between stones that are classified as pure limestone and those that are pure marble. The stone used on Tweed Courthouse fell somewhere between these two classifications. Although called marble, the stone is too coarse and granular to take a high polish. However, it has crystallized to

the point where it no longer has the characteristics of limestone.

The marble used in Tweed Courthouse came from quarries in at least two locations—Eastchester, New York, and Sheffield, Massachusetts—both of which lie in the Greenville stone belt extending from Québec along the line of the Appalachians into Georgia. Formed during the Cambrian period (500–600 million years ago), the formation is fairly consistent: a bed of dolomite (calcium magnesium carbonate ($CaMg[CO_3]_2$)) was formed over a layer of gneiss and under a layer of mica schist.

According to surviving contracts and receipts, the marble for the original portion of the building was purchased from the Eastchester Marble Company of New York and later the quarry in Sheffield, Massachusetts, which was owned by John R. Briggs, one of Tweed's cohorts on the Board of Supervisors. Nineteenth-century geologists determined that stones from the two quarries were essentially similar: coarse, white dolomitic crystalline limestone.

The Eastchester, or Tuckahoe, quarry was known for the size of the blocks that could be removed from it. It was said that blocks as large as 27 feet long by 4 feet 6 inches wide by 2 feet 6 inches deep and as heavy as thirty tons were quarried there.

Granite is an igneous rock formed of feldspars and quartz with smaller amounts of mica and hornblende. The foundation stone was referred to as Kip's Bay granite.

Examination of Masonry

At the beginning of the project in 1989, the exterior of the courthouse was badly stained and discolored; much of the stonework that projected from the face of the building—the window trim, column and pilaster capitals, and cornice with its modillions—had deteriorated, with pieces breaking off easily and falling to the ground. In order to determine the exact condition of the stonework and how much of it was salvageable, a preliminary cleaning was undertaken so that the facade could be examined in detail. Before the preliminary cleaning could be undertaken however, a visual inspection of the face of the building was carried out from the ground, roof, and open windows. At the same time, a laboratory analysis of the stone and its deterioration was made along with a review of previous cleaning treatments of buildings constructed of similar marble.

The visual survey, carried out with the aid of binoculars, indicated that the basic structural condition of much of the marble was very good, except for the projecting decorative elements. The blocks of stone that were the visible, outer facing of the thick masonry wall had not been heavily stressed. There were no indications that the foundation had settled or that the walls had moved. The failure of some of the window lintels, which became clearly visible after the building was cleaned, was not initially noticeable behind the heavy dirt buildup on the stone.

Deterioration was especially prominent on the most exposed areas of the facade, such as the cornice and the balustrade above it. Here the projecting stones were exposed to the weather on three sides, while the blocks that made up the main part of the walls were exposed on only one vertical side. The cornice and balustrade blocks also had exposed horizontal surfaces which were much more susceptible to water penetration caused by deteriorating mortar joints and movement of the blocks themselves. These exposed elements also experienced many more freeze/thaw cycles than did the flat wall areas, which were warmed from the inside. In the winter water entered the horizontal joints and froze. As the water changed to ice, it expanded and exerted pressure on the adjacent stone blocks, which caused the mortar joints to fail and the stone blocks to move. As the joints became wider, more water entered and froze, moving the blocks farther with each cycle.

Some blocks of stone in the cornice and balustrade

had moved more than one inch out of line, while others had split in half. Some of the stones were held in place with original iron cramps, while others were restrained by relatively recent steel cramps, which were badly rusted. Over the years there were many attempts to prevent water from entering the horizontal joints of the cornice and balustrade. Many of the joints were covered with bituminous coatings, which had cracked and failed.

An examination of the projecting elements—column and pilaster capitals, cornice modillions and dentils, and window-frame pediments and consoles—revealed that many ornamental elements had fallen or been removed. The abacuses of the capitals, for example, had lost their flowers and most of their acanthus leaves. These small, projecting elements had been particularly exposed and were therefore very susceptible to deterioration caused by weather and atmospheric pollutants.

The examination of the marble surfaces revealed many different conditions. The two types of marble had weathered differently, and even blocks of the same type of marble had weathered differently where their locations and exposures varied. Most of the facade of the original building had become a fairly dark gray, characteristic of Tuckahoe marble. Other blocks, from the Sheffield quarry, had remained quite white. The surfaces of many Tuckahoe blocks had numerous small holes where inclusions of other minerals such as iron once existed. Some of the Tuckahoe marble blocks that contained significant numbers of inclusions and had been installed in exposed locations, such as the top rail of the balustrade, were seriously deteriorated. The Sheffield blocks generally had smooth surfaces without holes or inclusions. Many blocks of both types of marble exhibited dark yellow or brown stains, especially where they had not been washed by rainwater.

In areas of the facade more protected from the flow of water, such as the lower moldings of the entablature and the joints in the rustication at the first-floor level, there were black crusts where the marble had converted to gypsum. In some of these areas, the gypsum and the stone behind it were so friable that they crumbled when touched. The corners of many ornamental elements and stone blocks were missing because the marble in these areas had been converted to gypsum, which then had been dissolved in water and washed away. There were numerous mortar patches filling areas at the edges where the stone had been lost.

The stone of the later south wing appeared more uniform and generally in better condition than the stone of the original portion of the building. However, many of the horizontal surfaces of the south wing had been treated with chemical bird-proofing agents in the past. These applications were unsightly, difficult to remove, and dam-

Cornice before cleaning and restoration. The deteriorated molding in the center is Tuckahoe stone, while the whiter and more round stone on the right is from the Sheffield quarry.

Detail of window entablature before restoration. Much of the marble element has been converted to gypsum, which can be removed by hand.

aging to the marble. They had formed thick, oily coatings on the surfaces where they had been applied and had stained adjacent areas of stonework. The coatings trapped dirt and provided vapor-impermeable barriers that did not allow water that had found its way into the stone beneath to escape.

The stonework of the facade was laid with fine mortar joints. In some joints the original lime mortar had deteriorated; in others it was missing to a considerable depth. These open joints allowed water to enter, further deteriorating the masonry through freeze/thaw action.

Because of the lack of adequate maintenance, vegetation was growing in masonry joints at the cornice level. Considerable amounts of pigeon excrement had accumulated on projecting horizontal surfaces, particularly on the south side of the building. The marble was coated in many areas with various other materials. There were numerous areas of bituminous coatings at the roof level, particularly around joints in horizontal surfaces, but also in areas where elements, now removed, had been flashed. A small area around the south entrance door had been painted black.

The granite at the base of the building was generally soiled and in many places had become dark gray or black. In addition, the surfaces of some stone blocks were flaking off in thin layers. Similar granite disintegration has occurred in other buildings where the stone had been kept saturated with water containing salts. The deteriorated granite on Tweed Courthouse was close to the ground, where it was constantly wetted by water from the soil rising in the stone by capillary action. This water contained salts from many sources: the soil itself, chemicals used on the plants around the building, ice-melting agents used on adjacent sidewalks, rainwater carrying pollutants from

the air, and rainwater runoff containing pollutants washed from the surface of the building.

Analysis of Surface Contaminants and Deterioration

Both the types of deterioration and the causing agents were identified and evaluated. Roger O. Cheng of the Atmospheric Sciences Research Center of the State University of New York at Albany assisted the architects in the characterization and identification of deteriorated stone collected from the building. This process of investigation involved research techniques utilizing various types of equipment, including an optical microscope with photomicrographic dispersive staining capability. An optical microscope, which is capable of magnification up to 100 times, is useful in studying the grain structure of marble cut into thin sections. Using index refraction oils with polarizing filters on the microscope allows the identification of soluble materials, such as gypsum, which are extracted from the marble samples. A scanning electron microscope (SEM) was also used. With appropriate coating technique and specimen preparation, the SEM allows a high magnification (10,000 times) of the structure of the material. A computer-based energy-dispersive x-ray (EDXA) yields the composition of the elements that make up the material. An SEM magnification of an area of the stone surface reveals the structure and composition of the material as well as any pollutants that may be on the surface. For instance, pollutants such as coal fly ash can be distinguished from oil fly ash; although both are relatively spherical particles, coal fly ash has a smooth surface, while oil fly ash has a pockmarked one. On an elemental basis, the EXDA reveals that coal fly ash has a high concentration of sulfur and iron.

*A cornice modillion before restoration. The black surface,
a dark gypsum crust, has broken away, revealing white, undamaged
marble. The breaking away of damaged stone located high on the
building was a major safety issue.*

Analysis of the Tweed Courthouse pollutants showed that the dark areas, or black crusts, on the building were gypsum, or calcium sulfate. The calcium carbonate ($CaCO_3$) in the marble changed to gypsum ($CaSO_4$) when it reacted with sulfuric acid, in the presence of heavy metals acting as catalysts to form gypsum, water, and carbon dioxide.

$CaCO_3 + H_2SO_4 = CaSO_4 + H_2O + CO_2$. H_2SO_4 (sulfuric acid) was formed by airborne sulfur pollutants—sulfur dioxide ($SO2$) and sulfur trioxide (SO_3)—that had united with water vapor. These sulfur contaminants originated from industrial facilities and automotive emissions, some of which may have been hundreds of miles from the building. The heavy-metal catalysts came from fly ash or unburned hydrocarbons from the combustion of fossil fuels from coal- and oil-burning power plants, automotive exhausts, and industrial emissions. Metals present in major concentrations in the marble samples from the courthouse included magnesium, nickel, vanadium, and iron; metals present in minor concentrations included chromium, aluminum, potassium, titanium, and copper.

There was an overall pattern of gypsum formation on the building, but it was more severe on the north and east facades, where there was more exposure to traffic. There have, however, long been hydrocarbon emissions that could have provided catalysts for the stone deterioration, including those from Thomas Edison's electrical generating station on Pearl Street from 1882, the Brooklyn Navy Yard, and various other industries in Manhattan, Brooklyn, and New Jersey.

Areas of the building that had been exposed to rainwater washing were clean. The water had dissolved the gypsum, and the pollutants on the surface had been washed away with it. Where the pollutants were the result of dry deposition on the surface of the stone, rainwater did not wash the surface. The crusts remained and held the pollutant against the surfaces, causing the stone behind it to deteriorate.

The EDXA spectrum analysis confirmed that the composition of the marble used in the courthouse varied and thus was from different quarries. However, all of the stones consisted of calcium carbonate, and many contained significant amounts of magnesium indicating dolomitic marble. Also many, but not all, contained significant concentrations of iron. These samples were the Tuckahoe stones, while the Sheffield marble did not contain iron. In addition, all of the marble surfaces examined contained high amounts of sulfur, indicating that the marble was slowly converting to gypsum.

The photomicrographs taken by the SEM showed the disintegration of the integrity of the marble into gypsum crystals, which have no cohesion. This change from calcium carbonate to gypsum accounted for the disintegration of the marble surface as the gypsum was washed away. Sometimes called "sugaring," this condition allowed the surface of the stone to be removed by rubbing it.

Cleaning Tests

After the initial examination of the exterior of the building and the laboratory analysis were completed, the architects determined that the exterior needed to be cleaned. The clean stonework could be examined in more detail to determine its exact condition and the potential for serious hazards.

Because of the unusual nature of the marble—two different semi-metamorphic marbles, one with iron inclusions—the most appropriate cleaning technique was not readily apparent. Other New York City buildings faced with Westchester County marbles had been cleaned previously with varying degrees of success. St. Patrick's Cathedral, constructed of marble from the Pleasantville Quarry in Westchester County—as well as from quarries in Maryland, Massachusetts, and Vermont—had been cleaned in 1978 using a long-term (twenty-four or thirty-six-hour) soaking with water, followed by a pressure (300 psi) wash using only water.

Brooklyn Borough Hall, constructed of Eastchester marble, had been cleaned using water-soaking techniques in 1984–86. The walls had been repaired with small blocks of a different type of marble; the iron inclusions in the original stone had begun rusting, turning the facade an orange-brown color and resulting in the need for new repairs, which remained white and stood out visually. A subsequent abrasive cleaning, using crushed glass, had been undertaken to correct the appearance.

The design for the cleaning tests for Tweed Courthouse took this information into consideration. With the assistance of Professor Norman Weiss of Columbia University, the architects proposed three types of cleaning tests—water cleaning, air-abrasive cleaning, and chemical cleaning—to determine the best method for the preliminary cleaning.

Various cleaning tests were carried out between July 6 and August 4, 1989, by Deerpath Construction Corp., Renewal Arts Corp., and ProSoCo, Inc. All tests were done under the direction of the architects and Professor Weiss. All testing was carried out in areas containing both the Tuckahoe and the Sheffield marbles, as well as areas stained with bird-proofing agents.

Cleaning with only water was selected because it is one of the least damaging methods that can be used on

Drawing of cornice showing diagonal cracks, which were a serious safety concern because pieces of the cornice broke away and fell to the ground.

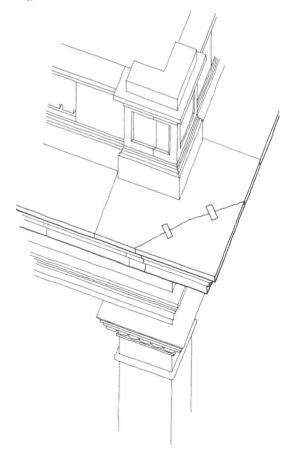

deteriorated stone. Water soaking is widely used in Europe for cleaning calcium carbonate stones and has proven to be successful in removing gypsum crusts similar to those found on the courthouse. The test was carried out with a gentle spray of water, in cycles of six hours on and six hours off, for forty-eight hours. At the completion of the test, the Sheffield marble had been cleaned of almost all of the yellow-brown stains, with only a faint trace of yellow remaining where the heaviest stains had been. The Tuckahoe marble, on the other hand, showed almost no effects from the soaking; it was lightened only slightly. This indicated that the gray on the surface was not gypsum, which would have been dissolved by soaking.

The soaking test was followed by another test in which the stone was rinsed with water at 500 psi. This removed some of the gray from the Tuckahoe marble and more of the yellow-brown stains from the Sheffield marble, which still retained a brown stain. This test was followed by a test that combined both water soaking and pressure rinsing. Although some of the stones were cleaned using the combination method, the Tuckahoe stone still remained gray and the bird-proofing stains persisted.

The next series of tests involved air-abrasive methods using three different materials: rice hulls, crushed limestone, and glass beads. Each was used at a low air pressure of between 20 and 25 psi, the lowest pressure that would carry the abrasive to the stone. The area cleaned with rice hulls still had a light-brown stain, and although the rice hulls appeared to be soft, the surface of the stone was damaged. Both the crushed limestone and the glass beads substantially eroded the stone surfaces, leaving them rough and scarred. Clearly, air-abrasive techniques were not appropriate for cleaning the courthouse facades.

Chemical testing, the third series of tests to be undertaken, began with the application of off-the-shelf alkaline prewash and acidic after-wash systems commonly used to clean limestone and marble. While these chemicals lightened the color of some of the stones, the treatments were less effective than pressure rinsing. The stone also turned slightly yellow, indicating that the alkaline pre-wash had reacted with the iron inclusions in the stone, causing it to rust. These systems did not dissolve or remove the gypsum crusts.

Based on these results, a dozen other systems, utilizing different chemicals for pre-wash and after-wash, were tried with varying degrees of success. They included an alkaline cleaner with ferrous-stain remover, a specially formulated alkaline crust remover, a poultice, and a gel alkaline cleaner, with an acidic after-wash cleaner of various dilutions.

Eventually it was determined that the most effective method was to use a gel that had recently been custom designed for cleaning interior marble and an acidic after-wash formulated for limestone and marble. This cleaning system, which was first used on the Tweed Courthouse project, cleaned both types of marble and left them white without any yellow residue. It also removed the gypsum crusts.

The bird-proofing that had been applied to the surface of the marble earlier in the twentieth century was removed by scraping with a metal blade, followed by washing with an organic solvent cleaner. Deep-seated bird-proofing and oily stains were removed by repeated applications of an organic solvent poultice.

Tests to clean the granite base were carried out using a standard acidic masonry cleaner at six different strengths. The application of this cleaner was followed by a water-pressure rinse. The completed tests ranged from stone that was not affected to stone that was completely cleaned. The solutions did not etch any of the panels.

At the conclusion of the tests, sample panels using the approved cleaning methods were prepared for use on the building. These panels served as the standard of performance that would be required of the contractor responsible for cleaning the entire building.

The cleaning tests demonstrated that the different stones on the building had been affected differently by exposure to the atmosphere, and that they reacted differently to the same method of cleaning. Thus a method effective in cleaning one type of stone often seemed to have little effect on the other, and a method effective in cleaning one type of stone in one location on the building was not as effective in cleaning the same type of stone in a different location. However, the major lesson was that a cleaning method that reportedly worked on one building constructed of a particular stone might not be effective on another project of similar stone, and might even be damaging to the stone. At Tweed Courthouse, the stone-cleaning program involved almost thirty separate test panels before an effective system was developed that did not damage the stone.

Cleaning tests were undertaken in 1989 to determine the most effective cleaning technique for the Eastchester and Sheffield marble, as well as the granite.

Cleaning sample panels on the west elevation of the building in 1989. It was found that a chemical cleaning system using an alkaline gel, followed by an acidic after-wash, was the most effective technique for cleaning the marble.

The Chambers Street elevation before the initial cleaning.

The Chambers Street elevation after the initial cleaning.

Cleaning

Using the results of the testing program, the complete cleaning of the exterior masonry of Tweed Courthouse was carried out between May 1 and November 7, 1990. Under the direction of the construction manager, York/Hunter City Services, Inc., the stone cleaning was performed by Renewal Arts Contracting Corporation. All areas of the facade were cleaned to meet the goals of allowing a detailed examination of the stonework and providing a more stable facade until the stone restoration work and a second cleaning could be performed.

As part of the cleaning process, scaffolding was erected that completely covered all walls of the building. The scaffolding provided access to within two feet of every surface of each facade for the cleaning contractor, as well as for the architects to monitor the cleaning process. After the building was cleaned, the architects and structural engineers used the scaffolding to inspect the entire exterior. The scaffolding also provided protection from falling pieces of stone. Sidewalk bridging was provided at all entrances to provide covered access to the building.

During the cleaning process a number of adjustments were necessary. Some were the result of further evaluation of the testing, and others were measures to speed the

progress of the work. These included slight modifications to the composition of the chemical agents, reduction of the rinse pressure, and changes of nozzle types. Initially, problems were encountered when high temperatures caused the rapid drying of some of the chemicals, resulting in a loss of effectiveness.

The architects monitored the cleaning process daily to ensure compliance with the specifications and sample panels. Many areas of the stone required two applications, and those areas that had been protected over the years from the washing action of rain often required three or more applications.

The alkaline cleaning agent had a pH of 14, and the acidic after-wash had a pH of 1.2, both exceeding the limits established by New York City for wastewater entering the river system (neutral pH is 7.0). Because city regulations require that wastewater have a pH between 5.0 and 9.5 and because one of the components of the after-wash, hydrochloric acid, is listed as a toxic waste, the architects specified that all wastewater be collected by the contractor, trucked off the site, and disposed of properly. They did this in accordance with regulations promulgated by the Federal Environmental Protection Agency and in accord with the Resource Conservation and Recovery Act passed by Congress in 1976 to protect human health and the environment from improper handling of hazardous materials. The contractor was also required to carry out a soil-testing program around the building throughout the cleaning process. Soil samples were also tested along the drip line of the scaffolding. All of the tests proved negative, verifying that the containment process had been effective.

Moldmaking and Casts

Because the edges of the sculptural stone elements of the facades had suffered extensive damage over the years, it was decided that molds and corrected casts should be made of selected examples before they were cleaned. These elements included column and pilaster capitals, modillions, pendants, and window brackets from the original building and a frieze panel, griffin, and window frieze from the Eidlitz wing.

Following specifications prepared by the architects, Gianetti Studios Inc., of Brentwood, Maryland, a firm with decades of experience with architectural sculpture and ornamental plaster, fabricated molds from elements in place on the building. The molds consisted of polyurethane supported by an outer plaster shell. Reinforced-plaster casts made from the molds were then corrected to produce elements as close to the original stone ornaments as possible. The reconstruction of the column and pilaster capitals, from which the acanthus leaves had been purposely removed a half-century earlier because of safety concerns, was especially challenging. The moldmaking and casting process began in September 1990 and was completed in January 1991. Both the casts and the original molds were turned over to the Landmarks Preservation Commission for warehousing until the stone restoration work began.

Comprehensive Inspection and Recording

After the exterior was cleaned, the architects began a block-by-block survey and evaluation of the stonework. A team from Robert Silman Associates, the consulting structural engineer for the entire duration of the project, surveyed the building independently. The surveys began in September 1990 and were completed in December 1990. The first step was the preparation of architectural drawings identifying each block of stone with a label consisting of two letters followed by a three-digit number that allowed each stone to be easily referenced. The first letter was E, S, W, or N, indicating the facade (east, south, west, or north), and the second letter indicated the section of that facade in which the stone was located. The numerals indicated the particular stone.

The architects also developed a survey form to record the characteristics, existing conditions, and recommenda-

tions for repair or replacement for each of the 10,000 stones. The characteristics of each stone included its dimensions, its color, its profile, and whether it had pronounced veining, bedding planes, or inclusions. The existing-conditions section of the form included information on the overall condition of each stone, on whether it was displaced, and on whether it exhibited delamination, exfoliation, block or edge loss, surface friability, cracks, previous repairs, gypsum crusts, or stains. The recommendations section included information on whether the block would need to be reset, retooled, replaced, repaired with a dutchman, or cleaned to remove deep-seated stains.

The survey team consisted of at least two members at any one time; they worked closely to help ensure consistency. At the completion of the survey, the leaders of the project team reevaluated each stone so that all findings would be consistent.

The comprehensive survey provided considerably more detailed and accurate information on the condition of the stonework than the preliminary inspection. The most significant finding was that there were more severe structural problems than had been evident in the preliminary inspection.

The most serious conditions affecting the structural stability of the building and public safety were found at the top of the structure, where many of the stone blocks had shifted and were cracked, warped, or otherwise damaged. Previous repairs, such as the use of ferrous cramps across the cracks, had deteriorated and compounded the problems. Several corner blocks were badly cracked or warped, requiring immediate attention. The large blocks at the ends of the cornice of the north portico were displaced. Failure of any one of the corner blocks, or of any of the corners as a whole could have disastrous structural and life-safety consequences. Horizontal displacement was also observed in stonework below the cornices.

The cornice consisted of large blocks of stone, each weighing 3,500 pounds and projecting 3 feet 8 inches from the face of the wall. The cornice of the original building had initially been surmounted with a stone balustrade, which provided a counterweight to the cornice blocks, thus making the entire entablature structurally stable. However, some of the balustrade was now missing, including a section where the south wing joined the original building, resulting in a potentially unstable and dangerous condition. In addition to the corner blocks, many other stones in the entablature were cracked and deteriorated. Many of the cornice modillions were deteriorated, and some were missing. This condition posed a serious hazard to pedestrians.

Below the cornice, many of the projecting elements— leaves and volutes of column and pilaster capitals, fluting on the columns and pilasters, window lintels, and pediments—were seriously deteriorated or missing. The removal of the leaves and volutes from the capitals of the north portico in 1943 indicates that the elements were dangerous at that time. The process of removing these and other stone elements may have introduced stress fractures in the remaining adjacent projections, many of which were narrow in cross section. The stone lintels between the columns and pilasters of the north portico were cracked near the midpoints of their spans. This cracking was caused by excessive flexural stresses in the stone, which has a relatively small capacity to resist tension; modern building codes do not permit stone to be used as beams in this manner. The comprehensive survey corroborated some of the conditions noted in the preliminary inspection. The south wing stone in the original courthouse was in relatively good condition, except for approximately forty percent of the blocks of the top two courses, which were deteriorated. Otherwise, only a few stones required repair or replacement.

The general condition of the stone on the original courthouse proved to be more deteriorated than expected. In addition, more than seventy percent of the stones forming the cornice were badly deteriorated, and more than seventy-five percent of the modillions required replacement. Most of the windowsills and heads were seriously deteriorated, and many of the balusters were seriously compromised or missing. The outer surface of many of the stones had worn away. The loss was less in finer-grained, more uniform blocks, and more in coarse blocks with a greater number of impurities. The extent of the loss was especially apparent where a surface contained hard inclusions, which, being more resistant to environmental forces, had worn less than the surrounding material and projected $\frac{1}{16}$ inch to $\frac{3}{16}$ inch from the face of the stone. This surface loss was caused by a number of factors, including abrasion by airborne particles, erosion by water and waterborne particles flowing over the surface, conversion of the surface to gypsum then dissolved by rainwater, and some acids in the rainwater.

The exposed edges and corners of many stone blocks had converted to gypsum and washed away. These losses ranged from gently rounded arrises to missing corners. Large sections of the projecting fillets on the edges of some column and pilaster shafts were missing, and there were long vertical cracks adjacent to the missing sections. The narrow cross sections of these elements made it likely that they were completely saturated with water that then froze and exerted pressure on the stone, causing damage. Differential thermal stresses between the projecting elements and the stone behind them, and stresses induced during carving, may also have been a factor in this deterioration.

The corners and edges of many of the rusticated stone blocks had been patched using plastic-stone (composite patching) repair techniques with a gray portland-cement mortar that did not match the stone in color or texture. Because the mortar was harder and less vapor-permeable than the stone, it inhibited the escape of moisture from the marble behind the patch. The trapped moisture froze and thawed, resulting in further damage to the stone.

The original joints between the marble blocks were thin; some were no more than $\frac{1}{16}$ inch thick and were originally filled with lime mortar, without any cement. A large number of these joints were open, and mortar was missing to a depth of at least 5 or 6 inches.

The granite blocks that formed the base of the building were in relatively good condition, and there were no apparent problems affecting the structural stability or the integrity of the masses of the blocks. However, the surfaces of some of the granite blocks had exfoliated to a depth of up to $\frac{3}{8}$ inch. This condition is typical of granite that is constantly exposed to water and salts. The surface exfoliation had not affected the basic integrity of the stone.

Based on the results of this survey, the architects and structural engineers recommended that when the pipe scaffolding was removed, scaffolding towers be erected at each corner as an emergency measure to support the cracked, deteriorated, or displaced corner blocks. It was further recommended that a sidewalk bridge be installed around the perimeter of the building for protection from falling pieces of stone. This recommendation was carried out by the Department of General Services in 1995, and the scaffolding remained in place until the restoration work began in 1999.

Planning the Stone Restoration Program

Unless the exterior stone on Tweed Courthouse was to be completely replaced, either the existing stone had to be conserved and consolidated with chemicals that penetrate the surface of the stone, or replacement stone had to be found. The replacement stone would have to match the existing marble in composition, color and markings, crystalline structure, light reflection, and weathering characteristics.

For centuries, builders have attempted to find substances that will arrest, and possibly reverse, the decay of building stones. Stone preservatives and consolidants have been used for hundreds of years, but despite recent research, no standard products have been tested over a period of time sufficient that they will guarantee to arrest or reverse stone deterioration without damaging the stone. Many products applied in the past have actually hastened the deterioration of stone, usually because they formed a relatively vapor-impermeable coating on the surface, retarding the escape of moisture. Water held within stone freezes, exerting pressure that causes the face of the stone to spall off. Many other products have been simply ineffective.

Preservatives and consolidants evaluated for use on Tweed Courthouse had to meet several basic requirements. First, the treatment had to have a history of previous use with some success on monumental buildings constructed of similar stone. Although some treatments that were successful in the past might be applied and evaluated in small, inconspicuous test areas, a prominent landmark such as Tweed Courthouse could not be used as an experiment for an unproven material. Second, application of the product had to be achievable under conditions that could be realistically fulfilled at the site. Many treatments developed in the laboratory require conditions that cannot be met easily except on the small scale required for sculpture or pieces of architectural ornament removed from a building. While some sections of the building could be enclosed to provide moderate levels of heat and humidity, it would not be possible, for example, to provide the controlled temperature and pressure required for the use of thermosetting acrylics, which have been used successfully on sculpture. Third, the process had to be affordable. This requirement eliminated consideration of such time-consuming, labor-intensive methods as the application of lime washes, which had been used with some apparent success on statues at Wells Cathedral in England.

Two methods of consolidation that appeared to meet the above criteria were treatment with barium hydroxide-urea, an alkaline earth consolidant, and treatment with ethyl silicates, an organo-silicate consolidant. Another method of relatively recent development that did not meet all of the above criteria, the use of polymerized acrylic resins, was also investigated.

Although barium hydroxide-urea had been tested on the coarse marble of the U.S. Patent Office in Washington, D.C., it was not used on that building. Ethyl silicates had been used on many monumental buildings in Europe, but tests on Tweed Courthouse before the preliminary cleaning indicated that there was a change in color of all marble tested. In addition, the Sheffield marble that was treated showed significantly lower vapor-permeability with a very slight depth of penetration in the material.

Acrylic resins had been used with considerable success on significant German monuments, such as Cologne Cathedral, which is constructed of sandstone. Their potential for use on Tweed Courthouse was limited for several reasons. The procedures are complicated and must be carried out under laboratory conditions. The stones cannot be treated in situ on the building; they must be removed and taken to the facility where they can be completely submerged in a tank, and there are very few facilities large enough to treat architectural elements. The facilities that can accommodate large objects are located in Europe and have a very limited capacity.

After reviewing the options available in the early 1990s for consolidating the stone, it was apparent that the technology for consolidating calcium-carbonate stone on the scale of Tweed Courthouse and with its level of deterioration simply did not exist, even if there had been an unlimited budget. Therefore, the only option was to use new stone for repair and replacement of damaged or missing elements.

Finding Replacement Stone

One of the major considerations in searching for replacement stone for a historic structure is the great variation among the individual blocks of stone. Some blocks may be white and almost completely uniform with a relatively fine grain, while other blocks may be gray with a larger crystalline structure. Some blocks may have prominent gray or blue/gray veining; others may have pronounced bands of inclusions. The fact that the stone varies to such a great extent has both positive and negative aspects. On the positive side, stone used for the replacement of a large section does not have to match the original exactly; it has to match it only closely enough to be within the range of the variation of other existing blocks. On the negative side, no one type of replacement stone would match all the blocks of the existing stone that required repair.

The first step in locating new stone to be used in the restoration of Tweed Courthouse was to investigate the original quarries at Tuckahoe, New York, and Sheffield, Massachusetts. The Tuckahoe quarry had been filled in decades ago, and the many neighboring quarries in Westchester County that once yielded similar marble had also been filled in and built over. After considerable research, the architects located the original Sheffield quarry. Although closed a century and a quarter ago, the quarry had not been filled in. It was still in private ownership, but all equipment and facilities used to extract, work, and transport the stone had been removed. Scattered around the site were over fifty large blocks of marble that had reportedly been extracted for use on the Washington Monument in Washington, D.C. When the Tweed Ring was exposed, the U.S. government canceled the contract because of Briggs's association with Tweed.

In 1990, after determining that it was not feasible to reopen the Sheffield quarry, the architects began looking for other sources of stone to match the marble at the courthouse. In addition to working with American stone suppliers, the architects went to the international stone exhibition, Marmomacchine, in Verona, Italy. Sources of white marble in North America, Europe, and Asia Minor were also investigated. Samples of possible replacement stones were placed on the roof of the courthouse, adjacent to the original stonework, for weathering tests.

Among the marbles considered for replacement stone were Georgia White, Georgia White Cherokee, and Imperial Darby, all from the United States; Thassos, from Greece; Bianco Lineato and Praly, from Turkey; and Kastle Light from Austria. When first quarried, all of these marbles were either white or light gray and bore some resemblance to the stones at the courthouse. Crystal size varied from fine to coarse.

The investigation of replacement stone also revealed that it was no longer possible to obtain blocks of stone that matched the size of the largest original blocks. The Tuckahoe quarry was known for its large blocks; some of the original cornice stones at Tweed Courthouse are 18 feet long, and the second-floor window-jamb pilasters are 14 feet in length. Today industry practices limit individual blocks taken from the quarry to approximately 8 feet and finished blocks to between 6 and 7 feet long, although in some spe-

cial cases blocks up to 10 feet long have been quarried. These limits are dictated by standard quarrying equipment, power stone-cutting equipment, methods of transportation, and handling methods used to set the stone.

Also investigated was the use of cast stone: a mixture of cement, stone aggregate, and pigments that is cast in a mold. Cast stone has a long history, both as an original material and as a substitute material. While it has been used with some success to replace limestone and sandstone—both sedimentary rocks consisting of aggregate and binder—it is not a good match for metamorphosed stones, such as marble with its crystalline structure, particularly marbles with mica inclusions and coarse grain structure.

The stone samples on the roof were periodically inspected by the architects to observe how each was weathering. In 1999, when the restoration campaign began, the stones had been exposed for almost a decade, and it was possible to determine which was the most appropriate replacement.

Most of the test samples had weathered very differently from the original stones, but the Georgia White Cherokee

Samples of marble from North America, Europe, and Asia Minor were placed on the roof of the building for weathering tests in an effort to find the most compatible stone for repairs.

Georgia Marble Company quarry in Tate, Georgia, which supplied the replacement stone for the restoration.

Blocks of newly quarried Georgia White Cherokee marble at the Tate, Georgia, quarry.

marble provided the closest match. Although the Georgia marbles are sometimes described as being very fine grained, the Georgia White Cherokee samples had a medium to large grain structure, which was closer to the Tuckahoe and Sheffield marbles. The Georgia White Cherokee samples were relatively uniform white in color with a slight mottling of gray. The marble also has a high compressive strength and excellent weathering characteristics.

Implementing the Stone Restoration Work

Once the city decided in 1999 to restore Tweed Courthouse, the first component of the work to be advanced was the exterior stonework. There were several reasons for this decision: including the extensive amount of work required to restore the exterior, and the long lead time needed to secure and fabricate replacement pieces. Also, because of the previous work, the architects had a great deal of information on the condition of the existing stonework, and were well prepared to quickly develop measures for its restoration.

The first step in the restoration of the exterior was to completely clean the building again using the methods and products identified in the 1989 testing and cleaning. The contractor for the cleaning, as well as the masonry restoration component of the project, was Brisk Waterproofing of Ridgefield, New Jersey. Once the cleaning was completed, the deteriorated mortar was removed from the joints, and the stonework was completely repointed with a mortar that matched the original in color, texture, and chemical composition. This provided a consistent appearance to the mortar joints throughout the building, and the stonework was made completely weather tight. A policy was developed for the conservation and restoration of the marble stonework. The highest priority was to provide facades that were safe and structurally sound.

In accordance with modern historic-preservation standards, as much of the original stonework as possible was to be preserved. Signs of age and wear were to be retained, provided that the stones were structurally sound. For example, deteriorated surfaces of flat blocks were left in place when only the appearance of the stone was affected. Similarly, sound decorative stones with missing edges and corners, or weathered detailing, were retained because they showed the natural aging process of the marble. Where there were badly deteriorated or projecting elements, such as the cornice, the architects in consultation with EDC and the construction manager decided to replace them entirely with new stone, so they would be structurally sound and safe.

Stones that were sound but missing significant elements or were badly disfigured were to be retained in

Damaged section of cornice and pendant after removal. The deteriorated stone was discarded and the sound material was recycled for use as dutchmen.

Fabricated from Sheffield stone, dutchmen were used to restore the window entablatures where localized deterioration had occurred.

Damaged stone removed so that a dutchman can be installed.

Upper section of exterior walls after restoration. The elements include original moldings, dutchmen, and new cornice modillion blocks.

place and repaired with new stone pieces, or "dutchmen," that were fabricated to match the original. In these situations, as well as when an entire element that was surrounded by similar units needing to be replaced, blocks of Sheffield marble and stone salvaged from the building were utilized.

Because the dutchman repairs were to be incorporated into existing stone blocks, exact matches were required so that they would appear as a single unit. Otherwise variations in color, veining, and texture would result in repairs that would stand out, making the building appear spotted. This was a complicated problem

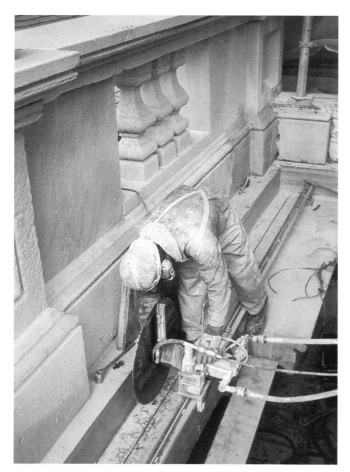

Removal of damaged cornice using diamond-tipped circular saw.

Corner of portico pediment after removal of damaged cornices.

Drilling holes and inserting new threaded stainless steel rods to anchor replacement cornice stones.

because the two different stones used originally varied in color and veining. Deteriorated areas requiring dutchman repairs included flat and fluted pilasters, columns, balusters, molded sill courses, chimneys, flat wall surfaces, and window jambs, heads, and sills.

The dutchman repairs were carried out by first carefully cutting away the deteriorated stone. The new marble patch, or dutchman, was then carefully fitted to the void in the block and fastened with threaded stainless-steel pins and epoxy adhesive. Because the dutchmen were precisely cut, the joints were inconspicuous.

The complete replacement of the cornice with new marble, an important structural and life-safety concern, was one of the most technically challenging parts of the entire restoration project. The scaffolding had to be designed and constructed to support the weight of tons of stone that had been removed and were waiting for the freight elevator to transport them to ground level and for new stone elements stacked and stored waiting

to be installed on the building. In addition rails were mounted on the scaffolding parallel to the walls to guide the diamond-blade radial saws being used to cut away the cornice to a depth of 3 feet, 7 inches. The raking and horizontal cornices of the pediments and north portico were also removed. The original cornice blocks served as models for fabricating the new cornice blocks made of Georgia White Cherokee marble, and were also reused on dutchman repairs. The new cornice blocks match the texture, dimensions, and profile of the originals. They are anchored to the building with ¾ inch diameter stainless-steel threaded rods that are 6 feet long. The rods extend from the midpoint of each new block through the building to the attic and are fitted with plates, washers, and nuts at both ends. Stone adhesive was applied to the intersection of the old and new stones, and the nuts were tightened to put the entire assembly in compression, resulting in the stable, strong, and safe cornice.

Installation of replacement cornice, along with new modillions and denticulated moldings, fabricated of Georgia White Cherokee marble.

Stainless-steel rods, plates, and fasteners anchoring the replacement cornice in the attic.

Blocks of Georgia White Cherokee marble being cut at the Nelson, Georgia, plant of the Georgia Marble Company.

Completed modillion stones before installation.

New modillion stones installed on the building.

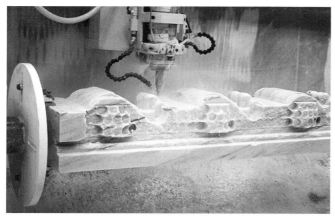

Cornice modillion stones were fabricated using computer-driven carving machinery at the Johnson Atelier studio in Mercerville, New Jersey.

Egg-and-dart pilaster capital moldings were rough-carved by machine and finished by hand at the Johnson Atelier studio.

Pineapple pendants were hand-carved by Traditional Cut Stone, Ltd. of Toronto, Canada.

Restoration drawing for one of the Chambers Street portico column capitals. Shaded areas indicate details that were removed in 1943 and which were replicated.

New Georgia White Cherokee marble was also used to replace rails, piers, and balusters of the roof balustrade; moldings, dentil blocks, and architrave portions of the entablature; modillions, and missing details from the Corinthian capitals of the fluted pilasters of the east and west facades. New stone was used for these repairs for structural and safety reasons and because these components were located at the top sections of the building and hence were less noticeable from the ground. The new stone elements were fastened using threaded stainless-steel pins and epoxy adhesive.

The newly carved replacement details were also anchored to the column and pilaster capitals with stainless-steel pins and epoxy adhesive. A team of stone carvers restored the capitals in situ under the direction of Shi-Jia Chen of B & H Art-in-Architecture, Ltd., of Brooklyn, New York.

The north portico entablature required specialized repair techniques. The system used, made by Cintec, included 7-foot-long stainless-steel anchors, surrounded by fabric socks inserted in oversized holes drilled up through the cracked architrave into the upper entablature. Fluid grout was then injected into the sock, providing a mechan-

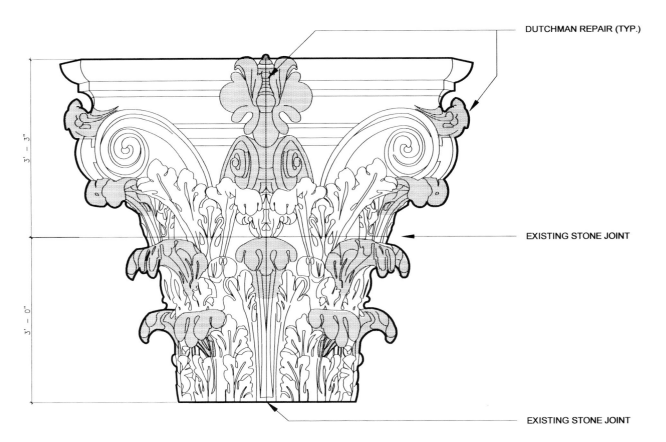

DUTCHMAN REPAIR (TYP.)

EXISTING STONE JOINT

EXISTING STONE JOINT

3' – 3"

3' – 0"

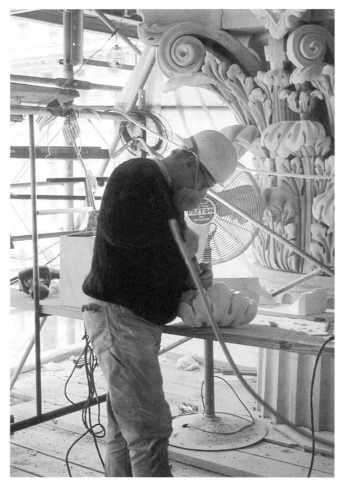

Missing details from the Chambers Street portico column capitals were hand-carved by workers from B & H Art-in-Architecture, Ltd.

Chambers Street portico column capitals restored with new decorative elements.

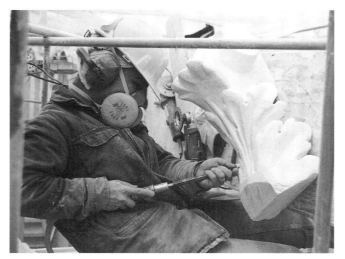

The newly carved details were anchored to the Chambers Street portico column capitals using stainless-steel pins and epoxy adhesive.

ical, as well as chemical, bond to the stone. The anchors were countersunk into the stone faces, and the holes were plugged with marble. Cintec anchors were also installed in the blocks forming the raking cornice and pediment ends, perpendicular to the rake, into the tympanum.

The amount of work required to fabricate the new replacement elements from new and recycled stone and the short amount of time available for construction resulted in the decision to utilize several stone fabricators, located throughout North America, to produce the components. The larger elements—such as the main cornice, the cheek walls for the Chamber Street stairs, and the roof balustrades—were fabricated at the Georgia Marble Company plants in Tate and Nelson, Georgia; this firm also reworked the original stone to be use in dutchman repairs. Smaller and more decorative components—such as the modillion blocks, the egg-and-dart moldings of the pilaster capitals, and the running lengths of cornice den-

Chambers Street portico with restored column capitals. The restoration of the pilaster capital on the right was still underway.

Elongated bead moldings were hand-carved by Traditional Cut Stone, Ltd. of Toronto, Canada.

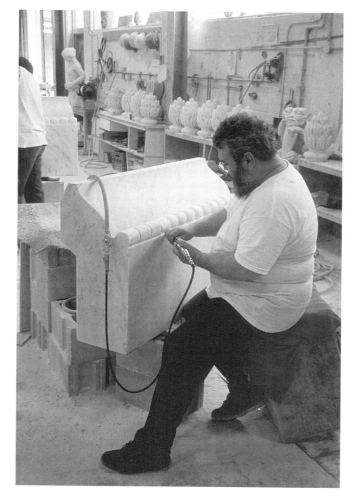

tils and related moldings that could be fabricated using computer-driven carving machinery—were subcontracted to Johnson Atelier of Mercerville, New Jersey. Features that required hand carving, such as the pineapples that originally hung from the corners of the cornice and elongated bead moldings, were produced by Traditional Cut Stone, Ltd. of Toronto, Canada. Granite Importers of Barre, Vermont, fabricated the new granite watertable stones and Chambers Street stair treads.

Marble made up ninety-five percent of the exterior walls, while the granite used in the watertable made up the remaining five percent. The granite had exfoliated, or delaminated, a condition that affected the appearance, but not the integrity, of the stone. To correct the problem, the granite was cleaned using the same pre-wash and after-wash chemicals used for the marble. The entire surface of the watertable was then ground down to a sound surface, removing the exfoliated material. The surface of the granite was then hand-tooled to replicate the original six-cut tooling. Joints between the granite blocks originally consisted of sheet lead packing, which was retained. New granite was used for the steps missing from the Chambers Street staircase and to extend the watertable walls of the reconstructed walls. The new granite matched the texture and color of the original granite.

Tweed Courthouse was one of the most extensive and complex stone restoration projects undertaken for a historic public building by the City of New York. The construction process required the close cooperation of the Economic Development Corporation, the architects, structural engineers, construction managers, contractors, fabricators, and suppliers, to restore the facades to a structurally sound and safe condition, while preserving the building's historic and architectural integrity. The shop drawings and sample submission process was complicated and extremely thorough. All totaled, there were 1,340 replacement and dutchman stones installed, using 344 recycled stones and 994 new Georgia White Cherokee marble blocks.

Reconstruction of the Chambers Street Stair

One of the last but most important elements in the restoration of the exterior of the building was the reconstruction of the Chambers Street stair. Once the main public entry to the building, this monumental granite-and-marble stairway originally led from the sidewalk on Chambers Street to the building's grand entry vestibule on the second floor. In 1942 much of the stairway was demolished to allow for the widening of Chambers Street between Broadway and Centre Street, thus providing an additional lane for traffic bound for the nearby Brooklyn Bridge. The relocated curb was 12 feet closer to the front of the courthouse, and this change dramatically altered its appearance. The front lawns were shortened to accommodate a new sidewalk, and the entry to the main floor of the building could no longer be reached from the street. A wall was built between the stair's truncated marble cheek walls, and a concrete slab was poured over the

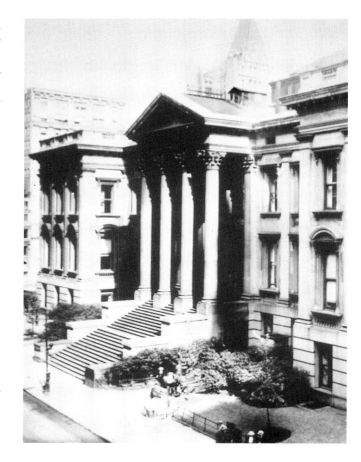

Chambers Street portico with original stairs leading to the entrance hall on the main floor.

Chambers Street facade after stairway was truncated in 1942. The public entrances to the building were relocated to the ground floor, behind the wall that replaced the stairway.

remaining steps near the top landing. A metal railing was installed at the perimeter of the landing and the cheek walls, reducing the once grand stairway to no more than a second-floor balcony.

As the planning for the restoration began, it became clear that the construction of a new stairway would be essential to the success of the project. The architects recommended that the historic configuration be reconstructed, in order to allow the public to experience the original entry sequence from the sidewalk through the large wood doors to the original entry hall and then through a low brick archway leading into the vast central rotunda. The stair reconstruction would also serve to increase fire safety by adding three additional exits from the second floor directly to grade level.

All of these benefits were, however, contingent upon the narrowing of Chambers Street to make room for the stairway and the relocated sidewalk. Reclaiming land taken to make room for the automobile is often a difficult task in American cities. Here the problem was solved by a demonstration project undertaken by the New York City Department of Transportation (DOT) at the request of the Department of General Services. Between February 14 and March 10, 1989, barricades were used to eliminate one eastbound lane of Chambers Street approximately 11 feet wide, simulating the effect of the restored stairway and the expanded sidewalk. Traffic characteristics were recorded and compared with those collected before the test. The results of this study, documented in a report entitled *Chambers Street Demonstration Project* (March 1989), included the following: traffic patterns and volumes remained unchanged; queuing and traffic back-up conditions on eastbound Chambers Street were unaffected; and travel speeds and intersection delays on eastbound Chambers and Duane Streets were not significantly affected. Based on the findings of this report, the Department of Transportation supported the stair restoration and the narrowing of Chambers Street and also cited the wider sidewalk space in front of the courthouse as an additional benefit that the project would provide.

Meanwhile, the architects oversaw the use of probes to verify existing conditions and to determine how much of the remaining portions of the stairway could be reused. Areas under the Chambers Street sidewalk were excavated to assess the condition of the foundations that had supported the portion of the stairs demolished in 1942. The probes revealed that the original footings still existed from a point approximately 18 inches below the sidewalk to a depth of about 9 feet. The lower 2 feet of the footings had been constructed of rough stone while the rest was brick. Both portions were determined to be in excellent condition and could be reused. Another probe was made at the landing between the two center columns of the por-

tico. Here a portion of the concrete slab was cut away, revealing that there was a void under the slab and that the uppermost original granite steps remained and were still in good condition.

With the information gathered from the probes and schematic designs done for the feasibility study, the architects began preparing detailed contract documents for the reconstruction of the Chambers Street stairs late in 2000. The existing stair and cheek-wall conditions were measured and drawn, and construction documents were created. The design called for new marble and granite-clad stepped cheek walls, and seventeen new granite treads leading from the sidewalk to the last remaining original treads. The matching of materials was crucial in order to provide a seamless transition between old and new stone. Georgia White Cherokee marble, already chosen for the new cornice and other facade work, was used for the marble cheek walls and capstones. Samples of many types of granite were compared with the basement walls and existing stair treads, but none seemed to be a perfect match. Finally, after additional research and samples comparisons, Sterling granite from Vermont was chosen. It provided an excellent match.

Final DOT approval for the narrowing of Chambers Street was received on August 2, 2000. This approval allowed the sidewalk to be shifted 11 feet into the street, removed the "No Parking" lane in front of the courthouse, and provided enough room for the stair extension and the enlargement of the building's front lawns. Because the stair reconstruction would have such a large impact on the appearance of a landmark building, the architects made presentations to the local community board and the Landmarks Preservation Commission to show how the proposed design would be constructed and

Original granite stair treads that were encased in the concrete platform construction in 1942, when most of the stairway was removed.

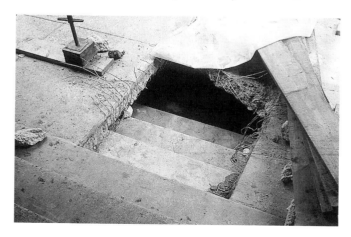

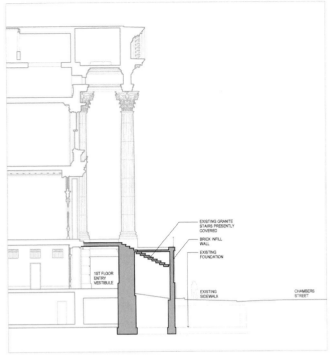

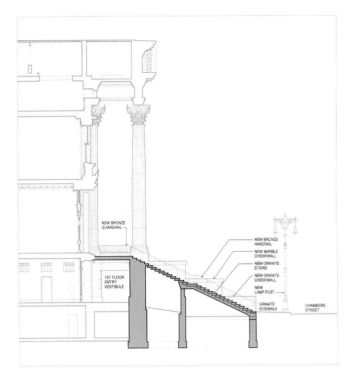

Cross sections comparing the pre-restoration condition of the original stairs with the restored main stairway. The original foundation

footings still remained after the removal of the lower treads and cheek walls, and were reused for the reconstructed portion of the stairs.

what its final appearance would be. Since the design of the reconstruction was based on photographic evidence of the original stair and would be built of matching materials, both the community board and the LPC strongly endorsed the proposal. These approvals were the final step required before construction of the new Chambers Street stair could begin.

In late April 2001 work began on the new stairway. The remaining original steps near the top landing were exposed and the sidewalk in front of the stair was removed, uncovering the tops of the existing masonry footings just below grade. A new concrete slab was poured over these footings, new concrete block (CMU) backup walls were built on top of the slab, and the voids in the blocks were grouted solid. At this point, the height of the lowest remaining original stair tread was surveyed to confirm that the new construction would meet it precisely, and the final tread heights were confirmed. Next, metal decking was laid to serve as formwork for a new stepped, reinforced-concrete substructure. After the concrete was poured, this substructure spanned the cheek walls and would support the seventeen new granite steps. Since restoration work was already under way on the front facade, the stairway had to be built around the scaffolding supports that were in place.

Concrete was poured around the supports, and the stair construction continued, timed so that the supports were cut and left in place after the scaffolding above was no longer necessary but before the stone steps were installed on the upper part of the stairway.

The stone cladding and the steps began to be set in place in July 2001. The cheek-wall cladding consisted of 3-inch-thick marble and 7-inch-thick granite supported by stainless-steel anchors attached to the CMU backup walls. The granite and marble stones were toothed into the existing stone of the remaining portion of the stair. On the marble faces of the cheek walls, two cornerstones were set to commemorate the restoration. The east stone was engraved with the building's original name, The New York County Courthouse, the names of the original architects, and the dates of their work on the building. The stone in the west cheek wall carries the building's more common name, Tweed Courthouse, and lists the city officials and agencies and the architects responsible for the 1999–2001 restoration.

As cladding was set on the cheek walls, the granite treads were also being set in place. Each new tread matched the existing tread profile and joint spacing exactly; each measured 7 inches in height by 14 inches in

Reconstructed Chambers Street stairs before the granite treads were installed and before the cheek walls were completed.

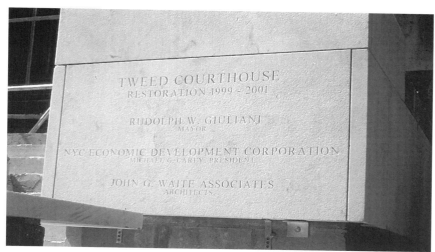

New marble dedication panels were installed at the first level of the cheek walls.

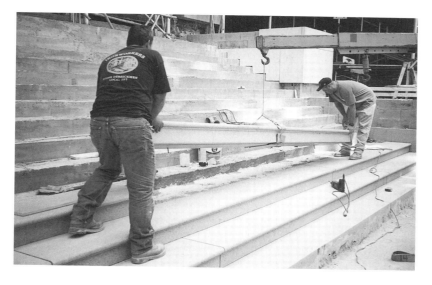

Installation of new granite steps to complete the reconstruction of missing section of stairway. Seventeen new treads were installed to complement the original steps, which remained in their original location.

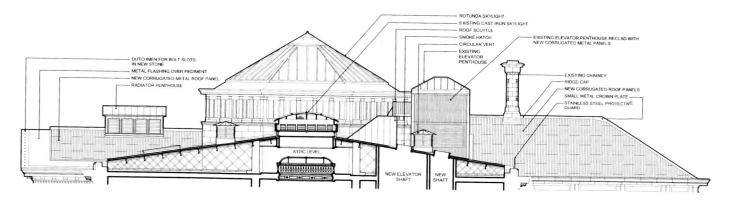

Opposite: The restored Chambers Street stairs, which are used as the main entrance to the building.

Cross section drawing looking east showing roof elements, including skylights, mechanical penthouses, and chimney that were restored. The main roof surface is corrugated terne-coated stainless steel that replicates the appearance of the original corrugated sheet-iron roofing.

depth, and up to 14 feet in length. The treads were set onto a 1-inch mortar bed and anchored to the concrete substructure with two stainless-steel pins. They were set in place from the bottom of the stair upward, with each tread overlapping the one below it until the seventeenth new tread was notched and slid under the edge of the lowest original tread. Next, the four enormous cheek-wall capstones, each weighing over 12,000 pounds, were put into place using a crane. The stonework was then pointed, and all the adjacent marble and granite was given a final cleaning. Bronze handrails were added on either side of the stairway and at the top landing. Although handrails did not exist historically on this stair, the new rails were sympathetic to the overall design and provided a level of safety required by modern building codes.

Completed by November 2001, the new Chambers Street stair helped to create an entirely new, inviting public entrance to Tweed Courthouse, attracting curious visitors who had to be turned away since work was still continuing in other parts of the building. The steps have since become a lunchtime destination for nearby office workers and tourists alike.

Roof

The roof of a historic building is usually an important visual element that helps establish its architectural character. In many public buildings constructed during the second half of the nineteenth century the roof incorporated advanced building technology and the newest materials. Today these materials are often no longer available or manufactured in the sizes or patterns that were used in

the past. It is often no longer possible to duplicate historic building technology, particularly flashing and jointing techniques, and in many cases this technology has proven to be unsatisfactory in keeping the building weathertight.

The challenge in restoring the roof of a historic building is first to determine how the original roof was configured, what materials were used, and how it was detailed. Once this information is known, an assessment of the significance of the roof can be made, and it can be decided whether the roof should be restored. As part of the historic structure report, information as to why the historic roofing failed should be collected and assessed.

Once the decision has been made to restore the roof to a particular condition, the next step is to determine whether the historic roofing materials are available or whether another material must be utilized. If the latter, the new material must replicate the appearance of the original. Similarly, the detailing—particularly flashing and jointing—must be designed so that the same appearance is replicated, utilizing sound modern technology that will make the structure weathertight and will permit the manufacturer of the roofing material to issue a warranty for the work.

The roof of the original courthouse, designed by Kellum, consisted of a series of shallow-hipped roofs surrounded by a balustrade. At the center of this roof was the octagonal rotunda opening, which was to be capped with the high iron dome that was never constructed. Instead, Leopold Eidlitz, who designed the hipped roof of the south addition, created the existing octagonal pyramidal skylight over the rotunda. The roof over the original parts of the courthouse had consisted of wrought-iron beams

Main roof covered with rolled asphalt roofing installed in 1978 as a temporary measure to preserve the building and to prevent further damage to the interior. This work was funded by The New York Landmarks Conservancy.

The original iron flashings had been removed from the stone eaves, resulting in open mortar joints that allowed water to penetrate the cornice area.

and trusses covered with corrugated rolled-iron decking, which formed the finished exterior surface, and Eidlitz followed suit. The entire roof, like the rest of the building, was thus constructed of noncombustible materials.

The original roofing consisted of corrugated rolled-iron sheets with a coating of an alloy of tin and lead to resist rusting. Known as terne-coated sheet iron, this material is no longer manufactured and the dimensions of the corrugation are no longer standard. The replication of such early machine-made materials, which utilized now archaic manufacturing technology, is one of the major challenges facing today's restoration architects.

In 1978, after more than a century of service, the original corrugated iron was removed. The shallow roof planes over the large central block of the building were covered with asphalt membrane roofing, and all other

Chambers Street portico roof after restoration with terne-coated stainless-steel corrugated roofing and eave flashings.

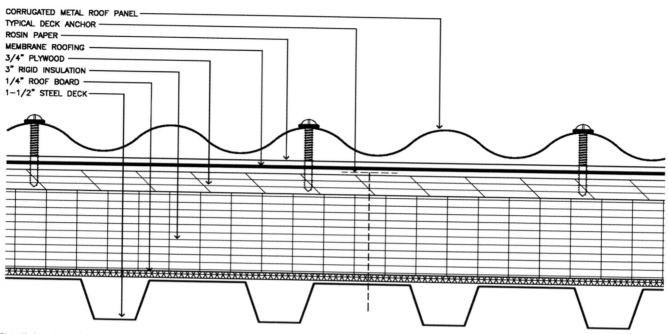

CORRUGATED METAL ROOF PANEL
TYPICAL DECK ANCHOR
ROSIN PAPER
MEMBRANE ROOFING
3/4" PLYWOOD
3" RIGID INSULATION
1/4" ROOF BOARD
1-1/2" STEEL DECK

Detail drawing of custom-rolled corrugated terne-coated stainless-steel roof system.

roof surfaces were covered with asphalt shingles. The asphalt roofing was supported by decking made of wood fiberboard impregnated with cement with a factory-applied asphalt felt membrane; the decking spanned the original iron roof purlins. After twenty years, this replacement roof was showing signs of deterioration, and when the restoration began in 1999 the roof surface was ready for replacement.

The intent of the restoration was to create a roofing system of better quality and longer life expectancy. The roof had to meet modern fire-code requirements, satisfy energy requirements, and allow for easy, long-term maintenance. Because the building is a prominent civic monument and is very visible from surrounding buildings and the Brooklyn Bridge, the plan was to match the appearance of the historic roof, thus restoring one of the major character-defining elements of the building.

At the beginning of the analysis process detailed measured drawings of the roof and attic spaces were produced. During this investigation an original piece of corrugated iron was discovered; it was 1 inch deep with 5 inches between the high points of the corrugation. Based on this discovery, the architects began to research materials and manufacturers that could match the historic profile of the iron. However, the standard corrugated shapes did not match the historic sample. Furthermore, the manufacturing process that produced the original corrugated shape was no longer commercially used. After an intense search,

the architects located a local manufacturer that could produce metal panels to match the exact profile of the original corrugated iron.

In conjunction with this search the architects investigated several options for the type of metal sheets to be corrugated, and TCS II by Follansbee Steel—a stainless-steel sheet coated with a zinc/tin alloy—was finally selected. The bare gray metal that patinas to a darker gray finish, offered the best color match to the historic roof, and eliminated the need for painting. The patina also provides a layer of protection against the corrosive atmosphere of the marine environment in New York City. Finally, because the steel has a low coefficient of expansion and can easily be soldered, it could also be used to line the gutters, providing a visually and technically compatible roof covering.

In order to ensure the best possible detailing, various sources were consulted, including a 1932 edition of graphic standards that contained once-common corrugated roofing details. One of the major issues was the positioning of the fasteners, either in the high points (ridges) or the low points (furrows) of the corrugation. Fastening at the high point, which was the desirable choice, would move the fastener—and therefore the hole in the roof panel—away from the natural flow of water. However, fastening at the low point seemed to offer a more secure connection to the underlayment, resulting in a more rigid surface for walking. In addition to providing a rigid surface, the fasteners had to counteract the suction force of the wind. The determining factor for the design of the fasteners in this case was the wind-pressure calculations. Based on these calculations, the final roof panels (approximately 10 feet long by 3 feet wide) were fastened at every corrugation across the top and bottom, and every other corrugation at five equally spaced intermediate rows. The specified fasteners, stainless-steel screws with an integral neoprene pad, provided a weathertight seal at the screw holes.

The custom-corrugated roof panel was only one piece of the entire roofing system. The existing structural system consisted of trusses formed by wrought-iron beams with a bottom cord-tension cable. These trusses rested on the interior and exterior masonry walls of the courthouse. In some areas, cast-iron columns, resting on girders, provided additional structural support. The 1991 feasibility report had recommended that all of the roof structure remain in place to minimize the amount of new framing and the amount of disruption to the existing structure. With a reevaluation of the test samples and probes, the structural engineer confirmed that this approach was still desirable. New steel beams were designed for limited areas where the existing structure would not meet current design-load capacities. Intumescent paint was also specified as a finish for all metal roof structural elements to provide protection against failure at high temperatures.

The restoration of the roof involved the application of several layers of materials. First, a 1½ inch-thick cellular steel structural deck was placed on the existing structural system. A ¼ inch-thick roof board with a water-resistant gypsum core formed the second layer; it would act as a fire barrier within the roof assembly. The third layer, a 3-inch-thick sheet of extruded polystyrene insulation, was then applied; it was designed in conjunction with the mechanical system to ensure the proper amount of thermal resistance. Next, ¾ inch-thick pressure-treated plywood was installed to act as the backup for the corrugated steel. This layer would be secured to the structural decking below, thereby creating a unified system. In addition, a rubber membrane was adhered fully to the plywood in order to create an additional layer of moisture protection under the corrugated metal panels. The rubber membrane was selected for its "memory": its ability to reform to its original shape even if punctured. This characteristic was crucial since the thousands of screws required to fasten the corrugated panels would penetrate this membrane. Finally, a rosin paper slip-sheet was inserted to prevent the bonding of the rubber membrane to the corrugated panels.

Skylights

Like the roof, skylights are often another important character-giving element for a historic public building. Historically, skylights have helped to define the exterior character of the building, and often they provided most of the illumination for major spaces inside. The character of illumination from a skylight greatly affects the perception of the space surrounding it.

Interior of one of the restored ridge skylights over a main staircase. The pattern of the hexagonal cast-glass blocks is important in defining the character of the restored skylight.

Rotunda skylight and elevator penthouse before restoration.

Rotunda skylight after restoration. A new skylight system with insulated, laminated glazing was installed over the original iron structure. In the foreground is one of the two cast-iron ridge skylights that illuminate the main staircases on either side of the rotunda.

Nineteenth-century skylights utilized materials and technology that created conditions prone to leaking. Consequently, skylights were often removed or covered over in an attempt to make the building weathertight. As nineteenth-century public buildings are being restored, it is usually desirable to restore the skylights so that they once again illuminate the major interior spaces.

Like roofing, the restoration of skylights involves research into the original configuration and materials, along with an analysis of why they failed. The restoration of skylights to their historic appearance, utilizing appro-priate modern technology and materials, is often a major architectural challenge. However, it is usually important to develop a solution that preserves and utilizes the remaining historic building fabric and restores the historic appearance of the skylights. It also should provide an effective, long-term, weatherproof solution for bringing natural light into the building.

The skylights at Tweed Courthouse created unusual situations for the roof reconstruction. The central skylight, with its elaborate internal iron-truss structure, spanned 50 feet between the octagonal bearing walls of the rotunda.

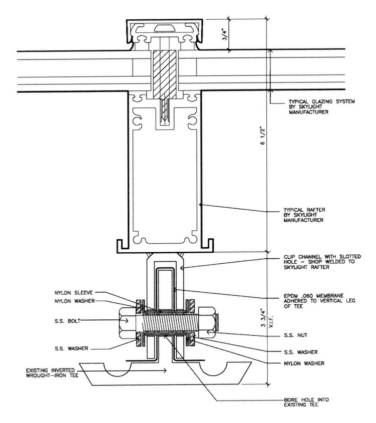

Detail drawing of new exterior skylight framing attachments to original cast- and wrought-iron structure.

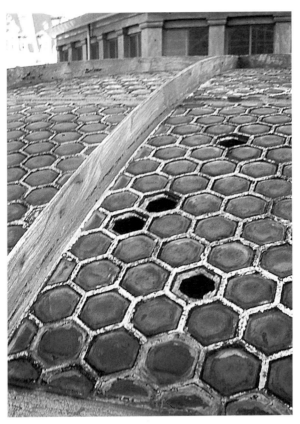

Detail of ridge skylight before restoration, with missing cast-glass blocks and original white lead putty that had failed. Previously, asphalt patching compounds had been installed as an attempt to stop the leaks.

The skylight held wired glass, which had replaced the original plate glass that was supported on iron ribs in the 1940s. At the beginning of the restoration work, rainwater was leaking through the skylight into the rotunda. The two large ridge skylights, located over the primary stairways at the east and west ends of the rotunda, were constructed of hexagonal glass blocks set in curved cast-iron frames, and they also leaked.

For the central skylight, a new glazing-support system was designed to fit onto the existing structure. Slotted channels, which could slip over the existing iron ribs, were fastened to the underside of the rafters of the new skylight. Fitted with an insulated, laminated glazing system, the new skylight replicated the historic condition with a new watertight and energy-efficient surface. The rafter caps and insulated metal panels at the top of the skylight were factory painted to match the adjacent stone.

For the ridge skylights, the original plan was to remove the original cast-glass blocks, clean the existing iron structure, and reset the glass blocks in a new bed of sealant.

However, during the initial removals, many of the glass blocks shattered because the surrounding bedding of white lead had become extremely hard. Instead, a second plan was devised: the original glass blocks were left in place, and the dirt and rust was cleaned from the joints. New cast-glass blocks were made to replace missing or damaged pieces. These new blocks were set with a silicone structural adhesive and the joints were filled with sealant. As a final precaution, a sheet of curved transparent acrylic was attached to the iron ribs, protecting the skylight from any water penetration. These ribs were finished with a dark-gray epoxy paint that matched the adjacent iron roofing.

The ridge skylights were designed in conjunction with the mechanical system. A plenum was created at a point below these skylights where the mechanical ducts would exhaust air through new louvers located at the base of the skylights. The mechanical system required that additional roof elements be constructed. Two penthouses, flanking the ridge skylights, were needed as air intakes, and another penthouse to house the large fans used by the emer-

Detail of restored cast-iron ridge skylight. The missing cast-glass blocks were replicated and all of the blocks were reset and caulked with a silicone sealant.

gency generator would be built over the ridge of the north pediment. Furthermore, two roof scuttles, a kitchen exhaust, additional air vents, and stacks for the emergency generator exhaust were needed. In all cases, these elements were located in places that historically had a penthouse or pipe, as seen in historic photographs.

The restoration of the roof and the skylights required careful coordination. One of the first steps in the construction process was the erection of a temporary roof over the entire building. This surface was supported by the scaffolding already in place around the perimeter of the courthouse and by numerous interior supports. It permitted the removal of the entire roof assembly down to the existing cast- and wrought-iron structure while protecting the rest of the building from the elements. In addition, the temporary roof allowed work to continue through the winter months—an important benefit given the aggressive schedule of the project. Because construction of the temporary roof required that a large crane swing over Chambers Street, the street had to be closed

during the erection process; thus the structure for the temporary roof was assembled, and later disassembled, over the course of only one weekend each time.

While shop drawings for the new permanent roof were prepared and reviewed, work on the attic was under way. The removal of the roof had revealed that many of the bricks at the tops of the masonry walls at the attic level were loose. The bricks were reset, creating a smooth surface that aligned with the slope of the existing roof structure. In addition, new steel framing was added, including the transfer beams that supported the rods that carried the new fire stairs. The entire roof structure was then primed and painted, and the corrugated decking was installed.

The construction of the roof system proceeded quickly. Each layer was custom formed to fit the complex shape of the roof and to fit around the scores of interior temporary roof supports. Other construction tasks were coordinated with the roof restoration process; for example, large pieces of mechanical equipment were installed in

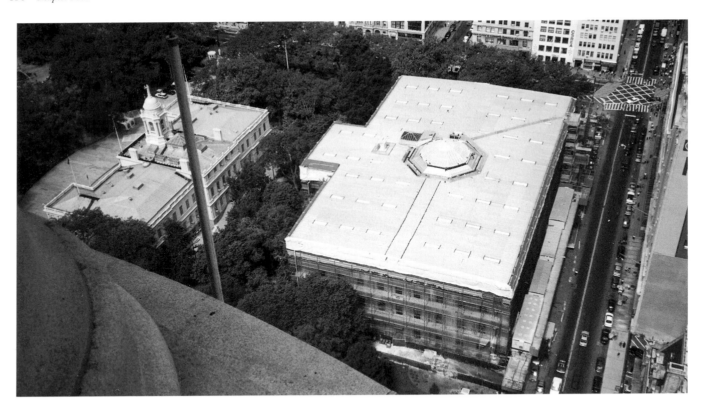

Temporary roof construction over the entire building, partially supported on the perimeter scaffolding. This construction allowed roofing, stone cornice, and structural work to continue through the winter by providing a weathertight enclosure.

Interior of temporary roof construction.

the attic on newly poured concrete floors prior to the completion of the roof. Once the rubber membrane was installed, the temporary roof could be removed because the rubber membrane would protect the courthouse from water infiltration while the final metal panels were being placed.

The corrugated steel, the final roof surface, was installed once the temporary roof was completely removed. The built-in gutters behind the perimeter balustrade and the sloping roof gutters were lined with terne-coated stainless steel. The new penthouses and other roof elements were clad in flat-seamed sheet-

After structural repairs were completed, a new corrugated steel deck was installed as the base for insulation boards, a waterproof membrane, and the final corrugated terne-coated stainless steel roofing system.

The roof with perimeter scaffolding in place.

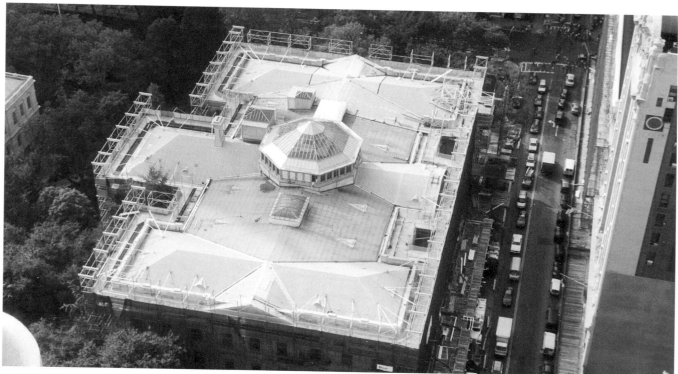

metal roofing. The top of the new cornice was covered with sheet-metal flashing to protect the joints and anchor locations in the stone. The corrugated metal panels were installed starting at the bottom of the roof to provide a positive overlap and staggered to alternate the seams. Large ridge caps and crown plates were con-structed over corners and edges. Finally, foam closure strips were installed at the open ends of the corrugated metal panels to protect against wind-driven rain and insects. By the end of the restoration, Tweed Courthouse had acquired a unique, durable, and truly brilliant roof.

Sitework

When undertaking an exterior restoration project it is extremely important to understand the historical development of the building and its landscape features as well as its immediate context. Archival research should include historic maps of the area, architectural drawings, photographs, and written accounts that document the building's original site and landscape configuration. Occasionally, archaeological investigations may be necessary to determine the presence, or absence, of significant subsurface features. A thorough chronology of changes to the site over time, including the addition and replacement of below-grade utility systems, should be developed and then used by the architects and engineers to make informed design and construction decisions pertaining to modern requirements, such as vehicle access and parking needs. Coordination with groundskeepers and municipal agencies is needed to ensure that proper maintenance strategies and future long-term capital improvement projects are considered and incorporated into a long-term stewardship program for the property.

The preliminary landscape restoration concepts for the areas of City Hall Park adjacent to Tweed Courthouse that were developed early in 1989 focused primarily on the reconstruction of the monumental stairs on the north facade of the building along Chambers Street. These proposed changes required the narrowing of Chambers Street, a four-lane street leading to and from the Brooklyn Bridge, and the widening of the sidewalk to accommodate the new stair construction. Other sitework included the restoration of the granite areaways, and some lawn and iron-fence replacement was also proposed.

Following the accidental discovery of the eighteenth-century African Burial Ground during construction of a federal government project at Foley Square in the early 1990s, the New York City Department of General Services authorized the architects to undertake a comprehensive archival research project to identify the history and use of buildings previously located on the site of what is now City Hall Park. Hunter Research Inc. served as archaeological consultants to the architects for the study, which revealed hundreds of buildings and landscape features, most no longer extant, that spanned almost three centuries of British, Dutch, and American occupation and included barracks, almshouses, cemeteries, and public buildings. The continuing evolution of City Hall Park had created an archaeological palimpsest, with great potential as a diverse and relatively intact cultural resource in lower Manhattan. This preliminary research and documentation proved invaluable; knowledge of the potential existence and possible locations of subsurface archaeological resources informed the early planning and design phases of construction work in areas along the Chambers Street sidewalk.

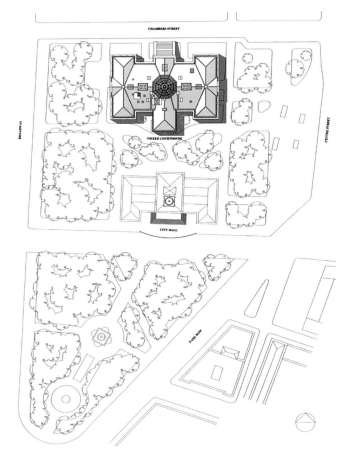

Site plan with Tweed courthouse at north end of City Hall Park. The main entrance to the restored building is from Chambers Street.

Two years before restoration work began at Tweed Courthouse, the New York City Department of Parks and Recreation undertook a capital campaign to restore City Hall Park and upgrade various utility and security systems at City Hall. This work included new paving, landscaping, irrigation, and power distribution throughout the park; the re-creation of a fountain, the park's historic centerpiece; gas lighting; pedestrian lighting; street furniture; and a new iron fence and gates along the perimeter of City Hall Park. The work in the park did not address the areas adjacent to Tweed Courthouse.

During the summer of 1999, as construction work by the Department of Parks and Recreation was being completed within the park, the Department of City Planning, the Department of Transportation, and the local community board met to discuss the proposed narrowing of Chambers

Street. This possibility had been studied internally for traffic-planning and legal implications by the Department of Transportation over the previous decade, and the concept was readily approved by all involved agencies. Final approval for narrowing Chambers Street was given following the submittal to the Department of Buildings. As part of the restoration work begun in 1999, a builders' pavement plan was developed to indicate the exact locations of new curbs and the proposed grading and drainage of both Chambers Street and the new sidewalk.

Coordination of materials and construction details was undertaken with the Department of Parks and Recreation, and the design was approved by the Landmarks Preservation Commission. This approach ensured that the paved and landscaped areas adjacent to the courthouse incorporated the design intent of the nearly complete park project. For the paved areas, granite and bluestone slabs were obtained from the same quarries and cut to the same dimensions to match the color, texture, and pattern of the sidewalks and pathways used in the park project. Cast-iron bollards and sections of metal-picket fencing and gates surrounding the park were fabricated by the same foundry. Installation details were similar, and the work was executed by the same contractors.

Sitework began with archaeological testing and monitoring, primarily under Chambers Street and along the north facade of the building. These were the areas where archaeological features were presumed to exist and where the majority of below-grade work for new utilities and landscape features was proposed. When significant archaeological features, including human remains, were encountered during the testing phase, the locations of utility pipes and conduits were rerouted, grades were modified, and the design of concrete footings was revised. In most cases the archaeological features that were uncovered remained intact and in place during construction, following extensive documentation and subsequent protection measures by the archaeologists. Construction resumed only after their efforts were reviewed and approved by the Landmarks Preservation Commission.

Following the relocation of below-grade utilities, most of the final grades were established in relation to the new sidewalk curb and the ground-floor entrances to the building, then granite and bluestone slabs were installed. This allowed several entrances to become accessible for wheelchairs without extensive modifications to the building or the addition of ramps or lifts. At the south entrance to the building where several steps that led from the building up to ground level, a short ramped walkway and a retaining wall were incorporated. Finally, two new doorways leading from the east and west fire stairs discharged onto landings and into restored areas of lawn at the back of the building.

Surrounding the perimeter of the building, new plantings were used to replicate the original landscape design that appeared in historic maps and photographs: broad lawns at the front, sides, and back of the building and trees in select locations. Delivery, sanitation, and recycling functions were consolidated and accommodated in a paved area adjacent to the west side of the building within the security perimeter of City Hall Park. This area can be monitored from a small booth within the landscaped perimeter of the site.

Integrated into the lawns were in-ground lighting fixtures that dramatically illuminate the exterior facade of the building and can be relamped easily when necessary. Full-scale mock-ups of the lighting design were conducted over several nights to determine the appropriate color rendition of the lamps. This feature lighting, which provides an extra measure of security to the exterior of the building, is complemented by additional down-lighting at the Chambers Street portico and by spotlights affixed to the replicated historic streetlights. Fisher Marantz Stone was the lighting consultant.

The landscape approach restored the original setting of the courthouse while accommodating modern functional and safety requirements including the lighting of the exterior. The restored building is an integral part of City Hall Park as well as a prominent civic landmark on Chambers Street.

As part of the archeological program associated with excavations for new utilities and landscape elements, significant below-grade features, including human remains, were encountered. This double burial was left in place and the utility line was rerouted to avoid it.

As part of the feasibility study, all of the original ventilation and heating shafts embedded in the masonry walls were investigated and documented for potential reuse in the new HVAC system. Over sixty shafts were located and investigated.

CHAPTER FIVE

Building Systems

Heating, Ventilating and Air Conditioning

As public buildings increased in size and scale during the nineteenth century, new technology was required for their heating, ventilating, and lighting. Fireplaces and small cast-iron stoves were not adequate to heat these larger buildings, and more illumination was needed than that provided by candles or oil lamps. As the century progressed, many new inventions addressed these problems. The rebuilding of the Houses of Parliament in London after the fire of 1834 provided an opportunity to develop technology for the heating and ventilating of public buildings. When the House of Commons was completed in 1852, it incorporated very advanced heating and ventilation systems.

The original construction of Tweed Courthouse included an extensive system of large and small air-distribution shafts, or chases, integral to the building's masonry bearing walls. Like the Houses of Parliament models, these shafts supplied air for heating and ventilation throughout the building. This system was one of the most comprehensive and progressive in America during this period.

Large shafts, triangular in plan and located at the four corners of the rotunda, extended the full height of the building, terminating in the attic. At the bottom of these shafts, in the basement, were large, rotating cast-iron fans that circulated air throughout the building. These fans pushed both fresh and recirculated air through trenches, or plenums, under the basement floor that led to a series of small rooms containing steam-heating coils and adjustable dampers, one in front of each opening in the vertical wall shafts. Fresh air was drawn into the system from four intake air wells located at grade level on either side of the north portico and on either side of the south addition. The intake air wells were identical in appearance to the light wells around the perimeter of the building. Similarly, air that had been circulated through the building was drawn down from the attic through the large rectangular shafts and mixed with incoming fresh air for re-distribution. This basic approach is still used in HVAC systems for large buildings today.

The wall shafts conducted heated air throughout the building, discharging the air through registers located low

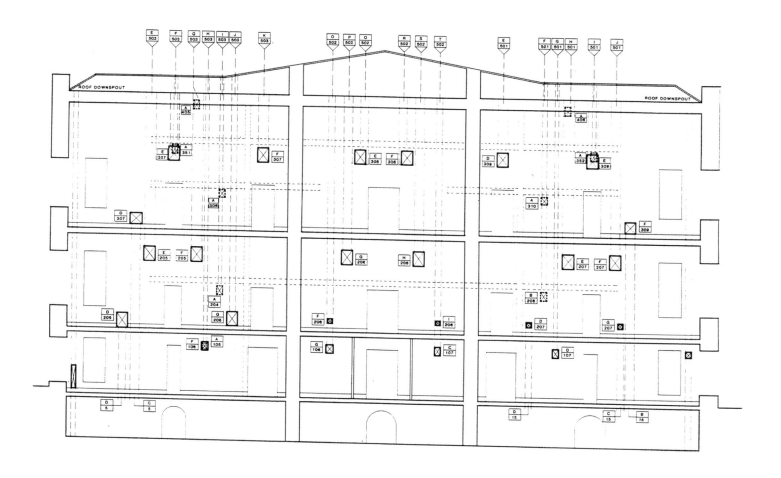

in the walls of each room. By means of natural convection and with the aid of pressurization from the fans, the warm air rose and was exhausted from the room through another set of registers, located near the ceiling, into shafts extending to the attic. Both the supply and return registers were constructed of cast iron and had operable louvers, which provided the means to control air distribution in each room. Decorative grilles made of porcelain enamel were set within the frames of the cast-iron registers.

When the courthouse was constructed, the quality of the indoor air was poor, largely because of the high levels of air pollution throughout the city resulting from the burning of coal for heating and power. Coupled with the lack of filtration within the building's air distribution systems, this pollution caused an early example of "sick building syndrome." Complaints were made at an early date that the air in the building was foul, and it was alleged that Chief Justice Monell died from "the evil effects of the malaria, which lurks in the walls of the building." One popular but inaccurate idea at the time held that interior brick surfaces could absorb and release harmful vapors in the air.

Early in the twentieth century four additional air-intake wells were constructed next to the original ones and connected with them. Intake airshafts were built to a height of 8 feet above grade in an effort to increase the amount of fresh air brought into the building. Shortly after that, a new steam-heating system with cast-iron radiators located under most windows was installed to replace the original air-distribution system, which was abandoned but left in place. Ventilation was provided by opening the windows. By the middle of the twentieth century at least one electric fan was being used in most rooms to assist in cooling, and by the 1980s window air conditioners had been installed in most of the building. Not only were they unsightly; their condensate caused the marble windowsills to deteriorate.

The introduction of modern HVAC equipment, ductwork, and piping into historic buildings is often difficult and complicated because of the size and complexity of modern systems. As a result, the desire to satisfy modern program and comfort requirements has often compromised the architectural character and significance of the building. In some cases the new systems have resulted in

TWEED COURTHOUSE MECHANICAL DIAGRAM

Outside air intake
Exhaust air discharge
Outside air intake
Emergency generator remote radiator

Rotunda Skylight

Portico

Chambers Street Stair

Air handling unit

Basement underslab ducts

Plenum collects fresh air for distribution
Air handling unit
Attic
Air handling unit
Third Floor
Emergency generator supplies City Hall
Second Floor
First Floor
Ductwork is integrated into original ventilation shafts in the masonry walls
Basement
Emergency generators located in basement vault

Schematic diagram explaining the new HVAC system that utilizes original ventilation and heating shafts. Air handling units are located in the attic and basement, and the building was divided into zones to pro- *vide maximum efficiency and flexibility. Hot and chilled water is provided to the building by the city's centralized heating and cooling plant located a block away.*

the further deterioration of historic building fabric. Therefore, prior to the design of new systems, it is important to understand fully the construction details of the historic building, including the exterior wall and roof details; to research the historic systems of the building to understand their design, their integration into the building fabric, and their past performance; and to conduct physical investigations to determine the feasibility of reusing the original distribution pathways for new systems. The available space within a historic building and the configuration of that space may either limit or suggest a particular HVAC system that would be most appropriate for the building.

An important element of the 1991 feasibility report was the design concept for the HVAC system. The goal was to provide the most efficient and effective system for the building without compromising its historic character and architectural significance. To begin the design process a preliminary survey of the building and site was undertaken, and the existing shafts in the masonry walls were carefully

documented for potential reuse. Next, meetings were held with representatives of the Department of General Services, the city agency responsible at the time for maintaining the building and its systems, and the Department of Buildings, the agency having regulatory authority over all city construction. As a result of these meetings, recommendations for a central heating and cooling plant were agreed upon along with critical life-safety and smoke-management objectives for the landmarked exterior spaces of the building, particularly the rotunda.

Tweed Courthouse is one of many buildings in the City Hall area that are owned and operated by the City of New York. In 1990 a long-range plan to standardize building-system equipment, centralize maintenance and operations, and reduce operating expenses for the area was being developed. A large-capacity, centralized heating and cooling plant located one block from Tweed Courthouse was proposed. Hot and chilled water would be circulated to the city-owned buildings in a below-grade, closed-loop piping system. Under this proposal most of the large equipment associated with a modern HVAC installation would be located away from the building, thereby minimizing the visual impact on the historic building and the adjacent landscape. This dual temperature "campus" system was also planned to include City Hall eventually.

By 1999, as the design and restoration of Tweed Courthouse began, the construction of the first portion of the city's central plant and dual-temperature water loop was being completed. Although the proposed use of Tweed Courthouse had changed during the decade after the feasibility report was prepared, the overall HVAC design concept remained the same. The detailed design of an all-air distribution system progressed, utilizing the city's central plant. The design of the system was based on the New Orleans Charter for Joint Preservation of Historic Structures and Artifacts, which provides guidelines for the intervention of new HVAC systems, with temperature and humidity controls in historic buildings that are to house museum collections.

Because Tweed Courthouse was listed in the National Register of Historic Places, it was exempt from the requirements of the New York State Energy Conservation Construction Code. Nevertheless, an objective of the restoration was to comply with the energy code as much as possible without damaging historic building fabric or compromising the historical and architectural integrity of the building. For example, insulation could not be added within the marble-clad exterior walls without destroying the decorative plaster interior finishes. However, the new wood windows and new roof system presented good opportunities to gain significant increases in the building's energy efficiency. These factors were identified and developed prior to the design of the new HVAC system so that the design criteria for the system could be based on the historic-preservation goals for the building.

The design of the HVAC system was under the direction of Imtiaz Mulla of ARUP. The design strategy for zoning, equipment location, and air distribution was developed to take advantage of the building's existing configuration. Primary air intake and exhaust for the entire system would be from the roof, and air handlers to distribute the treated air would be located in both the attic and the basement. Primary piping within the building from the dual-temperature water-supply loop to the air handlers would be routed through the basement and up the mechanical shaft constructed adjacent to the new service elevator. All fresh air was drawn in at attic level and distributed to the air handlers in the basement through the four large vertical shafts originally built into the walls surrounding the rotunda. Local distribution to and from each room would be through the many smaller shafts in the original masonry walls. This arrangement also allowed for temperature and

humidity sensors to be installed in the attic, not within the historic spaces.

In addition, the acoustical qualities and possible vibration impacts of the proposed scheme were studied extensively to determine their potential impact on the building. As a result, additional insulation was provided at all air handlers to decrease sound transmission throughout the interiors, because the plaster wall and ceiling surfaces are acoustically reflective. Vibration isolators to reduce noise transmission through the structure were provided for the air handlers.

An effective air-distribution system, utilizing the limited number and fixed locations of the original supply and return openings, was designed using advanced computer-simulated modeling techniques based on the principles of computational fluid dynamics. Known as CFD analysis, this approach utilizes software that models the movement of air within a space. It can be adjusted to reflect different variables, such as the rate at which treated air is supplied to the room, the potential occupancy of the room and resulting humidity, and temperature gradients at different locations

Installation of new HVAC ducts in former courtroom utilizing existing shafts.

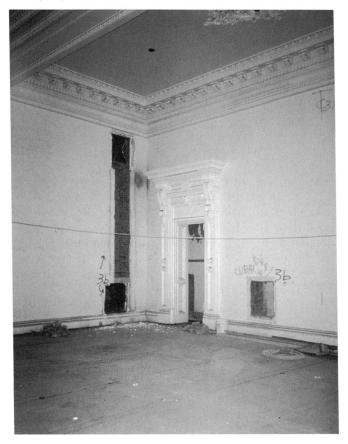

across a space. This analysis confirmed the validity of the HVAC design concept and determined which supply and return shafts and outlets should be utilized or modified. The analysis also aided in the design and positioning of the new louvers to control airflow, installed behind the original porcelain-enameled grilles. In order to make the original shafts with their rough masonry walls usable, new ductwork linings of flexible fabric were installed to reduce friction. In several rooms the locations of dampers and grilles were modified to improve the distribution of treated air based on the CFD analysis.

While the rooms in the main block of the building could be heated and cooled using the existing shafts, the spaces located in the south wing could not. Not only were the existing shafts serving these rooms too small; the externally imposed heating and cooling loads were greater than anywhere else in the building because of the large size of the windows and the southern exposure of the rooms. While the smaller shafts could provide conditioned air to the smaller secondary rooms, supplemental air distribution was required for the main spaces, because they have greater ceiling heights. Conditioned air was also distributed to the main spaces on the second floor through bronze grilles set within the border of the tile floor. These grilles were connected to ductwork mounted below the ceilings of the first-floor space. In the third-floor mezzanine space, black-painted grilles were set within the polychrome-brick ceiling vaulting, and the ductwork was installed in the attic level above.

Larger air handlers with greater heating and cooling capacity were installed to accommodate maximum future program flexibility, including large public gatherings. A building-management system, which can deliver precise control of a room's temperature and humidity from a central location through computer monitoring and controls, was also installed. This system connects the HVAC and fire-alarm systems so that emergency and maintenance personnel not in the building are notified of problems as quickly as possible.

Electrical

Tweed Courthouse was originally lighted by an illuminating-gas system incorporating chandeliers and wall brackets. Thomas A. Edison opened the first electrical power-generating facility, the Pearl Street Station, in 1882. Originally servicing only a few blocks of buildings along the East River above Wall Street, by 1887 the system was expanded to provide electricity to much of the rest of the city. Tweed Courthouse received electricity from this system by the turn of the century.

Many vestiges of the early electrical-distribution systems remained in basement and attic, including large and small distribution panels with exposed copper conductors. In many locations wire covered with cloth insulation was inserted in abandoned gas piping, which then served as the conduit. As the need for electricity increased as the building accommodated more and more offices, the existing electri-

As part of the work to install the new HVAC system, flexible fabric ductwork liners were provided to prevent air leakage within the rough masonry shafts.

New electrical conduit, installed as a grid, was laid in a lightweight concrete slab poured on top of the original iron-beam brick vault floor construction. The grid provides outlets at 15 feet on center, providing maximum flexibility for future use of the space.

Historic distribution panels with exposed copper conductors were still in use before the restoration began. Each panel board was a single piece of slate.

The basement before restoration, with a confusion of electrical wiring from many different periods. The system had never been designed in a comprehensive manner; circuits were added as needed to accommodate the changing demands of the building's users over time.

cal circuits were extended, and new distribution subpanels and additional circuits were installed. The development of the electrical system, as well as the various telecommunication systems in the building, had never been comprehensively considered or designed, resulting in a confusion of wiring and devices from many different periods. The building had never been equipped with a fire-alarm system or emergency lighting, and there was no provision for emergency power should electrical service be disrupted.

The original DC electrical service still powered the passenger and judges' elevators when the feasibility report was prepared in 1991. The restoration of the elevators and the replacement of the DC service began a decade-long phased program to remove and replace the entire electrical infrastructure of the building.

The first step in the process was the replacement of the existing electrical service and switchgear to provide greater capacity for accommodating possible future uses in Tweed Courthouse, as well as additional capacity for City Hall.

During the summer of 1999, concurrent with the planning and design of the electrical distribution system within the building, two large emergency generators and associated testing and cooling equipment were installed in a section of the basement of Tweed Courthouse. The generators were designed to have sufficient capacity to provide life-support and backup capabilities for critical equipment in both Tweed Courthouse and City Hall. Stainless-steel exhaust stacks for the emergency generators were threaded through two existing boiler flues so that they terminated well above the ridgeline of the roof. To cool the generators, remote radiators were installed in the attic and ventilated through a penthouse, which replicates the size and configuration of an original rooftop mechanical structure.

In the spring of 2000 the design for the electrical-distribution system for the building was completed, even though the final uses for the building and the resulting power-distribution quantities and precise locations still had not been determined. Because it was necessary to begin work immediately on the electrical system in order to meet the completion deadline of December 2001, the Economic Development Corporation decided that an electrical-distribution system would allow for a variety of uses in the building, including a museum, offices, and a conference facility. This approach allowed for maximum flexibility in future uses without extensive and costly modifications to the structure and the utility systems.

The concept for the design of the electrical system was based on dividing the building vertically into four quadrants. In each quadrant and on each floor existing small closets were converted into electrical rooms. From these rooms, which were aligned vertically from the basement to the third floor, electrical circuits were extended horizontally to all of the major rooms at the floor level. A grid of floor outlets, 15 feet on center with seven amps available at each location, allowed maximum flexibility for the use of each space. This grid was located within a lightweight concrete floor slab that was poured on top of the iron-beam and brick-vault floor construction. Additional outlets were located adjacent to the new fire stairs and restrooms.

Historic lighting fixtures were restored or replicated for use in the principal spaces of the building. Installed in their original locations, the chandeliers and wall brackets were attached to the original gas piping for structural support. The new electrical conduits inserted in the new floor construction above the fixtures were installed very carefully so that the original plaster ceiling medallions and cornices would not be disturbed. All historic lighting fixtures were wired, using separate circuits, to the emergency-light-

Electrical conduit for the historic lighting fixtures in the main courtroom in the south wing was installed above the stone ceiling. A lightweight concrete slab was poured to enclose the conduit and serve as the new floor slab for the replicated-tile floor of this room.

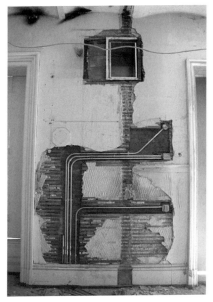

Electrical conduit for new fire alarm system devices, which were installed throughout the building.

ing panels, which were located in each quadrant. This arrangement eliminated the need for obtrusive, new emergency lighting fixtures; the historic fixtures serve as emergency lighting, automatically providing the required amount of illumination in the event of a power outage or other emergency. Small, discrete modern light fixtures were provided in a few locations to augment the historic lighting, in order to meet the code-mandated illumination levels. Illuminated exit signs were also installed where required by code.

Modern fixtures were installed in the fire stairs, restrooms, basement, and attic areas where lighting had not been used historically. Within each of the original courtrooms, provisions were made for the installation of ceiling-mounted track lighting should those spaces be used for museum purposes.

Because of its prominent location at the north end of City Hall Park, the building's facades were illuminated. Designed by Fisher Marantz Stone, the exterior lighting design incorporates large, in-grade fixtures coupled with spotlights mounted on adjacent streetlights and downlights above the entrance portico. The exterior lighting gives the building a dramatic presence at night, making it visible for a considerable distance along Chambers Street and from the Brooklyn Bridge.

A new internal-security system was installed as part of the electrical upgrade, as well as a complete fire-detection and notification system. Video cameras were installed throughout the building, and x-ray machines and magnetometers were provided at the main entrances. The security system, along with the fire-detection and fire-control systems, is monitored at a central facility within the building.

Plumbing

Originally toilets were located in a few small closets on each floor. Water was piped from the city's underground distribution system to four iron tanks in the attic, one tank supplying the closets in each quadrant, with water fed by gravity. Sanitary drainage piping extended to the basement, where it was connected with internal, cast-iron roof and basement window areaway drains to empty into a single sewer. Beginning in 1927, the entire plumbing system, including the fixtures, was replaced, and larger public restrooms were constructed on the main floor in what had been part of the original entrance hall. Over the years the plumbing system was reconfigured and extended on a piecemeal basis without regard to the integrity of the building's historic interior.

The redesign of the plumbing system began during the preliminary stage of design. Modern functional and code requirements called for public restrooms to be located on each floor. Two new public restrooms were located on opposite sides of every floor and, stacked, one above the other, in what had once been service rooms. This allowed the piping and valves to be concentrated in two vertical chases, thus minimizing the space required for these runs and eliminating the need for horizontal distribution and waste lines above the basement level. This arrangement makes maintenance work easier and more efficient.

The design for the new plumbing system accommodated the number of fixtures that would be required for the highest possible occupancy of the building allowed by code. Thus the new system would be adequate for any future use and density of occupants. All new restrooms meet the requirements of the Americans with Disabilities Act, including appropriate water-closet and lavatory fixtures. Service links and floor drains were installed in small service closets. There are new drinking fountains in public hallways.

A new drainage system was constructed underneath the basement floor. New storm and sanitary drainage piping was tied into the locations for the new cast-iron roof drains.

Images from a small video camera threaded through the existing sewer line leading from the building revealed that the sewer was intact and fully operational. Thus the sewer remains in use, eliminating additional underground piping and excavation within an archeologically sensitive area adjacent to the building.

The new plumbing system was designed to accommodate the installation of additional utilities, as well as the modifications of the existing systems, in the future. For example, sprinklers were installed in only a few locations within the building, and standpipes were located in the two new fire stairs and within the rotunda. However, the pumps and the supply piping were sized so that if the use of the

building changes in the future and additional areas have to be sprinklered, new branch distribution piping and sprinkler heads can be added without reconfiguring or replacing the existing system.

Similarly, provisions for piping and ductwork were made in the basement to allow the installation of a commercial kitchen in the future. An area of the basement floor slab was prepared so that it could receive a grease trap, and below-slab piping was installed and capped for a future connection. A kitchen exhaust flue was constructed from the floor to attic within the chase for the plumbing rises. This approach will help to avoid costly or inappropriate modifications in the future.

Typical restroom prior to restoration. These facilities were installed on a piecemeal basis during the twentieth century with little regard for the historic character of the building.

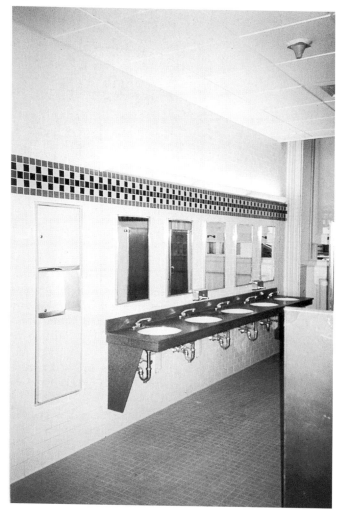

New restrooms were installed in two of the former service rooms on each floor. The new facilities meet modern code and accessibility requirements.

Conclusion

With the unprecedented nationwide interest in the preservation of old buildings in recent years, public agencies have found themselves increasingly responsible for the protection and continued use, or reuse, of historic public buildings. These efforts range from conserving and restoring museums and monuments to adapting historic structures for new uses completely different from their original function. Different projects require different philosophical approaches and technical methods, but there are fundamental principles that apply to all preservation projects. These principles include the following:

1. It is essential to understand fully the history and significance of the building. It is important to know how it was constructed; what materials were used, as well as the characteristics of those materials; what modifications have been made to the building over time; what is the nature of the existing building fabric; and whether the problems currently confronting the building are old or new. The most appropriate vehicle for organizing this information is often a comprehensive historic structure report.

2. The program for the building's future must be developed carefully so that the new uses do not result in major modifications that compromise the building's architectural integrity or remove significant character-defining features. If the building is restored to its historic form while also complying with modern building code and safety requirements, it will often be in a better position to accommodate a different use when the present use, in turn, becomes obsolete. In the case of Tweed Courthouse, had the museum use been imposed upon the building as proposed, major modifications would have been required; these changes would have seriously compromised the building's integrity and resulted in the loss of significant architectural features. Although the museum use may have seemed at first to be an appropriate use for a historic building, careful evaluation of the specific proposal indicated otherwise.

3. The composition of the project team is critical for the success of any architectural project, particularly one involving a historic building. All members of the team must have a clear vision of the goals for the project and a

Detail of iron framing for rotunda skylight.

clear understanding of their role in relation to the roles of the other team members. The owner of the property must provide effective leadership by giving strong and unwavering direction for the project and making decisions quickly and firmly. The architects and engineers must be experienced and skilled in dealing with historic buildings. They must understand the construction of old buildings and not be afraid to deal with their problems. The same architectural and engineering team members should remain for the entire project, from the initial evaluation and preparation of the historic structure report through contract document preparation and construction administration. The construction manager and contractors must be experienced with the preservation and restoration of old buildings so that they can plan and sequence the project to meet scheduling, cost, and quality goals.

4. The project must be planned carefully by the architect and construction manager so that a critical-path method can be followed to completion. A program of tests and probes will be needed to provide adequate infor-

mation on the construction and condition of the building and to handle unforeseen conditions once construction begins. The need for specialty subcontractors and suppliers must be identified at the beginning of the project. Multiple contracts are usually required for complex projects to provide control of costs and quality.

As part of the project-planning process, regulatory agencies must be involved in the project from the beginning so that they can function as partners, not as adversaries, with the design and construction teams. With the Tweed Courthouse project, the New York City Landmarks Preservation Commission, the New York City Buildings Department, and the Fire Department of the City of New York played significant roles in developing the design for the restoration of the building.

5. In planning the design of the preservation project, building and safety code considerations and functional requirements must be an integral part of the design so that the completed building will be safe and functionally efficient, with its basic integrity preserved. Close coordination between architects and engineers is needed to carefully integrate new mechanical and electrical systems into the building fabric. With Tweed Courthouse, the original heating and ventilating shafts in the masonry walls provided the key to inserting a new HVAC system that was code compliant and energy efficient, required low maintenance, and provided the amenities and controls found in new buildings.

Throughout the process the architects and engineers must remember that if they are successful, the building will last for centuries. Modifications should be reversible and as much historic building fabric as possible should be retained. Radical interventions that adapt the building to accommodate a specific use for only a generation before it becomes obsolete should be avoided. Radical modifications that compromise the integrity of the building and make it difficult to adapt it to other uses in the future pose a major threat to its long-term survival of the structure. New mechanical equipment should be installed so that it can be maintained easily and replaced in the future. Major pieces of equipment, such as boilers or air conditioning components, which can be a threat to the building if they malfunction, should either be located in secure areas of the building, outside the building in secondary structures, or in below-grade vaults specially constructed for this purpose.

The restoration of Tweed Courthouse provided an unusual opportunity to develop an effective and efficient process for the restoration of a significant public building so that it could continue to fill an essential role for the government of New York City. This effort was possible because there was sufficient funding to undertake the entire project at one time without having to divide it up into phases. There was strong political support for the project. The New York City Economic Development Corporation, an experienced and effective agency that had the ability to cut through bureaucratic regulations, was available to provide decisive leadership. These factors allowed the building's restoration to proceed on schedule, even though the eventual user of the building was not identified until after the work was substantially complete. Because the fundamental direction had been established for the restoration, the accommodation of the Department of Education in Tweed Courthouse required only the installation of furniture and the selection of finishes for these office spaces. This would not have been the case if the building had been substantially altered to accommodate the perceived needs for museum use.

The process that was developed for the restoration of Tweed Courthouse provides a prototype for other significant historic buildings that are to house public uses. Using this process, the modifications to the building to accommodate modern functional and code requirements can be carried out so that they also enhance and reinforce its historic and architectural integrity.

NOTES

Abbreviations used in the notes

NYCBAP	New York City, Board of Aldermen, *Proceedings*
NYCBEAM	New York City and County, Board of Estimate and Apportionment, *Minutes*
NYCBSP	New York County, Board of Supervisors, *Proceedings*
NYCBS	New York County, Board of Supervisors
NYT	*New York Times*

1. *NYT*, 27 Dec. 1861.
2. Kenneth Jackson, ed., *Encyclopedia of New York City* (New Haven and London: Yale University Press, 1995), 250, 882. Edward H. Hall, *An Appeal for the Preservation of City Hall Park, New York, with a Brief History of the Park* (New York: American Scenic and Historic Preservation Society, 1910), 9. Paul E. Cohen and Robert T. Augustyn, *Manhattan in Maps, 1527–1995* (New York: Rizzoli, 1997), 55.
3. Cohen and Augustyn, 52, 55. Mesick•Cohen•Waite Architects and Hunter Research, "African Burial Ground and the Commons Historic District, Archeological Sensitivity Study," (prepared for N.Y.C. Dept. of General Services, 1994), 2–320 (hereafter cited as "Archeology Sensitivity Study"). Hall, 8.
4. "Archeology Sensitivity Study," 2–8, 2–22.
5. Hall, 14. "Archeology Sensitivity Study," 2–63, 2–64, 2–65.
6. Hall, 10–17, 26. "Archeology Sensitivity Study," 2–58.
7. Hall 15. "Archeology Sensitivity Study," 2–61, 2–162. Jay E. Cantor, "A Monument of Trade, A. T. Stewart and the Rise of the Millionaire's Mansion in New York," *Winterthur Portfolio* 10 (1975), 165.
8. *NYT*, 27 Dec. 1861.
9. *Laws of New York*, 1857, Chap. 770. A similar county-federal government partnership was utilized in the construction of the courthouse in Canandaigua, New York, in the late 1850s.
10. NYCBSP, *Documents*, 1858, No. 6, reprinted in Landmarks Preservation Commission, "The Tweed Courthouse Historic Structure Report," n. d., 301–302 (hereafter cited as "HSR").
11. Ibid.
12. NYCBSP, 7 Jan. 1859, 14–20.
13. NYCBSP, 7 Jan. 1859, 20–21; 18 Jan 1859, 33–34. *NYT*, 19 Jan. 1859.

The *Times* called for repairs to be done on the city hall under a $50,000 appropriation ("that dilapidated ornament of the City to the condition it was in previous to the conflagration of last September"), stating that the sum "will do no more—so that all designs on enlarging it, by the addition of a new story, must happily be abandoned," and urged the City Hall Commissioners to "at once take steps for obtaining designs for the new City Hall, that the long-needed building may be commenced as soon as possible." It was "high time something were done toward re-collecting the scattered Offices and Courts that ought to centre in the Park," the *Times* declared. *NYT*, 23 April 1859, 28 April 1859.

14. NYCBPC 3 May 1859, 266–267; 7 June 1859, 358–360;12 July 1859, 465–470; 7 June 1859, 358–360; 12 July 1859, 465–466, 531. Special Committee on New County Court House, "Report on the Subject of Building the New Court House," published in NYCBS, *Documents*, 1863, No. 6, 71. NYT, 28 April 1859.
15. *NYT*, 28 March 1860, 13 Feb. 1861. NYCBP, 5 March 1860, 257; 19 March 1860, 282.
16. *Laws of New York*, 1861, Chap. 161.
17. NYCBSP, 16 April 1861, 524; 23 April 1861, 544; 7 May 1861, 614; 11 Sept. 1861, 248–255; 16 Sept. 1861, 324. The new law would force the Common Council to cede the land. NYT, 19 April 1861, 14 May 1861. Comptroller, New York County, *Annual Report*, 1862, published in NYCBS, *Documents*, 1863, No. 4, 119.
18. NYCBSP, 9 July 1861, 53; 25 July 1861, 113; 30 Aug. 1861, 200; 16 Sept. 1861, 324
19. *NYT*, 27 Dec. 1861.
20. *NYT*, 17 Sept. 1861.
21. NYCBSP, 24 Oct. 1861, 513–514.
22. Special Committee on New County Court House, 105–106.
23. Ibid., 107–108. *NYT*, 1 Nov. 1861.
24. Special Committee on New County Court House, 112–119. NYCBSP, 30 Oct. 1861, 573–574; 2 Nov. 1861, 583; 12 Nov. 1861, 638; 17 Dec. 1861, 785–786.
25. *NYT*, 21 Sept. 1861, 15 Dec. 1861.
26. NYCBSP, 27 Feb. 1866, 77. *NYT*, 17 Sept. 1861, 27 Dec. 1861.
27. *NYT*, 17 Sept. 1861, 27 Dec. 1861.
28. *NYT*, 27 Dec. 1861.
29. "HSR," 26. NYCBSP, 30 Aug. 1861, quoted in "HSR," 27. *NYT*, 27 Dec. 1861.

30. Adolf K. Placzek, ed., *Macmillan Encyclopedia of Architects* (New York: Free Press, 1982), s.v. "John Kellum." Cantor, 178–181. *NYT*, 27 March 1866. "HSR," 27–34.

31. *NYT*, 15 July 1865, 17 March 1866, 27 Dec. 1861.

32. *NYT*, 27 Dec. 1861. Clerk of the Board of Supervisors, *Annual Report*, 1862, in NYCBS, *Documents*, 1862, No. 14, 119.

33. NYCBSP, 18 March 1862, 252. Clerk of the Board of Supervisors, *Annual Report*, 1862, 119.

34. NYCBSP, 29 April 1862, 379. *NYT*, 1 June 1862.

35. NYCBSP, 29 April 1862, 377. *NYT*, 18 June 1862. Special Committee on New County Court House, 154, 157.

36. NYCBSP, 2 Sept. 1862, 153; 23 Sept. 1862, 217; 30 Oct. 1862, 424–425. *NYT*, 1 Oct. 1862.

37. *NYT*, 13 Dec. 1862, 24 Dec. 1862. NYCBSP, 11 Dec. 1862, 591–594.

38. NYCBSP, 16 Dec. 1862, 604–5; 6 Jan. 1863, 13–14; 8 Jan. 1863, 48–50; 20 Jan. 1863, 118; 23 June 1863, 809.

39. Contract, NYCBS and John M. Masterton, 17 Nov. 1863, Box 6 (Report of Committee on New Courthouse, Board of Supervisors, Minutes, 1863–65), File 2, Municipal Archives, New York City. NYCBS, *Documents*, 1866, No. 9, 329–338. NYCBSP, 23 Sept. 1863, 357–361.

40. NYCBS, *Documents*, 1866, No. 9, 319–328.

41. NYCBSP, 23 Sept. 1863, 357–361. NYCBS, *Documents*, 1866, No. 9, 319–328.

42. NYCBSP, 15 Nov. 1864 452; 1 March 1864, 307; 15 March 1864, 421; 10 July 1865, 32.

43. NYCBSP, 13 Feb. 1865, 352. Leo Hershkowitz, *Tweed's New York, Another Look* (Garden City, N.Y.: Anchor Books, 1978), 107.

44. *NYT*, 15 July 1865.

45. NYCBSP, 12 Dec. 1865, 584.

46. *NYT*, 26 Dec. 1865.

47. NYCBSP, 27 Feb. 1866, 75–85.

48. Ibid., 85–89.

49. Ibid., 89–91, 100. *NYT*, 28 Feb. 1866, 6 March 1866.

50. NYCBSP, 26 June 1866, 556–579. The findings of the investigation were published as NYCBS, *Documents*, 1866, No. 9.

51. NYCBSP, *Documents*, 1866, No. 9, 20. *NYT*, 27 March 1866, 17 Nov. 1866. NYCBSP, 26 June 1866, 556–579.

52. NYCBSP, 31 Dec. 1866, 662; 14 Jan. 1867, 19; 27 Feb. 1867, 172, 224; 8 May 1867, 313; 14 May 1867, 425, 449; 21 May 1867, 478; 11 June 1867, 557; 24 June 1867, 614; 1 July 1867, 30; 12 Nov. 1867, 316.

53. NYCBPS, 11 June 1867, 557; 30 July 1867, 155; 3 Sept. 1867, 207; 13 Sept. 1867, 256; 23 Sept. 1867, 269; 12 Nov. 1867, 316. NYT, 15 Dec. 1868.

54. *NYT*, 12 March 1867, 1 April 1867.

55. *NYT*, 12 March 1867, 1 April 1867; 22 April 1868. NYCBP, 23 July 1867, 70–71.

56. *NYT*, 25 Dec. 1866, 12 March 1867; 6 May 1867.

57. *NYT*, 17 Aug. 1867.

58. *NYT*, 15 Dec. 1868.

59. *NYT*, 15 Dec. 1868. NYCBSP, 5 July 1869, 10–11.

60. *NYT*, 4 April 1871.

61. Leo Hershkowitz, ed., *Boss Tweed in Court*, microfilm ed. (Bethesda, Md.: University Publications of America, c. 1990), vi. I. N. P.

62. Stokes, *The Iconography of Manhattan Island, 1498–1909*, Vol. 3 (New York: R. H. Dodd, 1915–1928), 751–752.

62. *NYT*, 11 May 1871.

63. Hershkowitz, *Boss Tweed in Court*, v-vi. *Dictionary of American Biography*, s.v. "William Marcy Tweed." Jackson, 1205–1206.

64. NYT, 8 July 1871, 20 July 1871, 26 July 1871. Alexander B. Callow, Jr., *The Tweed Ring* (New York: Oxford University Press, 1966), passim.

65. *NYT*, 21 July 1871.

66. Ibid.

67. *NYT*, 23 July 1871, 24 July 1871, 26 July 1871.

68. *NYT*, 29 July, 1871, 28 Aug. 1871. "The 'Times' and Tammany," Harper's Weekly, 12 Aug. 1871.

69. "The Lesson of the Frauds Continued," *Harper's Weekly*, 19 Aug. 1871.

70. Hershkowitz, *Tweed's New York*, 181–190.

71. Ibid., 194–204, 220. For an accounting of expenditures for the courthouse, see Board of Estimate and Apportionment, *Minutes*, 20 Feb. 1914, 893–897.

72. Hershkowitz, *Tweed's New York*, 220, 238, 248. *NYT*, 20 Nov. 1873.

73. Hershkowitz, *Tweed's New York*, 305, 318, 320.

74. Ibid., 323.

75. NYCBEAM, 25 Oct. 1871, 438.

76. NYCBEAM, 18 July 1872, 601–605.

77. NYCBSP, 11 Sept. 1873, 487; 16 March 1874, 223. NYCBEAM, 15 Feb. 1875, 815–819.

78. NYCBAP, 23 Sept. 1878, 578. Placzek, s.v., "Leopold Eidlitz." *NYT*, 29 April 1877, 20 Jan. 1879. In an article in the Jan. 20, 1879, issue of the *NYT* entitled "New-York's Great Peril," Eidlitz also challenged claims that cast iron was a fireproof building material.

79. NYCBEAM, 3 July 1875, 1535; 23 Aug. 1876, 1571; 25 April 1878, 81. *NYT*, 24 Oct. 1876.

80. NYCBEAM, 14 Jan. 1878, 6–7. *American Architect and Building News*, 2 (3 Feb. 1877), quoted in "HSR," 45. NYCBAP, 21 Feb. 1877, 305. *New York Daily Tribune*, 7 April 1877.

81. NYCBEAM, 25 April, 1878, 81. NYCBAP, 20 Aug. 1878, 323–324; 23 Sept. 1878, 576–580.

82. NYCBAP, 23 Sept. 1878, 578.

83. NYCBAP, 24 Dec. 1878, 752–753; 14 Jan. 1879, 35–37; 2 March 1880, 549–551; 20 July 1880, 176–177; 20 Jan. 1880, 99. NYCBEAM, 15 July 1880, 200; 16 Sept. 1880, 294.

84. NYT, 29 April 1877. *American Architect and Building News*, 3 (16 March 1878), 94, quoted in "HSR," 67, 69. *New York Daily Tribune*, 4 Aug. 1879.

85. "HSR," 69, 71. File for Building Permit 2902, Municipal Archives, New York City.

86. NYCBEAM, 16 June 1927, 6302–6303.

87. Dept. of Housing and Buildings, Alteration Application No. 1622, 1941, Municipal Archives, New York City.

88. *NYT*, 7 July 1974.

89. *NYT*, 14 June 1974, 7 July 1974.

90. *NYT*, 7 July 1974. *New York Post*, 14 June 1974, 22 June 1974, 23 Aug. 1974, 9 Oct. 1974, 30 Dec. 1976; Roberta B. Gratz, then a reporter for the Post, covered the preservation story and kindly provided copies of her articles.

BIBLIOGRAPHY

Allen, Oliver E. *The Tiger: The Rise and Fall of Tammany Hall.* Reading, Mass.: Addison-Wesley, 1993.

Barista, Dave. "Order Restored." *Building Design & Construction* (October 2003).

Bede, Elizabeth. "Cleaning and the Environment." *Building Renovation* "July/August" 1993.

Callow, Alexander B. *The Tweed Ring.* New York: Oxford University Press, 1966.

Burrows, Edwin G., and Mike Wallace. *Gotham, A History of New York City to 1898.* New York and Oxford: Oxford University Press, 1999.

Cantor, Jay E. "A Monument of Trade, A. T. Stewart and the Rise of the Millionaire's Mansion in New York." *Winterthur Portfolio* 10 (1975): 165–197.

Cohen, Paul E., and Robert T. Augustyn. *Manhattan in Maps, 1527–1995.* New York: Rizzoli, 1997.

Dunlap, David W. "The Grandeur That Graft Built." *The New York Times.* 9 March 2001, sec. B, p. 1.

Goldberger, Paul. "Beame Group's Proposal to Raze Tweed Courthouse Is Expected to Evoke Dissent." *The New York Times.* 14 June 1974.

Goldberger, Paul. "The Prize." *The New Yorker* (April 1, 2002): 72–73.

Grondahl, Paul. "Tweed Courthouse Tests Albany Firm's Restoration Skills." *The Times Union* (Albany, NY). 6 January 2002, sec. G, p. 6.

Hall, Edward H. *An Appeal for the Preservation of City Hall Park, New York, with a Brief History of the Park.* New York: American Scenic and Historic Preservation Society, 1910.

Hershkowitz, Leo, ed. *Boss Tweed in Court,* microfilm ed. Bethesda, Md.: University Publications of America, c. 1990.

Hershkowitz, Leo. *Tweed's New York, Another Look.* Garden City, N.Y.: Anchor Books, 1978.

Jackson, Kenneth, ed. *Encyclopedia of New York City.* New Haven and London: Yale University Press, 1995.

Kandell, Jonathan. "Boss." *Smithsonian* (February 2002).

Kolbert, Elizabeth. "Fellowship of the Ring." *The New Yorker* (May 6, 2002).

Linton, W. J. *House That Tweed Built.* Cambridge, Mass.: 1871.

Malone, Dumas. *Dictionary of American Biography.* New York: Charles Scribner's Sons, 1936.

Mesick•Cohen•Waite Architects and Hunter Research. "African Burial Ground and the Commons Historic District, Archeological Sensitivity Study." Prepared for New York City Department of General Services, 1994.

New York City, Board of Aldermen. *Proceedings,* 1874–76.

New York City and County, Board of Estimate and Apportionment. *Minutes,* 1872–79.

New York City and County, Board of Estimate and Apportionment. *Proceedings,* 1873–1937.

New York County, Board of Supervisors. *Documents,* 1858–68.

New York County, Board of Supervisors. *Proceedings,* 1859–74.

New York City, Landmarks Preservation Commission. "The Tweed Courthouse Historic Structure Report."

New York Times, 1859–79.

Placzek, Adolf K., ed. *Macmillan Encyclopedia of Architects.* New York: Free Press, 1982.

Popson, Colleen P. "The House that Tweed Built." *Archaeology Magazine* (July–August 2002).

Stokes, I. N. P. *The Iconography of Manhattan Island, 1498–1909.* New York: R. H. Dodd, 1915–1928.

"2001 Award of Merit: Restoration Project – Tweed Courthouse." *New York Construction News* (December 2001).

Youker, Darrin. "Restoring History." *The Sunday Post-Star* (Glens Falls). 7 April 2002, sec. A, p. 1.

Waite, John, and Nancy A. Rankin. "Tweed Courthouse: New Approach to Life Safety Management in a Landmark Public Building." *APT Bulletin: The Journal of Preservation Technology.* (2004): Volume XXXV, No. 1, pp.

INDEX

Page numbers in italic refer to captions. "CS" refers to captions in the color section.